THE DARK BOX

THE DARK BOX

A SECRET HISTORY
of CONFESSION

JOHN CORNWELL

BASIC BOOKS

A Member of the Perseus Books Group

New York

Published by Basic Books, A Member of the Perseus Books Group

Books published by Basic Books are available at special discounts for bulk purchases in the United States by corporations, institutions, and other organizations. For more information, please contact the Special Markets Department at the Perseus Books Group, 2300 Chestnut Street, Suite 200, Philadelphia, PA 19103, or call (800) 810-4145, ext. 5000, or e-mail special.markets@perseus books.com.

Scripture quotations are from the Holy Bible, Revised Standard Version, Containing the Old and New Testaments with the Apocrypha / Deuterocanonical Books: An Ecumenical Edition. New York: Collins, 1973.

Designed by Pauline Brown
Typeset in Adobe Garamond Pro by the Perseus Books Group

Library of Congress Cataloging-in-Publication Data
Cornwell, John, 1940–
The dark box : a secret history of confession / John Cornwell.
    pages cm
    Includes bibliographical references and index.
    ISBN 978-0-465-03995-1 (hardcover : alk. paper)—
    ISBN 978-0-465-08049-6 (e-book) 1. Confession—History. I. Title.
BV845.C67 2014
264'.0208609—dc23
                                                    2013042961

10 9 8 7 6 5 4 3 2 1

In memory of
Peter Carson
1938–2013
Editor, Publisher, Friend

I was so full of joy, submitting and humbling
myself before the confessor, a simple, timid
priest, and exposing all the filth of my soul;
I was so full of joy at my thoughts merging with
the aspirations of the fathers who wrote the
ritual prayers;
I was so full of joy to be one with all believers,
past and present . . .

—Leo Tolstoy, *Confession*, translated from
the Russian by Peter Carson, 2013

CONTENTS

AUTHOR'S NOTE

WHEN I BEGAN RESEARCH FOR THIS BOOK, I ASKED CATHOLIC friends: 'How long since your last confession?' I heard 'twenty years', 'thirty years', and an occasional 'two months'. Sometimes I was told 'Mind your own business'. It seems only right to state my own circumstance from the outset.

Brought up after the Second World War in London's East End by a devout mother of Irish extraction, I was instructed in the Catholic faith by nuns from the age of five. I made my first confession at age seven, the day before my first communion. On Saturday afternoons or evenings, all the family, including four siblings, joined the lengthy queues at our local church to confess our sins—all except my father, that is, who only became a Catholic to marry my mother.

In confession, as we were taught, you started by telling the priest how many weeks or months had elapsed since your last confession. You listed the sins committed since that last confession, then said a prayer of contrition. The priest would ask some questions to clarify the nature of the sins you had told him. He might also offer spiritual advice. You were obliged to feel genuinely sorry for having offended God, and to declare that you would try not to commit those sins again. If it was possible to make reparation to the people you had wronged, it was important to do so. The priest then imposed a penance—usually a few prayers—and said the words of absolution. We were told that absolution relieved us of the guilt for the sins we had confessed. We were taught that in the case of a mortal sin (a grave sin deserving of Hell), absolution lifted the dire penalty of eternal punishment. Nowadays, Catholics are commonly told that absolution reconciles them to God's love.

My father was convinced, like many non-Catholics, that confession allowed Catholics to commit sins, have them forgiven (and feel good), then commit them again. As a well-taught Catholic, I knew better. Absolution did not work unless you had a 'firm purpose of amendment'. That determination, we realised, was as fragile as human nature itself.

I served Mass at our local church every morning from the age of ten. At age twelve I admitted to our parish priest that I wanted to be like him—a priest. In retrospect, this was odd, for Father James Cooney—austere, desiccated, humourless— was hardly an attractive role model. My mother said that going to confession with him was like 'going on trial for your life'. But I had fallen in love with the ritual of the Mass and would spend hours in the privacy of my bedroom bobbing up and down before a makeshift altar, muttering mumbo-jumbo pretend Latin. The following year I was enrolled in a junior seminary—a monastic boarding school for boys, 150 miles from home, where I was to spend five years receiving a priv-

ileged education, including Latin and Greek, in preparation
for senior seminary.

I got on well with most of our priest-teachers, who worked
hard to bring us to a high standard of education. They were
generally kind men and exemplary models of priesthood.
One day, however, I was sexually propositioned by one of
our priests while he was hearing my confession. I realised
that externals of clerical piety are no guarantee of authentic
holiness. I would never again enjoy unalloyed trust in the
beneficence of priests, especially in confession. I nevertheless
proceeded at eighteen to the senior seminary, where I stayed
long enough to complete the course in philosophy of religion
and experience the rigorous priestly formation of that era,
including instructions that would shape a future confessor. I
was becoming a 'Catholic cleric'. My vocation had become a
matter of habit rather than choice. I had confessed every week
of my life—from boyhood to the age of twenty-one.

After seven years of seminary life, junior and senior, I
came to see that the priesthood was not for me. I knew in my
heart of hearts, and in my genitals, that I would not make it
as a celibate. Catching up with the world—music, dancing,
girls, lay clothes, making my own decisions after years of
seminary discipline—was not easy. My understanding tutor
at Oxford, where I had arrived to study English literature,
quipped one day: 'My dear fellow, you need to learn in life
how to take the smooth with the rough . . .'

I became convinced that Catholicism, for me at least, was
not an impetus for maturity and happiness. At the same time,

I was finding it difficult to reconcile Christianity with an increasingly positivist, scientific view of the world. As a graduate student at Cambridge, I finally, consciously, abandoned my Catholicism. For the next twenty years I would hover between atheism and agnosticism. But time, my dream life, and a gradual appreciation of the difference between religious imagination and magic realism opened the way to at least consider the *possibility* of a God after atheism.

Marriage to a devout Catholic who brought up our children in the faith, and nostalgia for the rhythms of Catholic liturgy, prompted a change of heart—not so much a return as a progression—although I remain circumspect. Notions of a vengeful God have been difficult to exorcise entirely. To this day, moreover, I have occasional, inchoate suspicions that these renewed quests for a once-rejected God mask a search for the lost abusers of one's childhood. This book, however, while written from the inevitable perspective of an individual member of the Catholic faithful, draws on a wide range of historical sources and the personal testimonies of fellow Catholics past and present.

PROLOGUE

IN THE EARLY PERIOD OF THE CHRISTIAN CHURCHES, penitents would confess in public those major sins that had excluded them from their communities—such as murder, idolatry, and adultery. The ritual of reconciliation into the community or congregation was seldom allowed more than once in a Christian's lifetime. It was not until the Middle Ages that all adult members of the faithful within Latin Christianity were obliged to tell their sins to a priest in private once a year. The penitent would kneel before the seated confessor, with the possibility of physical contact between the two. The practice of Roman Catholics entering a dark box to confess their sins did not begin until the mid-sixteenth century, following the Reformation and the fragmentation of Western Christendom.

The confessional box is a booth-like piece of church furniture containing a dividing panel. This panel physically separates the penitent, who kneels in the dark, from the confessor, who sits in the light. There is a grille set in the panel that allows for verbal communication; in theory, it obscures the faces of penitent and confessor from each other. Although most devout Catholics born before 1970 used to enter that box frequently, Catholic confession, whether inside the box or outside it, has been largely abandoned, despite pleas from the previous pope, Benedict XVI, and many of the world's bishops to revive the practice.

In this book I argue that the rejection of confession is a crucial symptom of a wider crisis within the Catholic Church. A gulf has opened up between official teaching and practice. An alteration across a broad front, described by some theologians as a 'paradigm shift' (in emulation of great sea changes in 'normal' science), has affected the way many Catholics understand sin, virtue, and the nature of God. This shift, in turn, has created new insights into the meaning of God's love and forgiveness.[1]

Over the past four decades, Rome has attempted to make confession more attractive. Today Catholics refer to the sacrament as 'reconciliation' (a term used in the early Church), and confessors tend to hear the sins of their penitents in the pews or the sanctuary, or on comfortable chairs in a parish room set aside for the purpose. Yet the more user-friendly circumstances of the sacrament have not brought back the penitents. From the mid-1970s, during the papacy of Paul VI, penitents were offered the option of group absolution—known as 'general' absolution; the initiative was quashed by John Paul II in 1983. Mortal, or grave, sins, he insisted, must be absolved in privacy after they have been told to a priest. (Mortal sins, according to orthodox doctrine, include not only the major sins, such as murder, grand larceny, physical

violence, and adultery, but also all sexual sins: using condoms, having sex outside of marriage, having homosexual sex,
divorcing and remarrying without an annulment, masturbation, and indulging in 'impure thoughts'.)

Confessions have been so poorly attended in recent
years that in many parishes the sacrament is only available
by appointment. Some priests will tell you that nobody has
sought the sacrament for months. If you go to a cathedral
church, you may still find queues of penitents waiting to be
confessed in the traditional confessional box; but this is an
isolated phenomenon. Many of these old-style confessants,
who are nevertheless as likely to be in their twenties as their
eighties, cling to a version of Catholicism that most Catholics
have abandoned. Many have come from parishes where their
confessions cannot be heard, or because they prefer to be
confessed by a priest who does not recognise them.

One practice that continues to be upheld throughout the
Church, however, despite the widespread decline of confession or reconciliation as a sacrament among adult Catholics,
is that of children making their first confession at age seven
in preparation for their first communion. A crucial theme
of this book is the phenomenon of obligatory confession in
early childhood. The story of its universal commencement
in the early twentieth century, the widespread oppression it
occasioned, and, scandalously, the opportunity it afforded a
minority of priests to abuse children sexually reveals the dark
face of confession's recent history.

———————————

In the library of Corpus Christi College, Cambridge, there is a handsome illuminated document, penned in black and red gothic script, entitled *Memoriale Presbiterorum*—an *aide memoire* for priests. Written in Latin and dating from the early fourteenth century, it has 218 chapters offering guidance to confessors on every aspect of confessional practice. The manual is typical of the many guides for confessors appearing throughout Western Christendom in the Middle Ages.[2]

One chapter, headed 'Concerning Children' (*Circa pueros*), offers this advice: 'You ought to know, confessor, that if a child be capable of wrongdoing, near to puberty, he is obliged to confess all his sins at least once a year.' By the time the *Memoriale* came to be written, a hundred years had passed since a great council in Rome decreed that all Christians in the Latin tradition must confess their sins at least once a year on reaching the 'age of discretion'—which, as this manual and many others implied, was around the time of puberty. The age for first confession in the Latin Christian tradition was therefore generally held to be between twelve and fourteen, a view that persisted down the centuries, with local and periodic variations, until the first decade of the twentieth century, when Rome issued a dramatic proclamation on the subject.[3]

Against the background of the eventful, and at times troubled, evolution of the practice of confession, this book culminates with the story of a historic experiment imposed universally on Catholic children. In 1910, the pope of the day, Pius X, decreed that first confession should be made not at puberty but at the age of seven—which meant that instruction on sin, and the different categories of sins, and the punishments due for sins in Purgatory and Hell, would begin at five or six. The decree also advocated weekly confession for Catholics of every age, instead of annual confession, the former norm for lay members of the faithful. Among the many unintended consequences of that experiment was the inculcation in young children of an oppressive sense of guilt and shame, especially for their bodies, and, for a significant minority, exposure to clerical sexual predators.

These charges are in stark contrast to the undeniable benefits—spiritual and psychological—that result from a mature individual's admission of remorse for having caused injury to others, and the subsequent forgiveness of the injured party, across a wide spectrum of religious practices and cultural contexts. One of the most beautiful arias in opera concludes Mozart's *Nozze di Figaro*—when marital discord, deceit and betrayal end with the husband begging for pardon, and the wife offering unconditional forgiveness. The poignant aria '*Contessa Perdono*'—'Countess, forgive me'—envelops the cast and the entire audience in a sublime ambiance of harmony and reconciliation. A similar poignant moment occurs in Shakespeare's *The Merchant of Venice* when Portia extols the power and beneficence of mercy as a type of divine grace:

> The quality of mercy is not strain'd,
> It droppeth as the gentle rain from heaven
> Upon the place beneath: it is twice blest;
> It blesseth him that gives, and him that takes.[4]

Poets of every era testify that the act of unburdening in a form of words and in public brings healing, or, as William Wordsworth put it—'timely utterance' gives 'thought relief'.[5] Yet the widely assumed instinctual universality and healing quality of the tendency to confess—or as young people might say today, 'fess up'—is a matter of debate. (How many marriages have been wrecked by a spouse's admission of having strayed?) Nor does Catholic confession—involving the patriarchal judgement of a priest over women and children— accord with voluntary exchanges of remorse and forgiveness within relationships where the parties have equal power.

For many centuries confession to a priest in the Catholic Church was obligatory—under pain of further sin. For centuries the Catholic sacrament of confession involved patriarchal authority, secrecy, and itemized lists of discrete 'sins' couched in formalised language. The 'telling' of sins, moreover, was normally divorced from the narratives and relationships of a penitent's life story. The role of the confessor was not that of a representative of an injured party, but of judge, healer, dispenser of penance, and representative of the divine.

The desire to be chastised for wrongdoing in a non-religious context can be traced through the works of many writers from Plato to Sigmund Freud, although Freud maintained that our conscious triggers for guilt hide deeper reasons, buried in the subconscious.[6] Penances imposed by Catholic confessors today are mild—a few prayers. These 'penances', however, are remnants of harsh self-mortification that once included fasts, pilgrimage, exile, and self-flagellation.

Yet the point of Catholic confession goes beyond absolution for wrongdoing. For many centuries confession has been deemed crucial for achieving holiness and Heaven. Of all Christian denominations, the Catholic Church has advocated the importance of confession as a means of salvation. Great saints, such as Teresa of Avila, have extolled confession's benefits as a means of achieving mystical union with God.

Spiritual writers within the sphere of the monotheistic religions emphasize the importance of the sinner making a decision for God: embarking on a conversion of life. The visible ritual of confession in the presence of a minister, however, makes such a conversion 'sacramental'—an outward sign of inward grace, sanctioned by the Church. Despite the unhappiness of the Protestant reformers with the medieval conduct of the sacrament of penance, confession would nevertheless be practised in a restricted form by the Lutheran, Anglican, and Episcopalian churches (as well as the Eastern Churches). These denominations mostly administer the ritual in cases where a penitent seeks reconciliation, or spiritual consolation, in crisis, such as in illness or in the face of death. Unlike the Catholic Church, they do not oblige a member of their faithful to confess in the event of having committed a 'serious' sin, nor do they maintain rules of annual obligation to confess.

Confession has merged with spiritual counselling across different Christian denominations, especially for people dedicated to a life in religion. In the Catholic tradition, moreover, the power of the priest to bestow absolution extends in cases of emergency to groups of believers, especially when the priest can offer spiritual consolation in time of peril. One of the heroes of the *Titanic* disaster was Father Thomas Beales, who had twice refused the opportunity to go into a lifeboat. He preferred to stay on the vessel, where he continued to lead prayers and absolve sins even as the ship went down. During the 9/11 attacks on the Twin Towers in New York, Father Mychal Judge was the first dead rescuer to be carried out. He was killed by falling masonry while hearing the confessions of the injured and dying. In time of war, moreover, Catholic chaplains have won praise for their courage in administering, at risk of their lives, absolution and last rites to the wounded and dying on the battlefields and at sea. There are countless instances of priests for whom confession is an occasion of compassion and inclusion. It has been revealed that Pope Francis, as archbishop of Buenos Aires, would go to the city's red-light district at night to give spiritual comfort to prostitutes, sitting on a roadside bench.[7]

And yet the Catholic history of confession is punctuated with evidence of a darker side. Confessors down the centuries, in the act of administering the sacrament, have been guilty of hypocrisy, avarice, sexual debauchery, and other forms of abuse. Theological disagreements over confession, as well as confessors' sexual and mercenary abuses, were prime reasons for Protestant indignation at the Reformation. The confessional box, separating confessor and penitent physically and visually, was invented in the Catholic Counter-Reformation to prevent the seduction of women. Sexual abuses nevertheless persisted. The whispering of secrets, invariably involving the marriage bed, would lead to new forms of confessional seduction. By the eighteenth century, anticlericalism, owing in part to antagonism between husbands and their wives' confessors, led to widespread neglect of the sacrament.

Pius X, later canonised an official saint of the Church, extended universal and frequent confessional practice to young children, believing confession and Holy Communion to be means of bestowing spiritual sustenance and protection on them in the face of secularism, materialism, and a form of heresy he termed 'Modernism'. The faithful responded: long lines of penitents, including young children now, were a feature of weekly confession-times in Catholic churches the world over. This was the Church familiar to Catholics from the First World War to the early 1970s, often referred to in nostalgic retrospect as a golden age of Catholicism. Catholic public and domestic religious practices increased—processions, pilgrimages, praying the Rosary, grace before and after meals, the Angelus, increased veneration of the pope. There was a surge in vocations to the priesthood—many candidates making their commitment, as I did, in boyhood.

In preparation for first confession, children barely out of infancy were taught the doctrine of 'mortal sin', which killed the soul and resulted in eternal punishment. Every sin of thought, word, and deed against chastity, or 'modesty', was mortal. Religious instruction at an early stage of moral development laid foundations of beliefs that were more akin to superstition than to faith, closer to fear than to love of

God. Adult disciplines such as fasting (from midnight on the day before receiving Holy Communion) were also imposed, often resulting in a child breaking the fast unintentionally. Children caught in this dilemma would go nevertheless to communion under social and familial pressures and suffer consequent guilt. They had been taught that receiving communion after breaking the fast was both a mortal sin and a sacrilege—compounded by a further sacrilege if the sin was not admitted in a subsequent confession.

Moreover, priests now had access to children on a weekly basis in the unsupervised intimacy of the confessional box. Many priests, because of the enclosed seminary education, lacked maturity as well as training in child psychology and pedagogy. In time, child victims of oppression would themselves become priests.

From the 1950s, and with gathering momentum during the period of the 'sexual revolution', a significant minority of priests was taking advantage of the intimacy of the confessional to groom young penitents for acts of sexual abuse. Current investigations reveal that priests were exploiting confession to test the vulnerability of children for sexual exploitation and to establish opportunities for abuse outside of the confessional. At the same time, the abusers would exploit confession to square their own offences with their pastoral lives. Priests who have served prison sentences for sexual crimes admit that they would seek out confessors to secure absolution while concealing the ages of their 'sexual partners' and their own priestly identities.[8] Lay Catholics have been angered by the knowledge that prelates right up to the Vatican have harboured or turned a blind eye to sexual deviants.

By the strict standards of papal teaching on sexual morals, Catholics who practise contraception, or who are living together outside of marriage, or who are practising homosexuals, are in grave sin. John Paul II insisted that the use of condoms, even by those infected by HIV/AIDS, is a sin. He also declared that grave sins can only be forgiven in confession. Yet the majority of practising Catholics go to confession rarely, if at all. In Europe the statisticians of Catholic practice have ceased to make enquiries about the reception of confession in their questionnaires. In the United States, the Center for Applied Research in the Apostolate (CARA) estimates that only 2 per cent of Catholics go to confession regularly. Anecdotal evidence for Ireland and the United Kingdom, as well as correspondents writing to me from Spain, Italy, France, Germany, and the Netherlands, suggests a massive collapse.[9]

The sense of sin taught to generations of Catholic children as an offence against God's rules barely survives alongside a virtual denial of sin. A recent convert informant, typical of many who were brought into the Church by traditionalist priests, tells me that she has been taught that missing Mass is a serious sin—a mortal sin, in fact, requiring absolution before receiving the Eucharist. In contrast, a pastor in his seventies, 'liberated' by the Second Vatican Council, tells me that he never speaks of sin: 'We have encouraged teenagers in our local Catholic school to see confession as an opportunity to talk about their *experience* of life, and their *difficulties.*' The occasional, and temporary, popularity of confession among groups of teenagers is clearly visible at World Youth Days when the young queue in the hundreds to be confessed. But there is no evidence that these teenagers continue to go to confession back at home, or that their sense of sin bears any relation to official Catholic teaching, especially on sexual matters.

UNDERSTANDING HOW CONFESSION has shaped Catholicism through the past century merits a rehearsal of confession's historical development, which forms the first part of this book. Confession in private to a priest (auricular confession) of minor as well as major sins (venial and mortal) evolved only gradually, and late in the first millennium, in remote monastic communities that had survived the barbarian invasions and the breakdown of civil society. Individual confession as we know it today grew out of one-on-one spiritual direction in religious communities. It was not until the thirteenth century that Rome commanded all members of the faithful to confess to a priest at least once a year under pain of excommunication, eternal damnation, and loss of the right to be buried in consecrated ground. The obligation to confess, imposed by Pope Innocent III and the Fourth Lateran Council in 1215, was as much a tactic in the war against heresy (an opportunity to question penitents on their orthodoxy) as a desire to call the faithful to greater holiness.

The practice of confession from the late medieval and early modern periods was to exert a potent influence on the development of Western ethics, law, and perceptions of the self. Confession gradually replaced trial by ordeal; and yet, in cases of suspected heresy, the Inquisition thought it legitimate to extort confessions (not the sacrament, but 'criminal' confessions) by torture. Catholic moral theology's obsessive interest in what happens between the bed-sheets helped shape our modern understanding of the language of the body and sexual behaviour. Ideas about the examination of conscience, and preoccupation with sins of thought and imagination, encouraged a deepening sense of subjectivity and individual moral agency. In the sixteenth and seventeenth centuries, believers died gruesome deaths—on both sides of the Reformation divide—for the right to practise confession or to refuse it.

The frequent confessions practised by my generation, and the generations of my parents and grandparents, nurtured an identifiable literary subgenre that extended from Paul Claudel and James Joyce through writers such as Georges Bernanos, Evelyn Waugh, Edna O'Brien, Tobias Wolff, and Colm Tóibín. Authors who were Catholic converts, such as Graham Greene, tended to exploit the drama of confession for the adult soul in peril. Others, including Frank O'Connor and Roddy Doyle, have expressed the comic potential of the confessional's dark box. For the poet Carol Ann Duffy, however, who recollected the confessions of her childhood, the confessional box was a 'dark cell' with suggestions of live burial, where a child would 'stammer' in fear of 'eternal damnation'. Sins were 'those maggoty things / that wriggle in the soul'. For another poet, the late Christopher Logue, the confessional booth was 'a dark, smelly, wooden crate of a place' where one retailed one's 'so-called sins to a hairy ear'. Logue complains: 'Proscription rather than examination, the cultivation of guilt, the awarding of punishment and blame—was cruel, abusive, even—if you countenance the thought—sinful in itself.'[10]

Logue declared that the universal practice of confession for young children was a form of psychological and emotional abuse. Moreover, the lowered age of confession from thirteen to seven would coincide with the age group of the young most affected by sexual abuse.[11] Pius X's initiative resulted in the frequent exposure of Catholic children to priests who had been removed from the normal, familial company of children for many years. It is significant that the rise in sexual attacks, from the late 1950s through the 1980s, coincided not only with the explosion of sexual permissiveness but also with the tendency for priests to hear confessions outside of the confessional box—in sacristies, parish rooms, and priests' quarters. Informants have spoken of confessions held in priests' bedrooms, on retreats, and in cars, and of being invited, at the age of seven or eight, to be confessed on a priest's lap.

Understanding the current crises in the Catholic Church, and its fate and its future, involves an appreciation of the chequered history of the powerful instrument of confession and the absolution of sins as seen by the laity, rather than through the doctrinal lens of theologians, or the pastoral perspective of priests, bishops, and popes. St. Augustine of Hippo believed that the authenticity of Christianity ultimately depended on the reception of its beliefs and practices by the faithful at large and the 'echo' it gave back to official doctrine. The Catholic faithful, en masse, have sent a definitive signal of dissent to the purveyors of 'official' doctrine on confession and the nature of sin.

PART ONE

A BRIEF HISTORY
of CONFESSION

One

Early Penitents and Their Penances

Wash me thoroughly from mine iniquity,
and cleanse me from my sin!

—Psalm 51

O N THE DAY KNOWN AS ASH WEDNESDAY, MANY Christians the world over sport a dark smudge on their foreheads in the shape of a cross. They are marking the beginning of the penitential season of Lent with a public display that harks back to the remote origins of the sacrament of penance. That morning they have received on the brow in memory of the crucifixion a sign in ash made from burnt palm leaves and olive oil, to the accompaniment of the words 'Remember that you are dust, and unto dust you will return!'[1] But there is an earlier tradition of marking the head with ashes that has its origins in Jewish and Christian rituals for the reconciliation of sinners.

The Hebrew prophets and poets dwelt on guilt, individually and collectively. 'My sin', wrote the Psalmist, 'is always before me.' And, 'I eat ashes like bread, and mingle tears with my drink.' Ritualistic contrition had antecedents in the Jewish Day of Atonement, involving a day and night of fasting. The tradition developed over many centuries and was originally a means of making reparation for mistakes and incorrect rituals in temple sacrifices. We read in Jonah how the Ninevites averted God's anger by wearing sackcloth and ashes and engaging in fasting and prayer. In time, the Day of Atonement, practised widely in synagogues in the absence of the Temple (after 70 CE), encouraged reconciliation with those whom one had wronged as well as sorrow for offending God. In the Jewish tradition, while sins against God could only be forgiven by God, sins against one's neighbour had to be forgiven both by that neighbour and by God. Repentance, according to the Sages, brought about acquittal and purity, allowing men and women to come close to God. The central meaning of atonement was this 'at-one-ment'.[2]

In the course of Jesus's ministry, we find him expressing a purer Hebrew prophetic tradition which required a change of heart rather than an external ritual. He said of Mary Magdalene: 'Her sins, which are many, are forgiven, for she loved much.' Critics who question the Scriptural origins of the Catholic sacrament of penance cite several examples—the woman taken in adultery, the prodigal son, the penitent thief, Peter's forgiveness for his denial of Christ—demonstrating the absence of an external agent, a priest or confessor, serving as mediator. James and John spoke of the need for all Christians to tell each other their sins.[3]

The principal rite of absolution of sins in the early Church was baptism, which was bestowed on adult converts. Baptism washed away the original sin of Adam and Eve. Atonement for sin had been achieved once and for all with Christ's sacrifice on the cross and was now completed for each individual in the waters of baptism. Nor was candidacy for baptism made easy. Catechumens—those preparing for Christian membership—were obliged to submit to long periods of prayer and austerity, and even to call on the services of official exorcists to cast out their demons.

Yet as the primitive Church grew and expanded, and members of the faithful fell by the wayside, rituals of reconciliation emerged as once-in-a-lifetime events. Christians often found themselves under threat and in a minority, fearful for their livelihoods and very lives. Those who committed serious crimes were a threat to the community. Christians were convinced, moreover, that Judgement Day would come sooner rather than later. Sinners stood in imminent danger of eternal damnation. In the early era of the Church, members of the faithful who had been excluded for grave sins were readmitted only after the completion of a series of painful public ceremonies.

The way back was harsh, melodramatic, and communal. Barefoot penitents—garbed in sackcloth, heads shaven, faces and skulls besmirched with filth—were summoned to approach the altar and the assembly's bishop at the beginning of Lent. After the congregation had chanted lengthy petitions to the saints, the penitents rose to confess their sins out loud: principally adultery, violence, and idolatry. In one ceremony the clergy and the laity cried out '*Indulgentia*' (Mercy), 'Release us from our misery!' 'Help all penitents!' St. Jerome wrote, of a widowed Roman penitent accused of adultery, 'The bishop, the priests, and the people wept with her. Her hair dishevelled, her face pale, her hands dirty, her head covered in ashes, she beat her naked breast and face with which she had seduced her second husband. She revealed to all her wounds, and Rome, in tears, contemplated the scars on her emaciated body.'[4] The readmission of penitents to the assembly, in many cases dependent on the communal decision of the congregation, traditionally took place on Maundy Thursday of Holy Week.

The evolution of ritual was not without problems. There were early rigorist groups who insisted that lapsed Christians should never be allowed re-entry. Casuistic arguments arose, especially over the circumstances of sexual sin—a focus of obsessive anxiety among early Christians. The influential second-century writer Tertullian, a lawyer by profession and a keen disciplinarian by temperament, was convinced that sex even between married couples polluted both body and soul. Women, moreover, constituted a permanent provocation to chastity. He saw them as indeterminate human beings. They were, as he expressed it in his *De Cultu Feminarum*, the 'Devil's Gateway', a breach in the citadel of the Church through which the secular world would enter to poison the chaste assemblies of male saints. Perpetual virginity in a woman was the highest virtue, in his view; even second marriage after widowhood was for him a kind of adultery. The delight of orgasm, he insisted, was shameful. 'In that final release of pleasure, do we not sense a loss of our very souls?' Tertullian argued that the principal sins—apostasy, idolatry, adultery, and homicide—were unforgivable, setting the scene not only for increasing exclusions from reconciliation, despite contrition, but debates about the extent and limits of adultery. So we find Bishop Cyprian of Carthage in 259 asking whether a consecrated virgin (a woman who had taken a vow of lifetime celibacy), guilty of a sin against chastity, was truly an adulteress, since she was not married. He concluded after much debate that she should suffer the same penalties as an authentic adulterer, as she had committed the sin against her spiritual spouse, Jesus Christ.[5]

ON A WINDSWEPT ROCK rising sheer out of the Atlantic some eight miles off the coast of Kerry, Ireland, stand the remains of a primitive monastery known as Skellig Michael, believed to have been founded in the sixth century. On this forbidding island, a community of monks lived a life of isolation, prayer, and penance for centuries. In such places, at the far-flung limits of Christendom, an early form of confession, as it would come to be known, was first practised.

With the invasions of the Visigoths and the Franks beginning in the fifth century, and the resulting breakdown of civil societies, the once-in-a-lifetime exclusions and elaborate reconciliations went into decline. Yet a form of repetitive, private contrition was emerging within monastic communities in Ireland, Scotland, and Wales, conducted by elders, abbots, and abbesses. The practice gradually spread outside the monastic setting as missionary monks from the north travelled south. This was the practice of 'auricular' confession in the making—confession 'into the ear of the confessor'. Hence the idea of sin as requiring the forgiveness of the community gave way to the confession of sins through the private ministrations of a confessor who might be a monk or a nun. A crucial difference between the old reconciliation and the new was the practice of confessing lesser, 'venial' sins as well as the grave, 'mortal' ones. The penances were no less harsh than in the past, but they became more systematic as bishops, abbots, and leading missionaries developed sets of penitential 'tariffs', including sleep deprivation, fasts, exile, and pilgrimages (alone or in groups), for a range of sins. Christian fast days today, the Catholic tradition of not eating meat (but welcoming fish) on Fridays, and the popularity of pilgrimages echo the penitential practices of the second half of the first millennium of Christianity. At St. Patrick's Purgatory Island in Donegal, Ireland, pilgrims to this day practise self-mortifications reminiscent of the penances of the sixth century. They pray all night in the island's church; the next day, they walk barefoot on beds of rock, praying as they go. They eat only a single meal, dry toast washed down with black tea, in the course of three days and nights.

Manuals of these early tariffs came to be known as the 'penitential books'. Among the most influential was *The Penitential of St. Columbanus*, who founded monastic communities in France, Switzerland, and Italy to become one of the great European missionaries of his age. Writing in about 600, Columbanus emphasised not only the sins of action and omission, and offences against others and the community, but also mental sins. Even if one had only desired 'in thought' to kill, to commit fornication, to steal, to feast in secret and be drunken, or to strike someone, he said, 'let him do penance for the great ones half a year, for the lesser ones forty days on bread and water.' He warned, moreover, 'just as we must beware of mortal and fleshly sins' before approaching the Eucharist, 'so we must refrain, and cleanse ourselves from interior vices and the sicknesses of the ailing soul before the covenant of true peace and the bond of eternal salvation.'[6]

As in the early centuries of the Church, the penitentials focused on sins of the flesh, which merited abstinence from intercourse for the married. In Columbanus's penitential, expiation of the sin of adultery in which a layman had begotten a child by another's wife required 'three years refraining from the more appetizing foods and from his own wife'. If a layman committed fornication 'in a sodomite fashion, that is, has sinned by effeminate intercourse with a male', the penance was seven years: 'for the three first on bread and water and salt and dry produce of the garden, for the remaining four let him refrain from wine and meat'. The regard for modesty in the teaching of Columbanus was extreme: '. . . if anyone, even while sitting in the bath, has uncovered his knees or arms, without need for washing dirt, let him not wash for six days, that is, let that immodest bather not wash his feet until the following Lord's Day.'[7]

The writer of the *Bigotian Penitential* of the eighth century was preoccupied with masturbation. If a priest by sinful thoughts 'has caused his sperm to flow', he must fast for a week. If he 'touches his member with his hand', he shall do penance for three weeks. 'He who often causes his sperm to flow by passionate thoughts', wrote the author, 'shall do penance for twenty days.' And there is more: 'He whose sperm flows whilst he is sleeping in church, shall do penance for three days. If he stimulates himself, for the first offence twenty days, for the second one, forty; if more often, fasts shall be added.'[8]

Women were to suffer exclusions in certain circumstances. 'During their monthly period women should not enter a church nor receive communion', states the *Bigotian Penitential*. 'He who has intercourse with his wife during her monthly period shall do penance for twenty days.' A pregnant woman, moreover, 'must abstain from her husband for three months before childbirth, and during the period of purgation afterwards: that is, forty days and nights.'[9]

As the penitentials multiplied, so did attention to the role of the confessor. One penitential warns of the crime of

telling tales outside of the confessing relationship. Categories
of sins were also developed, drawing not only on the Ten
Commandments but also the Book of Leviticus, the Letters
of St. Paul, and the wisdom of the individual author of the
penitential. The Seven Deadly Sins, those capital sins categorised in the early Christian period as symptomatic of the
Fall, were constantly invoked: anger, avarice, sloth, pride,
lust, envy, and gluttony. Intentional acts were contrasted
with unintentional ones: if the desire to sin was frustrated
only by lack of opportunity, it was deemed equivalent to the
act itself. Premeditated crimes carried greater penances than
those done rashly. For example, a murderer who had planned
his crime would be exiled for ten years, whereas one who
killed in the heat of the moment suffered exile for six. A sin
that had become a habit was punished more severely than a
single instance.

The status of the sinner was also considered, based on
degrees of responsibility, privilege, and education. A bishop,
for example, was deemed to carry more guilt than a priest or
layperson committing the same sin. Allowances were made
for the sick, the unemployed, and the poor. A rich penitent
was allowed to pay a substitute to do his penance for him.

Pilgrimage, an increasingly popular penance, was based on
a belief in the power and presence of the relics of saints. The
bones of Sts. Peter and Paul attracted the faithful to Rome as
the centre of Christendom, although the Eternal City would
also vie with Jerusalem. But whereas Muslims are obliged to
journey to one destination, Mecca, for the fulfilment of their
pilgrimage, Christians from the earliest era had a variety of

holy destinations, including not only supposed burial places of saints but sites of supernatural apparitions and occurrences.[10] For example, it was believed that St. Michael the Archangel had manifested himself in a mountain cave on Italy's Gargano Peninsula in 490. St. John Chrysostom, the early Christian Father, recommended the shrine of Job's dunghill, where 'many undertake a long pilgrimage, even across the sea, hastening from the extremities of the earth, as far as Arabia, that they may . . . kiss . . . the ground of such a victor'. The site of the burning bush beneath Mount Sinai was also popular. By the ninth century, one of the principal pilgrim destinations after Rome and Jerusalem was Compostela in Galicia, where, according to legend, the headless body of St. James the Greater had been miraculously transported from Jaffa in a stone ship. From the many accounts of pilgrimage, these journeys created not only an occasion of penance, but a rich experience of diversion, merriment, and sexual adventure. In the spiritual trade-off of the times, pilgrims could expect to be offered food and comfort from the locals along the way in exchange for special graces and blessings. For many, pilgrimage became a way of life.

The penances imposed on kings and princes tell a story of conflict between throne and altar. William the Conqueror was ordered by Pope Alexander II to build the abbey at Battle to expiate the killing of King Harold in 1066. A spectacular imperial penance was performed in 1077 by Henry IV, Holy Roman Emperor. In a titanic political struggle between Pope Gregory VII and Henry over who took ultimate precedence in Latin Christendom, Gregory, one of the greatest reform-ing popes of history, took the awful step of excommunicating Henry, thus undermining his secular authority among the German princes, bishops, and people. Finding his situation as excommunicate ruler untenable, Henry travelled in the depths of winter to confront Gregory, who was lodged in the castle of Canossa in a high valley of the Apennines. For three days and nights, Henry knelt in the snow outside the castle, barefoot and dressed in a rough wool shirt, pleading for absolution and reconciliation in a self-imposed act of penance and contrition. As Gregory noted, the emperor's lamentations 'provoked all who were there or who had been brought news of what was happening to such great mercy, and such pitying compassion, that they began to intercede for him with prayers and tears of their own.'[11] The pope finally acquiesced, opened the gates, and absolved Henry with the kiss of peace.

In the following century, England's Henry II was obliged to do penance to expiate the murder of Thomas à Becket. On 12 July 1174 he publicly confessed his part in the crime and submitted himself to receiving blows across the back from all eighty monks of Canterbury Cathedral.

With the spread of auricular confession came supplements to the penitential books to help priests in their pastoral duties towards penitents. The writings of Peter Abelard, the French eleventh-century theologian and philosopher, provide insight into the discussions and debates over confession in the early Middle Ages. He complained of the ignorance of confessors who did not understand the nature of the sacrament, or who failed to inform the penitent of the grounds of forgiveness, and thereby deceived them. Anticipating the corrupt practices of the high and late Middle Ages, he lambasted those bishops who tended to waive the penances in exchange for alms. The seriousness of confession, involving the destiny of individual souls, raised questions about the spiritual status of confessors—their suitability to guide souls.[12]

Another figure who wrote compellingly on this theme during the eleventh century was Peter Damian of Ravenna, an ascetic Benedictine monk who became a bishop and cardinal. Although known to be gentle on penitents, he was severe in his criticism of lax clergy, excoriating bishops for such pastimes as playing chess, and denouncing heads of monastic houses for their luxurious lifestyles. In his *Book of Gomorrah*, he drew attention to the clerical sexual abuse of adolescent boys. From the context it is clear that he was speaking of religious houses and monasteries where boys were housed as oblates and novices. He also paid significant attention to the suffering of victims of sodomy. He advocated celibacy for all priests while attacking homosexuality, mutual masturbation, the practice of sexual acts between the thighs, and anal intercourse. He believed that unbridled lust was a cause of lunacy.[13]

Two

Confession into Its Own

Full swetely herde he confessioun.
—Geoffrey Chaucer's Friar Huberd, *The Canterbury Tales*

IN THE YEAR 1191 CARDINAL-DEACON LOTARIO DEI CONTI di Segni was elected pope at the age of thirty-seven, taking the name Innocent III. His initiatives to encourage confession would shape the sacrament and its influence for centuries to come. He would make confession obligatory under pain of mortal sin.

Innocent, born into a wealthy patrician family, was a skilled canonist who had studied law in Paris and Bologna. He announced from the outset that he would exert the spiritual rather than temporal powers of his office, but he had ambitions in both spheres. He brought into constant use the epithet 'Vicar of Christ'—a role, as he put it, 'set midway between God and Man'—signalling his determination to elevate the rule of the papacy over both altar and throne. His political weapons of choice were the interdict (censure) and excommunication. In his quarrels with King John of England over ecclesiastical and monarchical authority, he declared the country's celebrated Magna Carta null and void.

Innocent centralised Church authority, downgrading the authority of bishops. He sought to improve the discipline of the clergy both within and outside of monasticism, and he guardedly encouraged the activities of the preaching orders—the Franciscans and Dominicans. He called a Fourth Crusade, which resulted in the sack of Constantinople and the collapse of any hope of reconciliation between Latin and Byzantine Christendom. He initiated a military crusade against the heretic Cathars of southern France. They were anticlerical and had declared that the sacrament of penance was a false doctrine. They taught that Mary was conceived of Jesus through her right ear. Pope Innocent's attempts to coax the Cathars out of their heresies through eloquent preaching failed; nor could they simply be ignored, since a central theme of their beliefs was the evils of the papacy. Innocent's campaign against the Cathars led to the slaughter of many thousands and made way for the expansion of the Inquisition in subsequent pontificates.

Innocent was nevertheless convinced that the Cathar heresies indicated a thirst for religious revival which he believed he could satisfy with a tranche of devotional reforms. In 1215 he convoked the Fourth Lateran Council. Among its provisions was the decree that all the faithful must attend confession and receive Holy Communion once a year. First confession should be made 'on reaching the age of discernment' by all members of the faithful 'of either sex'. Those who failed to do their Easter sacramental duties were to be 'barred from entering the church in their lifetime and to be deprived of Christian burial at death'. A familiar verdict of history is that Innocent was exploiting confession to seek out heretics. Yet he also hoped to encourage spiritual renewal and to establish the role of the priest as spiritual director of individual souls.[1]

The Lateran Council had additional recommendations about the adequate supply of skilled confessors. Innocent sought to implement these by appointing 'masters of theology' in every diocese. Bishops were ordered to oversee the formation of good confessors: 'If a blind man leads a blind man', he reminded his flock, echoing the words of Christ in Matthew 15.14, 'both will slip into a ditch.' Innocent's initiatives resulted in a flurry of activity at local levels, but there was a gulf from the outset between the ideals he advocated and the realities on the ground. The establishment of an educated priesthood would take generations, and there were many bad habits to be eradicated. Poorly paid holders of benefices all too often absconded, leaving their parishioners in the care of inadequate substitutes.

Whatever the spiritual advantages, the obligation to go to confession or risk excommunication meant that the Church had created a new grave sin, a new way in which individual souls could be excluded from the Christian community and merit Hell. But the requirement of annual confession also saw the decline of the old penitential tariffs, which were now giving way to more benign penances, such as prayers, special devotions, and payment of Mass stipends. Auricular confession became the norm in the Latin West. Examination of conscience and repeated contrition for daily failures became an essential feature of the devout soul's journey to God. And with this shift came a new genre of handbooks, treatises, and *summas* for confessors, setting out the subtle gradations of sins, dimensions of intention, motives, levels of contrition, and authentic purposes of amendment.[2]

A typical consideration in such work was the threefold distinction between types of sorrow. A penitent, for example, might repine for having spurned God's love; or for shame at having sinned; or merely for fear of Hell. Theologians were now wont to mull over the degrees and efficacy of these contrasting motives for repentance, querying whether the less commendable motive—fear of punishment in Hell—was sufficient for absolution. The disputes on this score would lead to a clash between the two great philosopher-theologians, Thomas Aquinas and Duns Scotus. Both agreed that the priest in valid orders had a central role in confession. But whereas Aquinas argued that genuine contrition was as necessary for absolution as the priest's verbal formula, Duns Scotus insisted that the efficacy of the sacrament was dependent on the confessor's words alone.[3]

Theologians argued about the spirit, letter, and intention of Innocent's decrees. Was it necessary, for example, to attend confession if one had not committed a mortal, or grave, sin? And who was to judge whether a sin was venial or mortal? Some scholars insisted that the very raising of such questions demonstrated the crucial importance of obligatory annual confession. The confessor could thereby 'enquire diligently', as the Fourth Lateran Council had put it, into the state of the penitent's soul. Aquinas opined that while it should not be necessary, according to God's law, to attend confession when one was not in a state of mortal sin, there was nevertheless an obligation to satisfy Church law. But disobedience to Church law, he intimated, did not involve turning away from God— the *sine qua non* basis of mortal sin.

An issue of major importance, and a source of debate both at the time and in subsequent centuries, was the age at which first confession and communion should be made. Experts in canon law in France and Italy argued that the age of discretion was at puberty or thereabouts; most pastors, in practice, were not prepared to administer the sacraments to the members of their flock until they had reached 'marriage age'. This was generally taken to be at about fourteen, with minor local variations.[4]

Attendance at confession, even annually, was subject to many adaptations and exceptions across Western Christendom, depending on local traditions, the prejudices and convictions of pastors and bishops, and the existence of religious houses. Complying with the new rule was hardest in rural parishes with a single pastor. The parish priest's workload increased exponentially with the new decrees, especially during late Lent and Holy Week, since many parishioners left their sacramental duties to the last minute. Priests complained of having to hear as many as three hundred confessions in a single day, hardly an ideal circumstance for a good confession. The priest usually sat on a chair in the sanctuary, the penitent kneeling beside him or in front of him. There were unruly scenes when people refused to wait their turn, and there was a tendency among penitents to eavesdrop. Overwhelmed by the numbers attempting to avoid excommunication as Easter approached, some priests would simply give general absolution to the entire congregation without hearing their sins. The stipulation that the faithful should confess solely to their own parish priest proved problematic. The better-educated parishioners refused to be confessed by an ignorant local priest, preferring to go to a monastic confessor of good reputation. Many were reluctant to confess to a priest who was known to them within their tightknit community. In some villages parishioners refused to attend confession despite the levying of fines, the threat of imprisonment, and the risk of excommunication.[5]

Confession as an instrument of enforced secular and spiritual regulation had by the early Middle Ages become a dominant feature of Western Christianity. In 1199, Innocent had established the tribunals of the Inquisition, which obliged those suspected of heresy to answer, under oath, every question put to them. Failure to take the oath indicated guilt. The period saw a decline, moreover, in trials by combat or ordeal in criminal cases, with greater faith placed in the efficacy of investigatory confessions (as opposed to sacramental ones) to reach a verdict of guilt or innocence. Under both secular and canon law (where heresy was involved), torture was allowed in order to extract confessions in quest of evidence.

Within sacramental confession, confessors were being taught to quiz their penitents rather than simply listen. Confessional manuals reveal that priests in the medieval period were expected to cross-examine penitents in a forensic manner, especially where adultery, incest, and masturbation were suspected. Masturbation, the single greatest obsession of the confessional manuals, was judged a more serious sin than the abduction and rape of a virgin, or straightforward adultery with a married woman. The theory of its evils was based on the idea that sperm contained homunculi; to spill human seed was therefore tantamount to homicide. Male penitents who failed to admit to masturbating were to be relentlessly challenged.

Jean Charlier de Gerson, chancellor of the University of Paris, writing in the early fifteenth century, counselled confessors to say to a penitent: 'Friend, do you remember when you were young, about ten or twelve years old, your rod or virile member ever stood erect?' And the confessor should pursue the matter, he advised, with further questions: 'What did you do, therefore, so that it wouldn't stand erect?' Finally, the confessor might say: 'Friend, didn't you touch or rub your member the way boys usually do?' It occurred, of course, to some insightful writers of the confessional *summas* that such officious questions might actually put ideas into the heads of penitents, leading them into sin. Yet the risks, according to other pastoral theologians, were worth taking to save all those who were hiding that vicious secret sin to their eternal damnation. One of the tricks of the trade, according to Gerson, was to affect a nonchalance when suggesting the dreaded sin of self-abuse, as if it were not sinful, in order to extract the confession, and only then to condemn that behaviour as abominable.[6]

Handbooks for confessors proliferated, offering obsessional analysis on the hierarchies, divisions, and subdivisions of sins. Under the sin of lust, for example, the penitent was invited to ponder at which points on the rising scale of sinfulness they might have offended: from kissing and touching right through to the rape or abduction of a nun—a sin of fornication aggravated by sacrilege. The encouragement of this subtle inward scrutiny of faults prompted anxieties in penitents that they might make inadequate confessions, committing, in consequence, the dire sin of sacrilege. Epidemics of 'scruples' (obsessive anxiety over minor imperfections) broke out in some religious communities, particularly among younger religious. In his *Imitation of Christ*, Thomas à Kempis has a tendency to both encourage and repudiate scrupulosity: 'Often also a person is hindered by too great a solicitude for devotion, and by some anxiety or other about his confessions. . . . Do not abandon Holy Communion for every trifling perturbation[;] . . . spit out the poison quickly, and then make haste to take the antidote'. While many laypeople were finding it difficult to submit themselves to confession once a year, there were those in the religious life who, under the tyranny of scruples, a spiritual condition comparable to hypochondria in medicine, were resorting to the sacrament with morbid frequency. There were even moralists who declared that scrupulosity was a sin, thus leading the sensitive soul to a never-ending spiral of further scrupulosity.[7]

Obedience and submission to authority were emphasised in the manuals of ascetical theology: 'If one does not freely and gladly submit himself to his superior, it is a sign that his flesh is not yet perfectly under control; for it often rebels and murmurs', wrote one. Or, again: 'Never think you have made any progress, unless you esteem yourself inferior to all.' The principle of the submission and obedience of the wife to the authority of her husband had parallels with obedience to superiors in the religious life. A husband was entitled, without sinning, to beat his wife in moderation, but she sinned if she attempted to correct or thwart him. A disobedient wife was guilty of mortal sin. Drawing parallels with the obedience owed by children towards their parents, submission to authority was obligatory in professional and public life even if one's superiors were sinners. Hatred expressed towards a superior was deemed a mortal sin.[8]

A CLERICAL CLASS OF SPECIALIST CONFESSORS, chaplains, and spiritual directors arose to care for communities of nuns and for every kind of guild, confraternity, and civic or military group. Chaucer's Prioress, whom we can take as typical of her ecclesiastical type, travelled with three priests. Catherine of Siena in the fourteenth century was accompanied by a team of clerics, including the English Austin friar William Flete. Wealthy widows with pious tendencies would take on personal confessors whose authoritarian relationship was virtually equal to that of a husband. An example in the thirteenth century was Elizabeth Queen of Hungary and her confessor Conrad of Marburg, an enthusiastic inquisitor. Married at fourteen to Louis IV of Thuringia, Elizabeth bore three children, but her husband died of plague while away on crusade when she was twenty. Elizabeth devoted her life to building hospitals and caring for the poor. She was given to fasts, long prayer vigils, and bizarre self-mortifications, such as taking female lepers into her bed—believing them to be representatives of Jesus. Conrad, who confessed Elizabeth frequently, took control of her feats of asceticism, the length of her prayer marathons, the details of her abstinence, and the extent of her almsgiving. He dismissed her ladies-in-waiting and hired two severe women who would slap her face. He increased her natural tendency to engage in self-mortification, and even beat her himself on occasion. She seems to have emulated his example, as she once thrashed an old woman patient in her hospice for refusing to confess her sins. Elizabeth died at the age of twenty-four. Her corpse is said to have exuded an odour of sanctity, and a cult dedicated to her memory developed rapidly.[9]

Preoccupation with the examination of conscience, with guilt, and with the need to confess was widespread in convents and monastic settings in the late Middle Ages, but the tendency also erupted into the streets and piazzas. The thirteenth century had seen the emergence of widespread associations of holy women, such as the Beguines of Germany and the Low Countries, who devoted their lives to prayer, almsgiving, and care of the sick. Their spiritual lives centred on confession and dependence on their confessors. In time, many thousands of women would be identified with the movement. They were not members of religious orders, took no vows, and lived 'in the world'. They reported supernatural visions and were said to have attained the higher realms of contemplative prayer. Many of their confessors became literary witnesses to their mystical states. James of Vitry's *Life of Mary of Oignies* exemplifies the horror of their sense of even trivial sin, hence their desire to confess daily. 'If it sometimes seemed to [Mary] that she had committed a little venial sin, she showed herself to the priest with such sorrow of heart, with such timidity and shame and with such contrition that she was often forced to shout like a woman giving birth from her intense anxiety of heart.' Papal encouragement of the Beguine movement arguably aimed to create an antidote to heretical repudiation of the clergy and the efficacy of confession. Certainly the Beguines' self-mortifications equalled anything performed by the Cathars. In a similar spirit, groups of flagellants would beat themselves while journeying across Europe, eventually in processions of thousands, preaching the need for acknowledgement of sin and repentance.[10]

In the early fifteenth century, the so-called 'Apostle of Italy', Bernardino of Siena, travelled through the peninsula to call the faithful to confession, citing the sins of gambling, witchcraft, sodomy, and usury. Peripatetic confessors followed in his wake. Savonarola, the visionary preacher and prophet of doom, also called the faithful to confession. He wrote a manual for confessors, but was later found guilty of heresy. Eventually he was hanged and burnt at the stake in Florence.

Yet by no means did all Catholics, or even all potential saints, conform to obligatory confession. An example was Catherine of Genoa in the late 1400s, who appears to have exerted unusual power over her confessor, Fra Marabotto. He was on hand for much of her life as a supporter and adviser, but he tells us that for a period of twenty-five years she did not confess her sins once. She thus blatantly broke the conciliar decree threatening excommunication for non-attendance. Marabotto was evidently anxious about this situation, but Catherine explained to him that she did not think that she had committed a sin during all that time and therefore saw no need to confess. Catherine's story not only reveals the failure of the official church to control confession-going universally, but her capacity to make a distinction between canon law and personal conscience. She became famous for her tireless self-sacrifice, but her austerities and aptitude for self-harm were equally notorious. On one occasion, in a bid to show empathy for a patient in her hospital, and at the same time chastise herself for the sake of chastisement itself, she sucked the pus from a plague victim. Not surprisingly, she caught the plague herself, but she survived. Her treatise on Purgatory argued that it was not a terrible place, but one of longing for the face of God—consoled by the certainty that one would in time be united with Him.[11]

The doctrine of Purgatory in the Latin tradition of Christianity was well established by the end of the twelfth century following a gradual genesis of half a millennium. Its basic tenets would continue through to the third millennium. The notion of Purgatory depended on belief in an intermediate afterlife occurring between death and resurrection on the Last Day. Those souls that could not attain immediate entrance into Heaven by virtue of a sinless life, yet did not deserve eternal punishment in Hell, were destined for a place where their 'venial', less grave sins were purged through suffering. The notion of 'venial' sins, and their contrast with 'mortal' sins, was confirmed and settled by the doctrine of Purgatory. During a person's life on earth, according to the emerging doctrine, it was possible to mitigate due suffering in the afterlife through prayers, pilgrimage, indulgences, and financial payments. Meanwhile, the living could employ the same penitential means (as well as purchased Masses) to intercede for purgatorial reductions on behalf of the dead. Belief in Purgatory endowed the Church, and the papacy, in particular, not only with extra spiritual powers, but with significant additional revenues. Much of the money was pocketed by members of the mendicant preaching orders, who were enthusiastic proponents of the doctrine. Indulgences, sanctioned by Rome, were not equivalent to absolution, but with the appropriate payment they could relieve an absolved penitent of remaining time in Purgatory. The indulgences could also be assigned to the dead, although not to those in Hell. Many of the faithful were sceptical about the efficacy of indulgences, which were seen as a kind of spiritual protection racket.[12]

———

THE LATE MIDDLE AGES saw the widespread spawning of criminal confessors. Chaucer, again, gives us an exemplar of the confessor-rascal. His Friar Huberd is a hypocrite who exploits his eloquence both to preach and to sexually seduce. Chaucer intimates that Huberd's chief interests are making money and having sex. He has a lurid past, having married off a number of women he made pregnant. He sells his absolutions, persuading his victims that his 'power of confession' is greater than that of a parish priest. And the more money paid out, the more efficacious the forgiveness: 'Instead of weeping and prayers, men should give silver to poor friars', he says. He spends his money on trinkets, which he keeps in his cowl to give to 'young wives'. Although a mendicant by vocation, he squanders money on fine vestments, rich food, and alcohol. The Friar has no time for the poor or the sick, preferring the company of traders and landowners. Chaucer makes it clear that he is not depicting all priests and confessors as corrupt. His Parson of a Town—'First he wrought and then he taught'—reveals the Friar's opposite. The Parson's

Tale is a homiletic 'meditation' on sin and the sacrament of confession, and significantly, it ends the telling of the tales.

Criminality among confessors was widespread and entrenched by the fifteenth century, as the records of ecclesiastical courts abundantly testify. Take the case of confessor Alonso de Valdelomar, of Almodóvar del Campo in Spain, who was brought before the ecclesiastical tribunal of Alcalá de Henares for rape, consorting with prostitutes, and gambling. Like Chaucer's friar, Fra Alonso had demanded money before hearing a confession, and he would withhold absolution if the sum fell below his expectations. He was also in the business of selling indulgences that 'were no longer valid'. Here, in 1520, is Antonio de Pareja of Cienpozuelos, whose behaviour was typical of that cited by reformers during the rising tide of Protestantism. Father Pareja was in the habit of soliciting his women penitents for sex. He cohabited with one of them in his priest's house, but threw her onto the street after she gave birth to his child. His accusers informed the tribunal that he had extorted money for celebrating Masses and had routinely broken the seal of confession. It emerged in witness statements that Pareja's 'evil and unscrupulous' pastoral style had led to most of the parish neglecting not only confession but even Sunday Mass.[13]

Take the case, in the same era, of the friars of San Bernardino at Chiari in the diocese of Brescia, Italy. The municipal leaders complained of the 'improprieties' the friars had committed while hearing the confessions of women in the privacy of their monastic cells. Then there was the priest of Gorgonzola who solicited sex from two female penitents at the same time. Or the charges against the parish priest of Limido, Father Geronimo Di Luciani: too lazy to hear confession, he would leave his parishioners unshriven even on their deathbeds. He was denounced to the local bishop for his gambling, cursing, and womanising.[14]

A Jesuit priest, Father Giacomo Carvajal of Milan, who was commissioned to write a report on the state of confession in his diocese in the mid-sixteenth century, before the Counter-Reformation got under way, expostulated that the abuses and corruption in the practice of confession in previous eras were too many to enumerate. In some rural areas, confessions had been heard by clerics in minor orders, or even by laypeople. The form of the sacrament was frequently ignored. Priests gossiped about what they had been told in confession. Money changed hands, bad advice was given, and heretical teachings imparted.[15]

At the dawn of the Reformation, however, there were other, more spiritual and theological objections to the sacrament arising from the spread of humanist thinking. Early in the reign of Henry VIII we learn, for example, of groups of earnest students who would meet at the White Horse tavern in Cambridge to argue about religion and discuss the ideas of Desiderius Erasmus, the Dutch Christian humanist. Like many other students and scholars in Europe, especially in the Low Countries and in Germany, these Cambridge students were excited by the stirrings of dissent within the Church. They looked forward to the prospect of offering the Scriptures in the vernacular to the people, and they wanted to purge religion of the excesses of control, violence, and superstition, including relics, alleged miracles, chantry Masses (commissioned at a cost for the souls of specific individuals), idolatry, and the sale of indulgences. Their dissatisfaction with the doctrinal basis of confession was a central contention, in particular the insistence on the mediation of the priest. There were suggestions that confession was unscriptural, blasphemous even: that the priest was coming between the soul and God. Thomas Bilney, one of the Cambridge leading lights, declared that on reading Erasmus, he believed he had 'met Jesus for the first time'.[16]

Erasmus, who never abjured his Catholicism, had written in his *Pietas Puerilis* that confession was not an authentic sacrament but an artificial, legal construct of the Church. The form of the book is a conversation between two students, Gaspar and Erasmillus. Gaspar insists that there is no need for a priest, no need of absolution: sins are forgiven when the penitent makes a direct act of contrition to Jesus Christ. The text brings to life the dissident conversations of the time.[17]

Erasmus and his followers would do much to lay the intellectual groundwork for the Protestant challenge to confession. Meanwhile, John Calvin was preaching in Switzerland against confession as a kind of butchery (*carnificina*). In Germany Martin Luther made a frontal attack on the theology of confession with the publication in 1520 of his treatises on the priesthood and the sacraments. That same year, he held a public burning of the *Angelica*, an important confessors' manual. The following year he wrote his *On Confession: Whither the Pope Has Power to Command It*. Priests, he taught, do not have the power to forgive sins; it is not penance that justifies us in the eyes of God, but faith. The Fourth Lateran Council, he declared, was 'the greatest plague on earth, through which [Rome has] bewildered the consciences of all the world, brought so many souls to despair, and degraded and oppressed all mankind's faith in Christ.' Confession, he went on, is a kind of rape, and the pope is the Antichrist who 'breaks open the bridal chamber of Christ and makes all Christian souls into whores.'[18]

Christendom was beginning to fragment, and the sacrament of confession, as defined and legislated by Rome, was a crucial centrifugal impetus. In England the question of the validity of confession was heatedly debated between the conservatives, who said the sacrament was instituted by Christ, and evangelicals such as Thomas Cranmer, archbishop of Canterbury, who said it was a human institution. The doctrinal disputes and antagonisms would soon become violent. During the reign of Elizabeth a few decades later, Catholic confessors would be hung and then drawn and quartered for hearing the confessions of devout Catholics.[19]

Three

Confession and the Counter-Reformers

So many abuses and such grave diseases
have rushed upon the church of God
that we now see her afflicted almost to
the despair of salvation.

—Secret report on the need for a Church council, commissioned
by Pope Paul III in 1536, quoted in John W. O'Malley,
Trent: What Happened at the Council

OR TWO DECADES OF THE MID-SIXTEENTH CENTURY, THE ancient walled city of Trent, high in the bracing air of the Tyrol, was the scene for the Church of Rome's response to the laxities and corruptions within Latin Christianity and the grievances and challenges of the Protestant reformers. A favoured Protestant metaphor speaks of the Council of Trent as the point at which Western Christendom broke into a delta of separated streams, with the Roman flood carrying off the filth and flotsam of the Middle Ages. Rome, however, speaks of that Council as the majestic continuation of Christianity's authentic mainstream, from which the Protestant churches broke away in heretical discontinuities.[1]

Pope Paul III had for eight years attempted to find the ideal location for the Council. Mantua, Piacenza, and Cambrai had been suggested and rejected. Trent held appeal because it was at a midpoint between the Papal States and the Germanic imperial territories. On 13 December 1545, the assembled prelates celebrated Mass in the city's Duomo, invoking the guidance of the Holy Ghost. There were four cardinals, including the Englishman Reginald Pole; four archbishops; twenty-one bishops; five heads of religious orders; and some fifty theologians and canon lawyers. The numbers would expand in time. It was a French prince of the Church, Cardinal Jean de Lorraine, who called on the assembly to acknowledge its responsibility for Christendom's woes: 'Whom shall we accuse my fellow bishops? Whom shall we declare to be the authors of such great misfortune? Ourselves; we must admit that much with shame and with repentance for our past lives.' Cardinal Pole declared, 'We ourselves are largely responsible for the misfortune that has occurred—because we have failed to cultivate the field that was entrusted to us.' Before departing from the council, he pleaded with the participants to read the works of 'our adversaries' with an open mind. They should not conclude, moreover, that because Luther said it, 'therefore it is false'.[2]

There were those who believed that the Council would last no longer than a few weeks. But it would take eighteen years for the conciliar documents to be signed off. There were to be fierce arguments, protracted suspensions, expressions of nationalistic hubris, even physical attacks. When a Franciscan bishop called a Neapolitan prelate a knave and a fool, the indignant Italian pulled out a fistful of the bishop's beard. In time the Council would settle down peaceably enough. Its work would shape the ethos and discipline of the Catholic Church for the next three hundred years and beyond.

There was a total of twenty-five sessions in three great sittings. The main business was to condemn Protestant heresies while clarifying Catholic orthodoxy across a broad span of doctrines. High on the agenda, and with the practice of confession in mind, was an insistence that the clergy should be better educated; seminaries must be established for clerical formation, with minor seminaries starting at the age of twelve. The disciplines for religious orders, male and female, were to be tightened. The roles of enclosure (keeping monastic inmates in, and the laity out) would be enforced to preclude the lax and scandalous habits that had developed through the Middle Ages. Nuns were instructed to make their confessions at least once a month.

Deliberations on confession began in earnest when the Council fathers moved temporarily to Bologna in 1547–1548, with the deficiencies of confessors topping the list of priorities. The bishop of Bologna, chairing the discussion, remarked: 'If we take pains to expel the wicked and ignorant priests, we can easily restore Christianity to its old splendour and dignity; if not, we will waste our energy in devising regulations and statutes.'[3]

The proceedings continued back at Trent, leading to the completion of the fourteenth session of the Council—which stated that confession had been given 'great consideration . . . so great are the number of errors relative to this sacrament'. Absolution and penance were necessary at all times for all men 'who had stained themselves by mortal sin'. The acts of the penitent, namely, contrition, confession, and satisfaction (making good the consequences of the crime, with reparation and penance), constituted the 'matter', which brings about 'reconciliation' with God as well as 'serenity of conscience and exceedingly great consolation of spirit.' The Council condemned the Protestant claim that forgiveness of sin was principally a question of faith rather than penance. For those who objected that confession created a sin-confession-sin cycle, the Council decreed that true contrition must be accompanied by 'the purpose of not sinning in the future'.

Against critics such as Erasmus, who taught that contrition in one's heart was sufficient for God's forgiveness, the Council declared that although perfect contrition might well reconcile a soul to God before the penitent performed the sacrament, 'a desire of the sacrament' was also essential. It was granted that, though fear of Hell was 'imperfect' (a kind of contrition labelled 'attrition'), such fearful sorrow was nevertheless 'a gift from God' and would prepare a soul for the desire for justice and the reception of God's grace.

Complete confession of all 'mortal sins', one by one, to a priest, who sat as judge and healer, was necessary for valid absolution, hence the need for 'diligent self-examination'.

Venial, or lesser, sins should be told in confession as a matter of piety, but might be omitted in confession without guilt. The Council confirmed that confession 'should be complied with by each and all at least once a year when they have attained the age of discretion.' Like the Fourth Lateran Council, the Council of Trent left the age of 'discretion', in actual years, unstated.

The enforcement of the decrees of the Council fell to the bishops and religious orders of the Church. Some were more creative and rigorous than others. Given the vast and complex cultural, social, and political differences across the continent, the Council hardly could have imposed universal conformity even had it tried. The obligation to go to confession on pain of excommunication, laid down at the Fourth Lateran Council, was reaffirmed. Registers were to be kept by parish priests. Failure to attend annual confession could mean answering to the Inquisition.

Within the diversities peculiar to local and national conditions, and against the background of hostility between Protestant and Roman Catholic communities, confession became a test of inclusion or exclusion across Europe. In the 1550s, not long after the fourteenth session of the Council, Duke Albrecht V of Bavaria used military troops to suppress Lutheranism within the region by imposing obligatory attendance at confession. Neighbours were encouraged to report on non-confessing fellow parishioners.[4] Elsewhere in Germany, in Passau and Geisenhausen, parishioners refusing to attend the sacrament were jailed.

In England, where Mary Tudor had acceded to the throne
in 1553 after the brief, iconoclastic Protestant reign of Ed-
ward VI, and Roman Catholicism was reimposed, mandatory
confession became a test of allegiance to the Crown and a
token of reconciliation with the old faith. During the Lent
of 1555, every adult in the country was instructed to confess
to their local parish priest—to 'reconcile themselves to the
churche' before Easter. An instruction issued by the bishops
warned that should any of the faithful disobey, 'every one
of them shall have process made ageynst him, according to
the Canons . . . for which purpose the pastors and curates of
every parysche . . . [are] to certify me in writing of every mans
and womans name that is not so reconciled.'[5]

In the archdiocese of York, priests were ordered to enquire during confession about specific articles of faith—
belief in the real presence of Christ in the Eucharist, the
supremacy of the pope, justification by faith alone or
through the sacraments—in order to detect lingering heresy. A measure of the strict enforcement, in May 1556 at
least fifteen Kentish people, such as carpenters, weavers,
and farm labourers, were arrested for what were deemed
heretical opinions and failure to confess. Five of them died
of starvation in jail by November of that year. Ten were
burnt at the stake in January 1557.[6] More fortunate were the
many other recalcitrant 'heretics', guilty of such crimes as
refusing to look at the elevated Host during Mass, who were
merely punished with public humiliation. One Margaret
Geoffrie of Ashford was forced to kneel in the chancel of the

parish church holding a rosary—symbol of Roman Catholic devotion—and disporting herself with reverence before the rest of the congregation.

It was all in vain. Under Elizabeth, who succeeded Mary in 1558, Catholicism became synonymous with Spanish and Popish treachery. Some 200 Catholics were executed in her bid to overturn Mary's reversion to the Catholic faith, 123 of them priests condemned as spies working in the interests of a foreign power. This was the era of priest-holes—secret hiding places in Catholic homes—and Jesuits flitting from house to house with the Eucharist. For the Elizabethan authorities, confession, with its seal and secrecy, enabled priests to encourage treason by 'reconciliation' among subjects who might well appear outwardly obedient to the state.[7]

———

AMONG THE ITALIAN PRELATES present at the Council of Trent was a cardinal who led a thoroughgoing reform of confessional practice throughout Roman Christendom. Cardinal Charles Borromeo has been credited with inventing the confessional box—an iconic piece of church furnishing to this day. Speaking to his diocesan priests, Borromeo would declare that confessors 'have the souls in their hands, as it were, and "speak to Jerusalem's heart."'[8]

Borromeo was endowed from birth with many ecclesiastical and aristocratic privileges. Nephew of Pope Pius IV, he had received the clerical tonsure at age eight, and at twelve he became the titular abbot of a monastery, which he attempted to reform with juvenile zeal. Tall, exceedingly thin, with an unusually prominent aquiline nose, Charles was awarded the red hat at the age of twenty-two and appointed Secretary of State to the Holy See. He was ennobled and wealthy in his own right, but the Church loaded him with even more titles and wealth. He became archbishop of Milan, protector of Portugal and Lower Germany, legate at Bologna, and archpriest of Santa Maria Maggiore in Rome. He was also granted many parish benefices. Nevertheless, it was said at his funeral that he slept on straw and adopted a regime of austerity and self-denial. Scholar, theologian, and canonist, he was an outstanding administrator in the preparation and proceedings of the Council. These abilities, in combination with a natural charisma and reputation for holiness, put him in good stead as he entered the archdiocese of Milan in September 1565.[9]

Milan was a vast province stretching from the Veneto to the Swiss Alps. The archdiocese, comprising eight hundred parishes, was in crisis, its priests sunk in ignorance (some knew so little Latin that they could not pronounce the words of absolution, let alone understand them). There were clerics in minor orders—in other words, not ordained priests—who heard confessions invalidly. Borromeo's hagiographer, Giovanni Giussano, wrote that the cardinal realised that his clergy 'could not have been more scandalous nor serve as a worse example.'[10] Priests wore lay clothes, carried weapons in public, and lived openly with their mistresses. Many priests were absentee pastors, either abandoning their benefices or letting them out to hire. Priests, Giussano wrote, were 'mean and almost detestable'. Their churches were often leased as storage barns for the crops of Lombardy; monasteries were available for hire as venues for balls and weddings. Calling a series of synods, councils, and other meetings with the heads of religious orders and auxiliary bishops, Borromeo moved to enforce the decrees of the Trent with vigour. First he focused on confession, for this, in his view, was a sacrament that involved more engagement between clergy and faithful than any other. It was a sacrament, he believed that had scope for far-reaching social and moral renewal.

In 1565 Borromeo commissioned the Jesuits in Milan to write a treatise, entitled 'On the Examination of Confessors', to explore the best way of ensuring the authentic administration of the sacrament and protecting the rite from future scepticism. Foremost in his mind was the issue that had driven the Donatist heresy of the fourth and fifth centuries: the belief that sacraments performed by a priest in a state of mortal sin were invalid. Theologians in the Middle Ages had insisted on the principle *ex opere operato*— that the state of a priest's soul did not affect the efficacy of the sacraments he bestowed. Yet dissatisfaction with sinful confessors, leading to widespread anticlericalism, had been cited as a chief reason for neglect of confession and a consequent decline in Mass attendance, participation in the Eucharist, and other devotions throughout the fifteenth and sixteenth centuries. As one parishioner in the diocese put it bluntly: 'I don't want to confess to one who is more of a sinner than I am'.[11]

While conscious of the need to avoid the Donatist position, Borromeo concentrated on the education and formation of future priests. There would be careful recruitment of candidates for the priesthood, frequent examinations, and chastisement of those who erred. And there would be visitations of parishes and religious houses, regular reports on progress, and tribunals for complaints. Above all, Trent had called for episcopal control of confessors, whether they were parish priests or monks and friars. Supervision and transparency were to be the order of the day. In Milan, which promoted itself as a model for dioceses throughout the Catholic world, special examinations were established for confessors. Only those who passed could receive a written licence to administer the sacrament.

Crucial to Borromeo's strategy was the publication of his *Avertenze* (Admonitions) to confessors in 1574.[12] These instructions outlined the scope of the bishop's authority—his right to set standards, impose conformity, reserve to the bishops the absolution of certain sins (especially those of priests), and withdraw licences, or 'faculties', to hear confessions. The instructions stressed the avoidance of familiar medieval abuses, such as sexual solicitation, sale of absolution, loose living, and ignorance of canon law. Borromeo was shaping a professional class of clergy which in time would be known as 'Tridentine' clericalism. His ultimate aim was to improve the spiritual lives of the faithful. Confession, for Borromeo, provided a window onto individual consciences, a crucial means of improving the moral lives of the faithful, which in turn, he believed, would improve civil society.

Mindful of widespread sexual abuse in the practice of confession, Borromeo resorted to a practical scheme to prevent confessors and penitents from coming into contact in the course of administering the sacrament. Before Trent, as we have seen, the priest would sit on a chair with the penitent at his feet—thus making it easy for the confessor to touch the penitent, and for the penitent to lean on the lap of the confessor. At times the confessor would hold the penitents' hands, or even encourage an embrace. Absolution, moreover, usually ended with the priest laying hands on the head of the penitent; eye contact was common, as evinced by warnings against its dangers in the medieval confessional manuals. The physical, potentially tactile, face-to-face proximity of the confessional relationship had offered ample opportunity for intimacy, and therefore 'occasions of sin'. Cases against soliciting confessors had come before the inquisitors involving kissing, touching penitents' breasts, and mutual masturbation during the very administration of the sacrament.[13]

We get an impression of the state of affairs in a report to the Roman Curia written in 1575 by Borromeo's former assistant, Niccolò Ormaneto: 'From all sides zealous people approach me to lament the great abomination of many impious men who violate the sacrament of penance by attempting to satiate their unbridled and bestial appetite with their spiritual daughters, during or outside the act of confession.'

Ormaneto faced the stark fact that it was not worldly pursuits alone—such as drinking, dancing, and immodest speech and dress—that acted as occasions of concupiscence, but the circumstance of the sacrament of confession itself.[14]

Against this unseemly background, Borromeo now commissioned an item of church furniture to set a physical barrier between confessor and penitent. In 1576, members of the faithful entering the Duomo in Milan were struck by the presence of several unfamiliar wooden booths. The confessional box had arrived. Borromeo's text on their design is to be found in a set of special instructions (*Instructiones fabricae et supellectilis ecclesiasticae*). The confessional was composed of a chair for the confessor and a kneeler for the penitent. The confessor was enclosed by wooden panels on three sides, but there was a door (or doors) left open into the body of the church, so that he would be on view to the faithful. The panel that divided the confessor from the penitent had a grille and a curtain. The primary significance of the design was to show the confessor in his guise as judge, with the penitent kneeling before him in an attitude of contrition and humility. The grille and the curtain emphasised 'custody of the eyes'. Although confessor and penitent communicated at close quarters, they were not meant to see each other (although an attentive confessor would have known who was entering the confessional next, or recognised the voice). The Borromeo confessional would be adopted throughout Western Europe, although it was to take a period of more than two centuries to become the norm; the expense of the items required for the box was an obstacle in the poorer parishes. Meanwhile, the habit of hearing confessions in the privacy of sacristies, the quarters of priests, and the cells of monks continued— although it was discouraged by diocesan bishops.[15]

Historians of ideas have pondered the significance of the confessional box as a symptom, or perhaps even a cause, of a shift in notions of the mind and self-consciousness at the dawning of the modern period.[16] According to this view, John Locke's description of the self as an 'empty cabinet' found its physical counterpart in the penitent's location in a cubicle. Isolation in the dark prompts a heightened sense of interiority. The confessional box thus encourages an image of the soul as essentially disembodied. In the dark box, penitents searched their consciences—those innermost thoughts known only to themselves and to God—sharing secrets with His representative, mediator, and judge on earth: the confessor. The advent of the dark box arguably prompted a shift of emphasis: from preoccupation with moral precepts and laws to an examination of subjective intentions; from the public or social nature of sin to the scrupulous examination of recollected motivation. Hence the confessional box had its part to play in a further shift within Catholicism from a consequentialist morality to interiorised, 'casuistic' soul-searching.

The box was meant to bring an end to the scandal of sexual solicitation, yet cases of sexual abuse of women brought against confessors appeared to be on the increase even as the Borromeo confessional became more widely used. This increase may well have been due to improved reporting of such incidents, especially in Spain. By 1561 Pope Pius IV had given permission to the Spanish Inquisition to prosecute the 'crime', as opposed to the 'abuse', of seducing women sexually in the confessional—*sollicitatio ad turpia*. But there was independent and general evidence that such sexual attacks were occurring despite, and perhaps even because of, the emergence of the dark box.

At a time when priests were being called to strict discipline in matters of chastity, celibacy, and sins of impurity, the new confessional apparatus was to become—for many confessors, it appears—a provocation to unchastity. Borromeo's *Avertenze* clearly acknowledged as much, warning that a confessor could find his 'soul stained after hearing the filth of others.' The advice is reminiscent of Jonathan Swift's satirical evocation in *Tale of a Tub* of the confessional box as a 'whispering office' for the purpose of 'evomition'. It was widely recognised that within the privacy of the confessional booth, the whispered sins, especially of married women—and especially the details of the bedchamber, recounted under cross-examination—could inflame the imagination of a confessor, leading to 'occasions of sin' on his part. Cardinal Thomas Cajetan, Luther's great antagonist, had warned confessors of the danger of probing too deeply into a penitent's sexual life. They should employ modest euphemisms: 'If . . . a woman confesses to having been known outside the natural vessel, this suffices; it should not be asked in what part of the body.' The Borromeo box, for all its physical barriers, still allowed for whispered pillow talk in the dark: the penitent's voice and breath up close to the confessor's ear. Many married women, suffering from domestic and marital frustrations, became addicted to the atmosphere of crepuscular intimacy. Confessors, for their own reasons and circumstances, were equally vulnerable. As the provost of Santa Fedele, a new Jesuit church in Milan, noted (arguing that the penitent should not face the grille full on, but sideways to it), there were distinct dangers in the circumstance of a 'woman's mouth being close to the confessor's ear'.[17]

IN THE CENTURIES FOLLOWING the Council of Trent, a variety of ecclesiastical and secular tribunals across Europe, including episcopal chancellories, the Holy Office in Rome, and the Spanish Inquisition, sought to enforce Trent's conciliar decrees. From Spain to France, Germany, and Italy, the surviving documentation provides an overview of the emotional and psychological dimensions of confessional practice even as bishops attempted to make confession a focus of regular Catholic practice and constrained clerics to new standards of discipline. In Spain, the scholarly work achieved by Professor Stephen Haliczer in the Archivo Histórico Nacional, especially in the Sección de Inquisición, is instructive. Haliczer, who presented his findings in *Sexuality in the Confessional: A Sacrament Profaned*, published in 1996, offers an insight into the broad scope of the problem of sexual solicitation. His research involved thousands of cases in this most Catholic of countries. The friars, or mendicant preaching orders (Franciscans, Dominicans, Carmelites, and Augustinians), were the greatest offenders. This is not surprising, given their licence to wander far and wide, largely free of episcopal jurisdiction. The friars had extensive access to convents of nuns, whose numbers in Spain increased from 25,000 in 1591 to 33,000 in 1747. Nuns, being obliged to make their confessions monthly, now had more frequent contact with confessors. Given the economic and familial pressures that sent many women reluctantly into the cloister, and given, moreover, the harsher rules of enclosure and asceticism laid down by the Council of Trent, it is not surprising that problems arose within the confessor-penitent relationship in religious communities of women. The Council of Trent had not only imposed virtual imprisonment on religious orders of women, but had also deprived them of sensory and imaginative stimuli. Even as Baroque music and painting flourished outside their walls, many communities were forbidden even to sing the Divine Office, or to display pictures and sculpture. From a twentieth-century perspective, it is clear that the dependency associated with transference in psychotherapy was common. It was customary for confessors to speak of penitent nuns as their 'spiritual daughters', and in one Venetian convent there was talk of 'marriages' taking place between friars and nuns. One Don Apollinario of Ravenna, giving witness to a tribunal, remembered how a Don Gregorio 'was given a nun as his spiritual friend, and apparently gave her a ring and they carried out certain ceremonies.'[18]

In a book for confessors published in 1644, Alonso de Andrade in Spain warned his readers that nuns became obsessed with their confessors, so much so 'that they neither thought nor spoke of anything else.' By the same token, a predatory confessor could carry out his attempted and successful seductions on vulnerable women unobserved. Mary Laven's study of nuns in Venice, where there were more than fifty convents during the early modern period, reveals the extent of the depravity of some convent chaplains even during the first flush of the Counter-Reformation. A contemporary commentator, Ippolito Capilupi, declared that one confessor-seducer existed 'alone, like a great Turk in his Seraglio'. Giovanni Pietro Lion (later beheaded for his crimes) had spiritual charge of a convent of four hundred nuns on the Giudecca. Capilupi wrote: 'When he confessed one of the nuns whom he liked, he would in the very act of confession try to draw her to his will with some pre-prepared speech, and by placing his hands upon her in order to excite the carnal appetite in her more readily; and if he found her at all opposed to his advances he would praise her greatly for her strength and constancy, and would seek to have her understand that he was moved to try her as a test of her goodness.'[19]

The phenomenon of sexual solicitation in the confessional during this period is perhaps inseparable from the background of clerical frustrations, inadequacies, and stress. Alcoholism among mendicant confessors was common. Take Fra Gaspar de Nájera, who, reportedly drunk in the middle of the day, attempted to seduce a fifteen-year-old girl in confession, then followed her from the church back to her home. Only after soliciting sex from nine female penitents was he brought before the Inquisition. In another case, reported to the tribunal in the Canaries in 1784, Fra Antonio de Arvelo, a highly intelligent scholar, was said to be so bored with hearing confessions under obedience to his superiors that he took to the bottle. He would hear confessions lying in bed, the worse for drink. He confessed to the Inquisition tribunal that he tried to guess his penitents' sins before they confessed them. Eventually he was denounced for attempting to draw women penitents into his bed.[20]

Some parish priests were in the habit of hearing the confessions of sickly female penitents in their bedrooms. In the 1580s Fra Gabriel de Osca was accused of soliciting four female penitents while they lay ill in bed. On one occasion he offered to soothe one Lucia Hernandez of what ailed her, placing his hand under her shift. When the hand wandered to her thighs, she screamed. On other occasions he reversed the tactic and invited women into his bedroom, where he allegedly lay sick, from which vantage point he was liable to pull the penitent into the bed with him.[21]

The Inquisition records show nevertheless that 41 per cent of solicitation cases in Spain in the seventeenth and eighteenth centuries were at least initiated from within the box. The presence of a screen did not stop assignations, and many of the confessionals were in any case rudimentary affairs. There were reports of screens full of holes, which allowed a priest to touch the faces of female penitents. We hear of a box in a Dominican convent which had a special opening so that the confessor could hold the hands of penitents. We have the story of José Borges of Valencia, who would use the confessional to make regular trysts with his lover. She would then meet with him later in the bedroom of the house of a widow friend of his. Then there was the prior of a Carmelite monastery in Ciudad Real who made dates within the secrecy of the box for subsequent meetings with his amour Maria Lopez Molina.[22]

Haliczer's study of sexual abuse in the confessionals of Spain puts the average age of women victims at twenty-seven. Children, whether boys or girls, were not abused in the confessional at that time only because the age of first confession was invariably after puberty. Outside of the confessional, however, we do see instances of sexual acts involving minors. For example, a Franciscan priest, José Nuela, was deprived by his superiors of the right to hear confessions after he was discovered masturbating in front of a young boy.[23]

Boys in the educational care of priests were not immune from abuse by priests, as shown by the scandal of the Pious Schools and their associated order of teaching priests, founded at the beginning of the seventeenth century in Rome by Father José de Calasanz. The harsh disciplinary regime, imposed mainly on boys from poverty-stricken families, can be surmised by Father Calasanz's warning that his priestly teachers should not draw blood from the noses and ears of their pupils, or leave bruises or cuts. One of the leading figures of the schools, a Father Stefano Cherubini, went beyond such masochistic punishments to engage in sexual abuse. We do not have the precise details of his activities, as he and his influential family burnt the documents that had been assembled to report him to the Holy Office. Calasanz, who was eventually canonized for his good deeds for poor youth, moved Cherubini from place to place, where he proceeded to reoffend.[24]

———————

ALTHOUGH CULPABLE PRIESTS and confessors appear to have gotten off lightly—with a suspension for a period of months or years from the right to hear confession—savage punishments were meted out to women who had confessed voluntarily or under torture to alleged sexual deviancy and witchcraft.

The Church had traditionally taught that masturbation was a more grievous sin than rape, since even in the case of rape, the semen was being deposited in nature's appropriate 'receptacle'. Female masturbation was deemed to yield a form of semen, too, according to the long accepted sexual biology of the period, hence the deed was every bit as evil as in the case of a self-abusing man. At the same time, mutual masturbation between women was held to be as wicked as sodomy between men. The Italian jurist Prospero Farinacci opined that when a woman 'behaves like a man with another woman she will be in danger of the penalties for sodomy and death.' Moreover, 'if she introduced some wooden or glass instrument into the [vagina] of another', she should be executed.[25]

In an attempt to clarify the true circumstances and morality of sexual acts between women, the late seventeenth-century Italian canonist Ludovico Maria Sinistrari wrote a treatise for the guidance of confessors. 'In practice, it is necessary for confessors to be able to discern the case in which women by touching each other provoke themselves to voluntary pollution and when they fall into the Sodomitical crime, in order to come to a judgment about the gravity of the sin.' Drawing a parallel between sodomitical men and women, he claimed that women with excessively large clitorises were capable of penetrating a female partner. Moreover, the enlarged clitoris, he argued, was a result of frequent masturbation from childhood. When a woman was suspected of 'sodomy' with another woman, he recommended that her clitoris be examined by a midwife. A large clitoris was taken as proof of the case, and the punishment was death by hanging followed by burning at the stake.[26]

As fear of witchcraft swept Europe with renewed vigour in the sixteenth and seventeenth centuries, affecting both Catholic and Protestant communities, confession was exploited to discover evidence of diabolism and sorcery in women. No doubt there was a small percentage of women who were practising benign magic, and an even smaller group engaged in maleficent magic, or *maleficium*. Yet of the thousands burnt at the stake (it is thought that as many as 65,000 women and girls were executed in Europe for witchcraft in the early modern period), the majority had been found guilty as a result of inquisitorial confessions obtained by torture, as opposed to sacramental confessions.[27]

Great doubt has been cast, in retrospect, on the existence of diabolism and witches' sabbaths—even some of the inquisitors of the day later questioned their earlier conclusions. Alonso de Salazar, having interrogated hundreds of alleged witches who confessed to diabolism, concluded in 1610 that their accounts were 'nothing but a chimera'. The Italian historian, the late Piero Camporesi, argued in his *Bread of Dreams* that the self-condemnation of many women in hunger-stricken areas of Europe was frequently affected by adulterated breads made with poppy seeds, mushrooms, and all manner of fruits, berries, and roots. The sixteenth-century Lombardy naturalist and doctor Girolamo Cardano, writing on the phenomenon of witches and sorceresses, observed that 'these wretched little women, living on herbs and wild vegetables . . . hardly differ from those who are thought to be possessed by the devil'. Even Joseph of Cupertino, who was eventually canonised as a saint, believed that he could fly, as did his devotees; yet the explanation for his flights probably owed more to his reputation as a 'maker of black bread' than supernatural impetus. Under cross-examination, women likely suffered a form of false recovered-memory syndrome, familiar to this day in cases of alleged ritual abuse. Above all, the accused women were routinely subjected to torture, a supremely unreliable basis for authentic confessions.[28]

One of the most remarkable confessors of the seventeenth century, and perhaps of any other, was the Jesuit priest Friedrich Spee, who blew the whistle on the Dominican inquisitors in Germany. A scholar and poet, he was employed by the bishop of Westphalia to hear the final sacramental confessions of women and girls, some as young as ten, before they were burnt to death. Eventually convinced that their extorted inquisitional 'confessions' were false, he wrote a tract, published in 1631, entitled *Cautio Criminalis* (Warning to Prosecutors). Writing anonymously and in eloquent Latin, he scorned the Inquisition and suggested that the judges should be liable for damages. Spee showed great courage in standing up to the era's tide of prejudice. His book made a significant contribution to the eventual decline and suppression of the witch trials. His readership, however, was less numerous than that of the popular *Malleus Maleficarum* (*Hammer of the Witches*) by the Dominican tormentors, which went through hundreds of editions in many languages. Spee was eventually discovered to be the author of the *Cautio* and was exiled to the Harz Mountains, where he ended his days writing elegiac poetry.[29]

———————

MANY 'HOLY WOMEN', known for their outlandish religious behaviour, including trances and excessive asceticism, also found themselves under investigation. Confessors played an important role protecting them from ecclesiastical censure. The era saw the blossoming of high spiritual aspirations, especially within austere religious orders. St. Teresa of Avila became an outstanding reformer in her order of Carmelites while pursuing her own personal spiritual perfection. Her efforts led to a form of mystical abandonment which was described by her fellow Carmelite, St. John of the Cross, as the 'Dark Night of the Soul'.[30]

Teresa insisted that a good confessor was essential for progress in the spiritual life. She preferred, she said, an intelligent and scholarly confessor to an ignorant saint. She went through a number of confessors, not all of them convinced that she was an authentic mystic. One, Gaspar Daza, a saintly man given to missionary zeal and work among the poor, eventually refused to confess her. He thought her voices and visions were bizarre, if not the work of the devil. She commented on his departure: 'I do not think that my soul would have prospered.' He was followed by two Jesuits, one old and one young, who both reassured her that her visions were genuine. It was not until she met Father Juan de Prádanos, however, that she rose to new heights of mystical experience. The key to his confessional instruction was that she should abandon a particular friendship as a matter of self-denial. Following his advice, albeit reluctantly at first, she was granted an ecstasy that would be immortalised in Bernini's famous sculpture. 'There came upon me', she wrote, 'a rapture so sudden that it almost carried me away—something so sure that there could be no mistaking it. This was the first time that the Lord granted me the grace of ecstasy.'[31]

Unfortunately, Father Prádanos fell ill and died, but he was followed by yet another confessor, the youthful Father Baltasar Alvarez, who was inexperienced in the ambit of high spirituality. When Teresa reported fresh visions and voices, and in particular, the actual, physical presence of Jesus, he was sceptical. He recommended that she get out more, read more widely, and seek distractions. He became increasingly dubious about her experiences, suspecting that they were diabolical. He was finally convinced of her authentic mysticism, however, after he began to have visions himself. She would keep Father Baltasar for three years, but while he was absent for a period, she took on a substitute confessor, who was convinced that she was possessed by demons and in need of exorcism. With the return of Baltasar, she began to perform levitations, witnessed, it was said, by her community. Other advisers and confessors followed, including Peter of Alcántara (one day to be made a saint), who dwelt in a cell just four and a half feet in length, and who slept no more than an hour and a half a day, breaking his fast only once every three days. He kept constant 'custody of the eyes' to guard against lust, and wore a spiked 'discipline' around his middle. He was said to have given Teresa much spiritual comfort and confessed to her in turn. After his death, he continued to appear to her, offering further spiritual direction.[32]

A fine line between genuine mysticism and florid neuroses bordering on psychoses is manifest in the repertoire of strange stories that erupted during the period. Some religious women, such as Mary Magdalen de Pazzi, reported experiencing unbearably high temperatures (interpreted as the 'furnace of divine love'), stigmata, odours of sanctity, and visions of devils (one was said to sit on Teresa's breviary to distract her from prayer). Confessors, including highly placed prelates, at times administered spiritual direction to charismatic women who, by today's state of knowledge, were likely suffering from a range of illnesses—bulimia, anorexia, and forms of self-harm sufficiently injurious to make them bedridden, sometimes for years. The confessors wrote up curious, semi-hagiographical accounts of these subjects, often judging their symptoms—including visions, voices, and 'lights in prayers'—as on the borders of the diabolical and the authentic. It is perhaps no coincidence that the seventeenth century saw the initiation of Pope Urban VIII's 'scientific' procedures for canonization, a more empirical approach than was used in earlier centuries. A hundred years on, Pope Benedict XIV would draw up a list of saints who allegedly did not eat, attempting to distinguish between those who were holy women and those who were 'possessed'.[33]

Professor Rudolph Bell, in his 1985 book *Holy Anorexia*, argues that such borderline holy women exemplified the consequences of a new regime of male-dominant Tridentine clericalism; that women seeking the highest levels of sanctity, independent of the cloister and stricter codes of canon law, were driven neurotically in on themselves. Invariably such women had suffered from the envy, even hatred, of prelates who objected to their powers of spiritual insight and spiritual counselling. Whatever the case, their stories reveal a role in the early modern period for the confessor as diagnostician and therapist: now advising, now critiquing, the penitent as patient—hovering between adulation and suspicion, superstition and scepticism. Among the well-attested biographies, we find, for example, the seventeenth-century saint, Margaret Marie Alacoque, a French nun of Paray-le-Monial, who founded the devotion to the Sacred Heart of Jesus. Margaret would deliberately eat cheese knowing that it made her vomit, and by her own admission she ate the vomit of sister nuns.

––––––––––

HISTORIANS HAVE TENDED to impose a grand unifying narrative on the Counter-Reformation era, claiming widespread conformity of belief and practice, as if the Catholic faithful had begun to march in unified and disciplined step. Yet despite the powerful influence of the Council of Trent on Catholic orthodoxy and militancy for subsequent centuries, Catholic culture and practice were marked by considerable variety, local discretion, and original manifestations of vibrant religious and artistic imagination. Latin Christianity was in a process of revitalisation in every dimension of its life—including art, architecture, music, poetry, and spirituality.

New religious orders were founded that were prepared to engage a rapidly changing and expanding world. These included the Jesuits under Ignatius Loyola, and the Oratorians under Philip Neri. A new spirit of evangelism, and rivalry with Protestant opponents, drew Catholic missionaries to the Americas and the Far East. In almost aggressive rebuttal of the Protestant denial of the real presence in the Eucharist, the great Baroque churches drew the eyes of their congregations to the tabernacle at the centre of the high altar, where resided the 'sacred species' of the preserved Eucharist. Basilicas, cathe-drals, and other large churches boasted imposing and ornate confessionals.

Meanwhile, the drive to demonstrate Catholicism's posses-sion of the moral high ground would lead to intense academic explorations in moral theology. The major preoccupation of Catholic moralists was with distinctions between mortal and venial sin. Moral theology, following the Council of Trent, would focus with casuistic intensity on the refined complexi-ties of intentions and conscience. These approaches to moral and pastoral guidance would lead to heated conflicts between schools of moralists with far reaching consequences for the confessional.

Four

Fact, Fiction, and Anticlericalism

He who acts in obedience to a learned
and pious confessor, acts not only with
no doubt, but with the greatest security
that can be had upon earth,—on the
divine words of Jesus Christ, that he
who hears his ministers is as though
he heard himself: 'He that heareth you
heareth Me.'[1]

—Alphonsus Liguori, *The Way of
Salvation and of Perfection*, 1767

FROM THE FOURTH LATERAN COUNCIL IN THE THIRTEENTH
century to the Council of Trent in the sixteenth, and
beyond to the Vatican Council of 1869–1870, the Church's
moral theology did not enjoy a separate existence within
theology as a whole. While there had been two rich seams

of moral and ethical teaching available to theologians—
the legacies of Augustine and Thomas Aquinas, with their
foundations in the thought of Plato and Aristotle—much of
what passed for moral theology had focused on the confessor-
penitent relationship in the sacrament of penance.[2]

Moral guidance, especially when given to members of
religious orders and priests, was synonymous with spiritual
direction. Such advice centred on ascetical practices and
prayer; individual poverty of spirit and obedience; rules relating to obligations to fast, attend Mass, and receive Holy
Communion. Matters of sexual transgression in thought,
word, and deed were crucial. There was scant emphasis in
Trent, and hence in subsequent seminary education, on how
the lay faithful should live their moral lives in light of Scripture, or reflection on a positive Christian moral theology: the
fostering of the virtues or the common good, ideas inherent
in the theology of Thomas Aquinas.

Ever since the period of the penitentials, restitution and
reparation to those wronged—by theft, say, or libel—had
been advocated as a condition of absolution. Yet the chief
focus of interest had been the state of the individual sinner's
soul, not the victims of sin. There was, indeed, the work of
the great Spanish moralists of the sixteenth century—Francisco
Suárez, Francisco de Vitoria, and Bartolomé de Las Casas—
who had had enlarged on themes of natural law relating to
warfare, international law (especially on questions of conquest and colonialism), and property rights. Aspects of their
work anticipated the great encyclical of Leo XIII (*Rerum*

Novarum, 1891) on Catholic social teaching. But as the moral theologian and professor John Mahoney has pointed out: 'This social teaching has, until fairly recently been aimed to quite a large extent at the defence of the individual in society, as in the arguments traditionally marshalled to justify and defend the institution of private property'. He added that the Church's official and humanitarian teachings had concentrated more on the individual's response 'to the divine command not to steal, . . . often in the context of his eternal fate' than the 'context of the social well-being of others.'[3]

Against this background, the early modern Catholic confessors and seminary pastoral theologians were preoccupied with 'what morally may I do or not do to avoid mortal sin?' (Or, as the novelist David Lodge, four hundred years on, would put it in the title of his satirical novel on Catholic sexual morality, *How Far Can You Go?*) Hence, in the era that followed the Council of Trent, there was ample scope for conflict between those who pursued the most stringent principles in judging what constituted mortal sin, on the one hand, and those who were inclined to be more permissive, on the other. A rigorist standpoint, Jansenism, emerged in France and the Lowlands in the seventeenth century, based on the book *Augustinus* by the Louvain theologian Cornelius Jansen, published in 1640, two years after his death. Jansen's followers advocated the strictest moral standards, ultimately basing themselves on the darker, more negative elements in Augustinian thought, with an emphasis on the corruption of Original Sin. A fiercely antagonistic debate arose between the Jansenists and the Jesuits, whom the Jansenists accused of morally harmful laxity, indicting their 'casuistry'—alleged chop logic, allowing greater latitude in moral opinions and judgements. The disputes fragmented into a chaos of viewpoints, resulting in Jansenism's polar opposite, Quietism, which recommended contemplative passivity aimed at achieving unity with God. A key characteristic of Quietism was its opposition to active strivings in one's moral life.[4]

A major focus of conflict between moralists, moreover, was the principle known as 'probabilism', which meant that a confessor should recommend a solution to a tricky moral case by invoking the most lenient judgement on offer, even if it was held by a single pastoral theologian. Probabilism was defended by many Jesuits. Much time was expended on test cases, such as whether it would be breaking the fast on an official fast day (Good Friday, say), leading to mortal sin, if one were to eat tiny quantities of food frequently through the day, which might amount to more than the normal fast-day allowance of the single main meal.

In the end, papal authority weighed in, condemning the extremes of both Jansenism and Quietism, in 1653 and 1689 respectively.[5] In time, the wider disputes were eased, if not entirely settled, by the influential works and teaching of Alphonsus Liguori in the 1700s. Son of an aristocratic family in Naples, Liguori was a man of wide scholarship and artistic talent. He was an accomplished harpsichordist, having practised the instrument for three hours each day during his youth. He had trained originally as a lawyer, but after witnessing a rigged court case in Naples he devoted himself to work among the poor, both in the city and the countryside—where he discovered that the peasants were sunk in ignorance of the faith. After ordination to the priesthood, he founded the Redemptorist congregation, dedicated to parish mission work, retreats, preaching, and, above all, hearing confessions. He wrote more than a hundred works—mainly instructions for priests and works of apologetics against the Church's enemies. His lasting legacy, however, was his *Theologia Moralis* (*Moral Theology*), which went through nine revisions during his lifetime, and a vast number after his death. There are many thousands of editions and translations of his various works on morals in existence.

Liguori was dedicated to the task of preparing priests as confessors. His achievement—for better or for worse—was to limit the scope of Catholic moral and pastoral theology to the questions, scruples, and judgements that arise in the confessional. He succeeded, however, in promoting an uneasy peace between the rigorists and the laxists. As we shall see, his prestige and influence would shape the textbooks in moral and pastoral theology into the first half of the twentieth century, and, in consequence, the guidance given to confessors up to the Second Vatican Council (1962–1965). Among his many reflections on the supreme importance of confession, and the need for souls to be moulded by their confessors, was his recommendation of blind obedience to one's confessor. Pius IX would declare him a 'Doctor of the Church', and in 1950 Pius XII would proclaim that the teaching of Alphonsus

Liguori was the 'most thoroughly approved' and 'safe norm' throughout the Church. The pontiff also declared him patron of moral theologians.[6]

BEFORE HIS DEATH IN 1787, Liguori noted that attendance at confession was in steep decline. His impression of the reason for the collapse, based on personal experience of parish life in Italy's cities and rural communities, was that rigorist confessors were routinely withdrawing absolution from their penitents. Other reasons were not difficult to discern. Sexual solicitation had continued to give confessors a bad name, and there was a perception, on the part of men, that confessors were coming between themselves and their women. Anticlericalism was spreading throughout Europe, partly because of a growing resentment over the power that priests wielded over women in confession. The anticlerical sentiments grew especially in France, where Voltaire, along with other Enlightenment philosophers, had prepared the ground with their claims for the supremacy of reason over faith and accusations of clerical corruption. The French Revolution dealt a further massive blow to the Church in France, which had been closely associated with the privileges of monarchy and aristocracy. Some 20,000 priests were laicised under threat of death or imprisonment. Parishes were abandoned in their thousands, and some 30,000 religious sent into exile. The Mass and the sacraments virtually disappeared.

An entire literary genre of anticlericalism arose, featuring abusive confessors. Whatever the truth of the alleged scandals, the reputation of the Catholic priesthood was being undermined on a broad front. A typical exponent was Antonio Gavin, a Spanish ex-priest and former confessor of Irish extraction. He had been a member of a 'moral academy' set up by the Inquisition in Saragossa in the second half of the seventeenth century to investigate allegations against confessors. In 1713 he left the priesthood, in disgust, so he claimed, and travelled to England. His book *A Master-Key to Popery*, aimed at the Protestant prejudices of an English readership, purports to expose an array of abuses in the confessional. There would be many editions in German and English, as well as a French edition, which circulated in Spain for a number of years before it was placed on the Vatican's Index of Forbidden Books.

Among other allegations, he claimed that young people learned in confession about sins unknown to their consciences; that confessors cross-examined married women inappropriately about their sexual lives; and that confessors insinuated themselves with families for monetary gain. Among many cases, Gavin cited a young woman whose family had been bullied by a confessor. They made him her guardian, and left the family fortune to him. After the death of the father, the priest seduced the girl and left her destitute. In desperation she became the mistress of an army officer, but he was killed while on service in Catalonia. Turning to religion for consolation, she found herself a new confessor, who said that he would arrange a suitable marriage for her if she would give him the jewellery left by her soldier-lover. This she did, whereupon he ordered her to sleep with him, threatening to turn her over to the Inquisition if she refused. In summary, Gavin claimed that 'confessors are the occasion of the ruin of many families, many thefts, debaucheries, murders, and divisions'.[7]

Much anticlerical material was clearly fictitious and even tongue-in-cheek. Denis Diderot's *La Religieuse*, the narrative of a fictitious nun, Suzanne, was written originally as a joke perpetrated on an aristocratic friend. The 'author' was pleading with the Marquis de Croismar to release her from a convent where she was imprisoned. It was eventually published as an epistolary novel in 1796, after Diderot's death, and was an immediate commercial success.

A typical literary anticlericalist author in the next generation was another former Spanish priest of Irish extraction, Joseph Blanco White of Seville, who had been ordained in 1800 at the age of twenty-five. In 1810, disillusioned with Catholicism (by his own admission, in consequence of abuses in the confessional), he went to England, studied theology at Oxford, and joined the Anglican Church. He became a close friend of Samuel Taylor Coleridge, who admired his poetry, and the Anglican theologian John Henry Newman, who was then a Fellow of Oriel College. So popular was White among the Fellows that he was granted membership in their Common Room. In his book *The Preservative Against Popery*, White inveighs against the tyranny of confession over families, and women in particular, because of sexual solicitation. He had stories, including the tale of a Franciscan confessor who fell passionately in love with a woman penitent, then murdered her on learning that she was to be married. Newman, even after deciding to become a Catholic, was convinced that White was sincere, and that he had left country and friends 'all for an idea of truth, or rather for liberty of thought.'[8]

Many other writers in the jaundiced anti-Catholic genre followed. Juan Antonio Llorente—an Enlightenment convert, bibliographer, and archivist—tells the story of a Capuchin confessor who persuaded some thirteen holy women (*beatas*) that he was in receipt of a supernatural vision telling him he was obliged to satisfy their sexual needs.[9]

By the mid-nineteenth century, fictional accounts of Catholic clerical seductions and debauchery had become popular on both sides of the Atlantic. Rebecca Reed's *Six Months in a Convent*, a lurid account of her time in an Ursuline convent in Charleston, Massachusetts, appeared in New York in 1835. It was a runaway best-seller. She died of tuberculosis shortly after the book's publication, and it was believed that her death was caused by the privations she had experienced in the convent. The success of Reed's book was partly attributed to the anticlericalism of a wave of immigrants from Ireland and Germany. The 1834 Ursuline Convent Riots near Boston also played a role. Rumours had spread that a girl was being kept in the Ursuline Convent against her will. Rioters set the convent on fire in a bid to secure her release.

Against this background, there followed a notorious anticlerical, anti-Catholic work of fiction masquerading as fact. Entitled *The Awful Disclosures of Maria Monk: The Hidden Secrets of a Nun's Life in a Convent Exposed*, it derived partly from the gothic novels of the late eighteenth and early nineteenth centuries and the success of Reed's earlier book. Maria Monk's first-person story alleged that she had been incarcerated in the convent of the Religious Hospitallers of St. Joseph in Montreal for seven years. She became pregnant, she claimed, by a priest from the neighbouring seminary, which had a connecting tunnel into the convent. The baby was strangled, according to the account, and dumped in a lime pit in the basement. The political and cultural historian Richard Hofstadter has written that Maria Monk's novel was 'probably the most widely read contemporary book in the United States before *Uncle Tom's Cabin*'. The book would spawn myriad imitators, of which the novel *Priest and Nun: A Story of Convent Life*, published in New York in 1871, was an example. In an attempt to establish the book's authenticity, its anonymous author included a prefatory note claiming that in order to depict 'the insidious principles of the Roman Church' and the 'inner of life of the modern nunnery', the work was 'strictly based on facts'.[10]

The facts, fictions and factions of alleged clerical abuse had led in 1851 to the curious trial of John Henry Newman, friend, as we have seen above, of White's. After becoming a Catholic priest, Newman founded an Oratorian house (following rules laid down by Philip Neri) at Edgbaston in Birmingham, England. While he was overseeing the building of the house, he was obliged to refute rumours, prompted by a speech in the House of Commons, that Catholic religious houses were designing basement 'cells' for nefarious purposes. Richard Spooner, member of Parliament for North Warwickshire, had delivered a speech on the Religious Houses Bill, suggesting that a large religious convent in Edgbaston had 'fitted up the whole of the underground with cells, and what were those cells for?' To which the House resounded with 'hear, hear'. The mayor of Birmingham was accordingly called upon to inspect Newman's basement area, and confirmed that the site was innocent.[11]

To combat the ugly rumours about Catholic priests, Newman impugned the wayward Protestant imagination. Citing the cliché of Catholic institutions, such as the slander that all convents and monasteries were places of torture and sexual perversion, he turned the image against the Church's antagonists. It was the Protestant imagination that was a grim convent or workhouse where the 'thick atmosphere refracts and distorts such straggling rays as enter in.'[12]

In a crowded lecture in Birmingham, Newman ill-advisedly accused one Giacinto Achilli of sexual depravity. Achilli was a former Italian priest of the Dominican order who had apostatised in Italy and escaped to England. He had been touring the country denouncing the Catholic Church for abuses in the confessional and other crimes. In September 1851 Achilli instituted criminal libel proceedings against Newman, which could result in an unlimited fine or imprisonment. Unfortunately, crucial evidence against Achilli in the keeping of Cardinal Nicholas Wiseman was not to be found. Newman lost the case and received his sentence on 31 January 1853. The fine was £100, a derisory figure; but Newman was also obliged to bear the costs of the case, which amounted to more than £14,000—about a million pounds at today's value (about $1.5 million in US dollars). The judge rebuked Newman, declaring that he 'had been everything good' when he was a Protestant, 'but had fallen' on becoming a Catholic.[13] Such was Newman's popularity among wealthy Catholics that he raised the money easily enough with a margin to spare.

THE ANTICLERICALISM of the mid- to late nineteenth century was exacerbated by the clergy's resistance to the rise of secularism and the consequent conflict between the Catholic Church and the governments of the emerging nation-states of Europe. In France, where anticlericalism was at its height through the second half of the century, there was a widespread perception of the clergy as manipulative in the confessional, if not always abusive. There were also widespread charges of hypocrisy. The title of a book by Michel Morphy, published in Paris in 1884, was *Les mystères de la pornographie cléricale; secrets honteux de la confession, immoralités, obscénités, et guerre aux prêtres, corrupteurs de la jeunesse* (Mysteries of clerical pornography, the shameful secrets of the confessional, immoralities, obscenities, and the war against priests, corrupters of youth). Later in the century anticlericalism flared anew in

France following the Church's disgrace for its anti-Semitic attacks on Alfred Dreyfus, the wrongly accused and imprisoned Jewish army officer. Dreyfus was charged with treason and sent to Devil's Island: the case divided the nation. Those representing the right-wing segments of the Church insisted on his guilt even after his reprieve.

At the same time, priests were prompting anger throughout France because of their campaigns against the new styles of dancing, such as the polka—which encouraged touching and embracing. Confessors were counselling married women against collaborating with their husbands in popular forms of birth control, such as mutual masturbation, coitus interruptus, and anal intercourse. Priestly interference in matters of the marital bedroom was depicted in Marcel Jouhandeau's novels, for example, and clerical hypocrisy was vividly dramatised by Stendhal (*Le Rouge et le Noir*) and Octave Mirbeau (*Sébastien Roch*).

———————

As ANTI-SEMITISM, and, in particular, allegations against Catholic confessors, spread on both sides of the Atlantic, the posthumous reputation of an unusual priest in France was gaining national, and eventually international, attention for his remarkable feats as an ascetic and confessor. Jean-Marie Vianney was parish priest of the village of Ars, a poor farming community near the city of Lyons. Born in 1786, Vianney was a man of meagre education but profound piety. He found his seminary formation difficult, as he was a slow learner. He often spent part of the night flat on his face in church, with only snatches of sleep on the stone floor of his bedroom—using a log for a pillow. He whipped himself daily with a metal scourge, spattering the walls with blood. For food he would boil a pan of potatoes once a week and live off them until the final ones were black and rotten. He performed his fasts and self-mortifications, he declared, in order to rid the parish of the devils that inhabited it. On one occasion he reported that a devil had beaten him up in the church during the night.[14]

Convinced that his parish was sunk in wickedness, he set about a campaign of spiritual renewal. He cut down the trees in his orchard so that children would not be tempted to steal his apples. He declared war on the taverns and the occasional dances and fiestas. Week by week from the pulpit, he preached against the sin of dancing, declaring that the doors of the taverns were the entrances to Hell. Finally he acquired money from a wealthy pious local to pay off the owners of the taverns in order to close them down; but he did not rest until he had banned dancing, which he believed to be a prelude to every carnal temptation.

From this point he managed by sheer force of personality and eloquence to turn the village into a kind of spiritual concentration camp. With little left to distract them, the parishioners attended church daily and confessed frequently. In the end he was hearing their confessions for up to fourteen hours a day. He was credited with special discernment, and was given to informing penitents that they were 'damned'. Often he would be in floods of tears as he heard confessions. In time, the stories of his holiness and insights spread throughout France, and pilgrims began to travel to the village to be confessed, or just to catch a glimpse of the extraordinary wraith-like man. In the year of his death in 1859, some 90,000 pilgrims came to the village.

One of his keenest admirers would be Pope Pius X (elected in 1903). Pius X would see Jean-Marie Vianney as an extreme exemplar of the suffering endured by French pastors. Pius kept a statue of the famous confessor on his desk during his pontificate and beatified him in 1905. The popes of the twentieth century, from Pius X to Benedict XVI, celebrated Jean-Marie Vianney as the leading exemplar of a parish confessor. Pius XI canonised him in 1925. In 2011, Benedict XVI nominated Vianney Patron of the Year of the Priesthood.

PART TWO

THE CHILD
PENITENTS

Five

The Pope Who 'Restored' Catholicism

I suppose the greatest reform of our time
was that carried out by St Pius X . . .

—J. R. R. Tolkien, letter to his son Michael, 1 November 1963

AFTER THE DEATH OF LEO XIII IN 1903, THE CARDINALS IN the conclave to elect a new pope broke a centuries-long tradition by choosing a prelate of working-class origins who had never worked in the Curia, had no experience of Church diplomacy, and was neither a theologian nor a canon lawyer. Giuseppe Sarto, at sixty-eight years of age, was unknown outside of Italy and had never been abroad. He took the name Pius X in honour of his 'great predecessors of that name'.[1]

He was born in 1835 in Riese, a rural district in the Treviso Valley north of the Veneto region—at that time part of the Austrian Empire. His mother was a seamstress, his father a local government messenger. Unsubstantiated accounts claim that Sarto's forebears were of migrant Polish extraction (his pale, harmonious features are reminiscent of John Paul II). Ordained in 1858, he spent the first quarter-century of his ministry as a curate and parish priest, with administrative duties in the diocese of Treviso, where he also acted as the seminary's spiritual director. At the age of forty-nine, he was appointed bishop of Mantua, a backwater diocese where he busied himself re-establishing the seminary and making parish visits. The year he took over the diocese, only one seminarian was ordained; there was an acute shortage of priests.

Leo XIII made Sarto a cardinal in 1893 and awarded him the See of Venice, which carried the grandiloquent title 'patriarch'. The diocese was smaller than some of the greater metropolitan parishes. He immediately revealed an aptitude for reactionary politics by warning the faithful against the Radical Democrat city councillors of Venice. He banned orchestral music, women singing in choirs, four-part choral motets, and clapping in church, advocating a return to the austere simplicity of Gregorian chant. He attempted to forbid clergy and laity from visiting the city's first great art exhibition because, he claimed, it displayed a picture offensive to religion. A sign of things to come, he closed down the college for lay students attached to the seminary to prevent seminarists from coming in contact with the laity.[2]

On the death of Leo XIII, Sarto was not the first choice of his fellow cardinals during the conclave. The former secretary of state under Leo, Cardinal Mariano Rampolla, had been an early favourite. The emperor of Austria-Hungary, Franz Joseph, had attempted to exercise an ancient right to veto, in order to prevent Rampolla's election via an intervention made by a Polish cardinal. In the event, the vote was going against Rampolla anyway, and in Sarto's favour. The conclave had discerned in Cardinal Sarto a pastoral, 'holy man' pontiff. French Cardinal François-Désiré Mathieu, a member of the Curia, wrote: 'We wanted a pope who had never engaged in politics, whose name would signify peace and concord, who had grown old in the care of souls, who would concern himself with the government of the Church in detail, who would be above all a father and shepherd.'[3] One of Pius X's first acts was to forbid under pain of excommunication any future attempt to influence the conclave. After his election, Sarto proclaimed his motto, 'To restore all in Christ.' He chose as his secretary of state the suave Anglo-Spanish prelate Rafael Merry del Val, although the latter was not yet forty years old. A consummate diplomat, and highly intelligent, Merry del Val spoke a number of languages and had an enormous capacity for administrative work.

Sarto impressed all who met him as an unusually charismatic and holy individual. Just forty years after his death, he would be canonised—he was the only pope to be made a saint for three centuries, until the canonisation of John XXIII and John Paul II. Many testified to his saintliness at the beatification and canonisation tribunals, emphasising his deep faith and his sweet nature (although, as we shall see, there would be a striking exception in this regard). One day the memory of Pius X would become a rallying point for those who opposed the Second Vatican Council, believing it had undone the Church that he had 'restored' and defended so vigorously.[4]

Pius X had a great love of the priestly vocation, which he deemed an estate higher than that of the angels. He retained throughout his pontificate the characteristics of a devout parish priest. He was unassuming and loathed protocol. He dispensed with much of the daily ceremonial pomp and frippery that surrounded the papal office. He was at times absent-minded—he wiped his pen on the sleeve of his white cassock, and he tended to wear the papal triple crown askew. He did away with the *sedia gestatoria*, the chair in which popes were traditionally carried, and abandoned his predecessor's habit of eating alone. He took snuff and smoked cigars. Early newsreels show a slow-moving man of medium height, his paunch carrying all before him; there is an impression of watchful indolence. He had a lineless face and wistful eyes. His thatch of thick hair had turned silvery white in youth.

Yet this devout, avuncular exterior hid a bullying streak. Pius X could not abide contradiction.[5] An astute autodidact, he had studied well beyond the spoonfed seminary courses of his youth. He was smart, yet he had never been exposed to peer-group exchange and challenge within a university. He had a brooding capacity to demonise those who questioned matters of faith. Sarto did not like intellectuals, especially clerical ones. He would more than live up to his reputation for sanctity and as a model for ideal priesthood. He has been less recognised for his schemes to strengthen the Church for the twentieth century. Seeking to bolster the clergy, he instituted new rules for seminaries, disciplinary action against 'modernising' priests, a universal clerical oath of mental allegiance to papal teaching, and a worldwide surveillance system that reported 'liberal' priests back to Rome. Culprits were punished by removal or excommunication, their books and writings banned. He would be remembered for lowering the age at which children make their first communion; he is less remembered for a more historic decision—to insist that children also make their first confession at the same time. There was to be a powerful symbiosis between the two sets of measures—obligatory confession for children, and a highly regimented priesthood that itself would one day be composed of the products of premature confession.

WHAT WAS IT THAT DROVE Pius X's relentless determination to recreate, some might say 'reinvent', the Catholic Church at the beginning of the new century? As Pius X looked out upon the world from the purview of the Apostolic Palace in 1903, he saw enemies on every side: without, as well as within. In his first encyclical, *E Supremi Apostolatus*, issued on 4 October 1903, he wrote apocalyptically: 'Society is at the present time, more than in any past age, suffering from a terrible and a deeprooted malady . . . apostasy from God'. He went on: 'There is good reason to fear lest this great perversity may be as it were a foretaste, and perhaps the beginning of those evils which are reserved for the last days; and that there may be already in the world the "Son of Perdition" [the Antichrist] of whom the Apostle speaks.'[6]

Ever since the Reformation, the papacy had struggled to cope with a fragmented Christendom, the challenge of Enlightenment ideas, and the profound political and social changes that had followed the French Revolution: liberalism, secularism, science, industrialisation, and the evolving powers of nation-states. Through two pontificates preceding Pius X's reign, Catholicism had suffered a series of hammer blows as the states of Europe appropriated domains, both spiritual and geographical, that were once the preserve of the Church. By 1870 the papacy had lost the last vestige of its temporal power: the Eternal City itself. Pius IX became a prisoner in the Vatican. The march of secularisation, even in Italy, was unstoppable. Outdoor devotions were banned and religious communities dispersed. The government instituted civil divorce, secularized schools, and removed Holy Days from the calendar. In Germany, in response to allegations that Catholic citizens had divided loyalties, Bismarck instituted the Kulturkampf, the so-called cultural struggle between the state and religion. Religious education was put under state control; the Jesuits were exiled; seminaries were subjected to secular interference. In Belgium, religious orders were banned and Catholics were expelled from the teaching profession; religious orders were banned in Switzerland; schools were sequestrated in Austria; and in France, there was rampant anticlericalism and the eventual separation of Church and State. In 1901 the Waldeck-Rousseau government in Paris forbade religious orders to teach, and entire religious congregations left the country. In the government expropriation of Church property, clergy and religious were evicted from their houses and community buildings. As it happened, Pius X felt more secure with the total separation of sovereignties: the Church in France now stood aloof, the pope unquestionably its supreme head.

If Pius X had limited power to control the enemy without, there was much he could do to manage the perceived dangers from within. He would write in his 1910 encyclical *Editae Saepae* that the peril existed 'in the very veins and heart of the Church'. He would seek to eradicate the rot inside the Church while fortifying the faithful against current and future shocks in the outside world. Speaking to the conclave cardinals immediately after his election, he declared his intention to 'defend [the Church] with strength and gentleness'.[7]

Pius X was not alone in thinking that the faithful, lay and clerical, had already been seduced and corrupted on every side by secular influences, including indifference, scepticism, lukewarm faith, lack of devotion, a failure to practise the faith, and a tendency to lapse. On the eve of his election, the prominent Italian statesman and devout practising Catholic Senator, Tancredi Canonico, had commented on the malaise among the laity and clergy alike. 'The life of the Church has come to a standstill', he wrote. 'It is rare to hear the vibrant and vivifying note of the spirit. The secret has been lost of the word that moves the soul to its very root and creates the Christian conscience therein.'[8]

In his defence of the Church, Pius X pursued a dual strategy: the strengthening of the faithful, including men, women, and especially children; and the reform of the clergy. He would fortify the faithful by encouraging them to flood their lives with sanctifying grace through frequent reception of the sacraments of communion and confession. And it must start young, with a thorough catechesis and inculcation of devotions that would last a lifetime. He would strengthen the clergy by promoting discipline, mental obedience, and strict allegiance, legally as well as in spirit, to papal teaching. Both lay and clerical Catholics must hold the clerical estate in high regard—with self-esteem on the part of priests, and due deference on the part of the laity. The ultimate test of strength overall, however, would be an insistence on the recognition of authentic Catholic identity—an 'integralist', total acceptance of Rome's definition of what it meant to be a good Catholic. There would be no room for the half-hearted, the unorthodox, the *non praticant*, liberalism, local discretion, or dissidence.

His first priority in bolstering a priesthood worthy of its ministries was to transform the seminaries. He was convinced that the Church's internal problems stemmed, in part, from poor initial training. He ordered a monastic-style regime to ensure life-long holiness and dedication.[9] Seminaries were destined to become highly disciplined hothouses shut off from the world and its corruptions and temptations. Seminarians were obliged to wear cassocks and Roman collars at all times, and their vacations at home were severely curtailed, since they might otherwise breathe a secular, less clerical air. The pope put the greatest stress on obedience to superiors and the external signs of piety, purity, and innocence. Many of his 'reforms' were reapplications of the norms of the Council of Trent, which had fallen into neglect.

Pius X decreed that seminaries should exclude outside influences. Lay teachers, secular books, and newspapers were banned (from the 1930s and into the 1960s, the same went for radio and television). Seminarians were obliged to walk out of the seminary confines in groups (in Rome the group, or *camerata*, typically consisted of five men). Seminarians were no longer allowed to attend courses in secular universities; nor were lay students allowed inside the seminary. Women must not enter the enclosure, and seminarians were not to be involved with the local community. In the presence of women, seminarians were advised to practise 'custody of the eyes'. They must avoid 'special' or 'particular' friendships within the seminary community. In order to encourage seminarians and priests to ever greater heights of asceticism, the pope advocated that they should become 'prisoners to the confessional' in the manner of Jean-Marie Vianney—the austere, self-flagellating French country priest we met in Chapter 4. Pius X regarded Vianney's lack of education, and his struggles with his studies, a commendable circumstance. Pius believed that a learned priest stood in danger of being a proud and potentially unfaithful one.

The emphasis on a monastic-style obedience in seminary formation would give rise to a new ethos of clerical piety that ran the risk of discouraging initiative, independence, and emotional maturity. Seminarians found themselves cut off from family life and the presence of women; they had little knowledge of children and their stages of emotional and intellectual development. They were released from domestic and financial responsibilities. The French novelist Georges Bernanos, who had attended seminary in the full flush of Pius X's reforms, wrote of the experience, 'It made schoolboys of us, children to the very end of our lives.'[10]

PIUS X BELIEVED THAT intellectual pride lay at the root of the clerical rot. This pride, he believed, was a consequence of the dangerous influence of the phenomenon he labelled 'Modernism', an amalgam of unspecified heresies corrupting the clergy throughout the world. The way in which he chose to deal with this heretical contagion would have far-reaching consequences for the ethos of the priesthood and for confessors of the future. Pius X's strategy was to promote acquiescence to Rome's every utterance, punishing, by demotion or exclusion, any priest who was believed to be tainted with the Modernist 'poison', as he termed it. Clerics would come to live in daily consciousness of being watched and reported. Fear of transgressing Rome's teaching, and the belief that one was under surveillance, would dominate the Catholic clerical mind.

Modernism did not exist as an organised conspiracy. Yet so fanatical was the Vatican's fear and loathing of its influence that it was soon credited with being a movement comprising hundreds of thousands of 'members'. As with the McCarthyite Communist witch-hunts in post–World War II America, fear prompted widespread paranoia. The Modernist 'conspiracy', however, was no more than a small, loosely allied constituency of Catholic scholars and thinkers who had attempted to come to terms with intellectual forces shaping contemporary culture. How could one reconcile Charles Darwin's theory of evolution with the biblical creation story? How should one understand the Church's claims of immutability in view of the facts of its historical development? How could one square belief in the divine inspiration of Holy Scripture with the latest exegeses, disputed provenance, and unreliable authorship? There were political dimensions, moreover, which had arisen during the 1890s in the United States among Catholic scholars who sought to make connections between Christianity and democracy. In Rome such thinking was deemed not only suspect but heretical. Labelling the initiative 'Americanism', Leo XIII had quashed the tendency in an apostolic letter in January 1899. The work involved 'great danger', he opined. It was 'hostile' to Catholic doctrine and discipline inasmuch as 'the followers of these novelties judge that a certain liberty ought be introduced into the Church'.[11]

At the eye of the Modernist storm was the French priest and Scripture scholar Alfred Loisy. Among his alleged heresies was his suggestion that the Book of Genesis was not literally true, but poetic. Ironically, his main purpose was to combat Protestant scholars who would do away with the notion of divine inspiration altogether. Hence, his 'Modernism' was a means of fighting 'modern' Protestant fire with 'modern' Catholic fire. His books were greeted with enthusiasm by seminarians and their teachers in France and elsewhere (before Pius's seminary reforms began to filter through), creating excitement and debate. Rome believed that 'Modernism' was spreading unchecked throughout the Church, and Loisy's works were placed on the Index of Forbidden Books. In England, however, his book *The Gospel and the Church* had been welcomed by two independent Catholic thinkers: Baron Friedrich von Hügel and the Jesuit George Tyrrell. Von Hügel would remain cautious in his published writings, but Tyrrell would make his own bold reflections in the spirit of Loisy, particularly on the need to reconcile theology with science.

Pius's loathing of the Modernist 'conspiracy' can be measured by the violence of his language against clerics who cautioned charity and understanding of these 'heretics'. 'They want them to be treated with oil, soap and caresses', he once declared, referring to those who counselled reasoned discussion with the accused. 'But they should be beaten with fists. In a duel, you don't count or measure the blows, you strike as you can. War is not made with charity; it is a struggle, a duel.'[12]

As more and more works were placed on the Index of Forbidden Books, Pius became increasingly assertive. On

17 April 1907, he delivered a papal denunciation of the Modernist heretics who sought to destroy the Church. Their errors, he thundered, were 'not a heresy, but the compendium and poison of all the heresies.' He published his declaration *Lamentabili Sane* later that year, condemning sixty-five Modernist errors. He decreed that it was heresy to question the existence of the sacrament of confession in the early Church. Moreover, it was heretical to state that the words of Christ in John's Gospel (20.23)—'If you forgive the sins of any, they are forgiven; if you retain the sins of any, they are retained'—did not refer to the sacrament of penance. Yet, according to Loisy and like-minded scholars, such 'heresies' hardly resembled their own views on these matters; Pius was merely rehashing stock Protestant objections to the doctrine of confession.

Pius followed his declaration with the anti-Modernist encyclical *Pascendi*, also in 1907. This document established the dogmatic, centrist tone of papal teaching through the twentieth century up to the Second Vatican Council. It set out a strengthened definition of papal primacy, asserting that theological disputes within the Catholic Church were not academic matters, to be settled by scholarly peer-group debate. Instead, they were moral matters to be definitively resolved by papal authority.

Six

Pius X's Spy-Net

[Pius X] approved, blessed and encouraged
a sort of freemasonry in the Church,
something unheard of in ecclesiastical
history.

—Cardinal Pietro Gasparri, testimony during the beatification
process for Pius X, quoted in Owen Chadwick,
A History of the Popes, 1830–1914

DETERMINED TO IDENTIFY THE EXTENT OF THE MODERNIST
threat and to eradicate it early in his reign, which began
in 1903, Pius X sanctioned a secret organisation, linked both
to the Department of Extraordinary Ecclesiastical Affairs in
the Secretariat of State, under Cardinal Rafael Merry del
Val, and to the Consistorial Congregation under its prefect,
Cardinal Gaetano de Lai.[1]

The man who established and ran this clandestine operation was Umberto Benigni, a stout, bespectacled, highly ener-
getic monsignor working on foreign affairs in the Secretariat of

State. A former Catholic news service and newspaper editor, he had won the confidence of the pope and an inner circle of reactionary cardinals. Benigni had a gift for languages as well as highly honed polemical and journalistic skills. His paranoid tendencies were combined with a capacity for verbal aggression and a gift for caricature. He was particularly antagonistic towards 'dissident' Church historians. He declared that for Modernist historians, 'history is nothing but a continual desperate attempt to vomit. For this sort of human being there is only one remedy—the Inquisition.'[2]

Benigni's scheme was nothing less than a modern-style Inquisition—to ferret out dissent wherever it might exist, and report it back to appropriate Vatican departments to be dealt with. His operation, which officially did not exist (it never appeared in the Vatican yearbook, *Annuario Pontificio*), was code-named 'Sodalitium Pianum' (Sodality of Pius); the pope's code name within the system was 'Mama'. The 'Sodalitium' was set up in a private apartment outside the Vatican, although Benigni continued to work in the secretariat in the mornings. In addition to being a 24/7 espionage service, it doubled as a propaganda operation for the planting of anti-Modernist items in the Italian and foreign press, including exposés and slurs against dissident individuals. Benigni founded a newspaper called *Corrispondenza Romana* that specialised in attacking liberals. He was its secret editor-in-chief, and its funding came from the pope himself. Benigni's undercover network, staffed with a team of nuns, was partly a spy network and partly a news and public relations organisation. It employed the latest in copying machines and telegraphy, and its volunteer informants, or 'stringers', operated throughout the world. Benigni commissioned the clandestine photographing of documents on private premises and the interception of private correspondence, and he pressed double agents into service. His tactics extended to aliases, disguises, and Watergate-style breaking and entering.[3]

The key purpose of this activity, much of it criminal, was 'delation' (from the past participle of the Latin *deferre*: 'to bring down, report, accuse'), the process of reporting back to Rome all instances of alleged doctrinal unorthodoxy, liberalism, dissidence, and so-called Modernism. In time, the accused spanned the lowliest seminarians right up to princes of the Church, the cardinals. The cardinal archbishops of Vienna and Paris were delated, and so was the entire scholarly Dominican community at Fribourg University in Switzerland. The taint of Modernism could include being overheard speaking favourably of 'Christian democracy', or being seen reading a newspaper that expressed liberal views, or being overheard questioning an item even of devotional as opposed to doctrinal belief, such as miracles and apparitions of the Virgin Mary. Sneaks and tittle-tattlers now became righteous informers and saviours of the Church. A chance ill-advised word in the refectory or common room, a lapse in a sermon or lecture, could find its way back to Rome. The consequence could be dismissal from a seminary or religious order, demotion or removal from a diocesan office, the loss of a post of academic responsibility, or exile to a distant village curacy.

More important, and long-term, was the effect on the ethos of the clergy. There arose a fear of speaking one's mind, or even asking certain questions; priests and seminarians were careful not to be known to read outside of the narrow confines of approved seminary courses. A realisation emerged that Rome was ever and everywhere observing and capable of punishing.

It would take seventy years for Catholic readers to discover that even the youthful future John XXIII had been 'delated' to the Vatican after being seen reading a suspect book. His grovelling letter of exculpation to the Holy Office reveals that even the best of men were degraded by the process.[4] In the secret tribunal testimonies that preceded Pius X's beatification, Cardinal Pietro Gasparri, Secretary of State in the Vatican during the 1920s, asserted: 'Pope Pius X approved, blessed, and encouraged a secret espionage association outside and above the hierarchy, which spied on members of the hierarchy itself, even on their Eminences the Cardinals; in short, he approved, blessed and encouraged a sort of freemasonry in the Church, something unheard of in ecclesiastical history.' Pius XII chose to ignore this damning testimony, which was given under oath by the most powerful prelate of his day. Endorsing his papacy, Pius XII made Pius X a saint on 29 May 1954, describing him at the ceremony as 'a glowing flame of charity and shining splendour of sancitity'.

But the long-term impact of Pius X's reign of moral terror went further—into the very minds and hearts of the clergy. In an act of extraordinary coercion, Pius X decreed that all clergy, from diaconate upwards, should take an oath denouncing Modernism and supporting the encyclicals *Lamentabili* and *Pascendi*. The oath, which further shaped the new clerical ethos, is sworn to this day in modified form by all Catholic ordinands and all priests; it is also repeated by those accepting theological teaching posts in Catholic institutions. The oath commits the individual to mental acquiescence in Rome's teaching, including the sense in which Rome might interpret such teaching at any time. Pius was manoeuvring the clergy to a point where there was no room for individual conscience and judgement, no wriggle-room for special cases or context. The oath constrained the cleric to self-excommunication should he break it, even within his innermost secret thoughts.[5]

The Anti-Modernist oath imprisoned the minds of Catholic priests for the twentieth century, creating for many a virtual schizophrenia between the individual voice of conscience and the mental assent of the oath taker. Habits of secrecy, hypocrisy, and strategies for squaring the circles of emotional, moral, and intellectual life would become endemic among the clergy, as later testimonies will reveal. The predicament was reminiscent of George Orwell's 'doublethink' in *Nineteen Eighty-Four*, which he described as 'to know and not to know, to be conscious of complete truthfulness while telling carefully constructed lies, to hold simultaneously two opinions which cancelled out, knowing them to be contradictory and believing in both of them, to use logic against logic, to repudiate morality while laying claim to it'. The moral schizophrenia involved helps to explain, in part at least, the states of mind discovered in priestly child sex offenders, who would attack children one day, and say Mass the next.[6]

———————

MEANWHILE, IN 1904, and in strictest secrecy, Pius X had launched a project that was to transform the legal structures of the Catholic Church. The scheme would take thirteen years and involve some 2,000 scholars. It would not be completed until three years after Pius X's death.

Canon law, the ecclesiastical laws of the Church, had been gathering over many centuries in a vast array of rules, regulations, and statutes as well as case law covering everything from marriage annulments to the consecration of churches, concordats, and treaties. Organised by date rather than by theme, canon law was a legal jungle. From the outset of his pontificate, Pius X issued a directive to his canon-law subordinates to create a 'Code of Canon Law'. Ironically, for the pope of Anti-Modernism, he was calling for nothing less than a manual of ecclesiastical law based on the modern formula of the Napoleonic Code of 1804, which had played such an effective role in the modernizing of France. The code was to be applied throughout the Church, each priest possessing an identical copy.[7] It was, in essence, a handbook setting out the lines of responsibility, authority, rules, and penalties for members of the clergy. It was to transform Catholic allegiance to papal authority.

According to Ulrich Stutz, a distinguished Protestant canon lawyer of the period, 'Now that infallibility in the areas of faith and morals has been attributed to the papacy, it has completed the work in the legal sphere and given the Church a comprehensive law book that exhaustively regulates conditions within the Church, a *unicus et authenticus fons* [a unique and authentic source] for administration, jurisdiction, and legal instruction—unlike anything the Church has previously possessed in its two-thousand-year existence.'[8] Among the Code's provisions, there was a blurring between the ordinary and solemn teaching authority of the pope, a confusion that the First Vatican Council of 1869–1870 had tried to avoid. Henceforth, papal encyclicals would be regarded with virtually the same authority as infallible dogma. Heresy and error were now conflated: 'It is not enough to avoid heresies, but one must also carefully shun all errors that more or less approach it', stated the text. 'Hence all must observe the constitutions and decrees by which the Holy See has proscribed and forbidden opinions of that sort.' All teaching of the Holy See, even though it is not strictly 'infallible', must be received with 'internal and intellectual consent and loyal obedience'. Thus the Anti-Modernist oath was absorbed into the Code of Canon Law.[9]

The code constrained not only the clergy but also the laity through a series of decrees and regulations aimed at undermining intellectual freedom and curbing peer-group ecumenical discussion: 'Catholics are to avoid disputations or conferences about matters of faith with non-Catholics, especially in public, unless the Holy See, or in case of emergency the [the bishop of the] place, has given permission.' Judgements concerning theological orthodoxy were to be entrusted exclusively to the Holy Office. No priest could publish a book or edit or contribute to a newspaper, journal, magazine, or review without permission of the local bishop. Every diocese would have its own censors, who were obliged to make a special profession of faith. The names of the censors were not to be divulged until the bishop had endorsed the work.[10]

Seven

The Great Confessional Experiment

> At an early age—I was scarcely eight years
> old—I had to go to confession. . . . And
> the very next thing we were told was,
> 'That is a sin, and now your guardian
> angel is crying because of you.' I cannot
> forget the way we were threatened and
> terrified with the 'evil spirit', the devil
> and hell.
>
> —Anonymous, quoted in Mary Collins and David N. Power, eds.,
> *The Fate of Confession*, citing Ludwig Fertig, *Zeitgeist und Erziehungskunst*

PIUS X's INITIATIVE TO FORTIFY THE FAITHFUL AGAINST THE evil forces of the world began with a decree on Holy Communion, published on 20 December 1905. The sacrament, he declared, ideally should be approached 'daily', since its chief purpose was to help communicants 'derive strength to resist their sensual passions, cleanse themselves from the stains of daily faults, and avoid these graver sins to which human frailty is liable'. Hence its primary purpose was 'not that the honour and reverence due to our Lord may be safeguarded, or that it may serve as a reward or recompense of virtue bestowed on the recipients.' The Eucharist, the pope went on, was 'the antidote whereby we may be freed from daily faults and be preserved from mortal sin.' From the outset, then, the focus was as much on avoidance of sin as on spiritual flourishing and full participation at Mass.[1]

As a result of failure to attend communion regularly, Pius X opined, 'piety . . . grew cold'. Disputes had arisen, he declared, 'concerning the dispositions with which one ought to receive frequent and daily communion; and writers vied with one another in demanding more and more stringent conditions as necessary to be fulfilled.' The result was that people 'were content to partake of it once a year, or once a month, or at most once a week.'

The papal encouragement to partake frequently, even daily, in communion was to be broadcast with impressive results, through sermons, retreats, parish missions, and visitations. Special confraternities and sodalities of the Eucharist were formed; Eucharistic congresses were held in many countries, and a constant flood of articles on the Eucharist appeared in the Catholic media. Yet a major problem soon became apparent.[2]

Throughout the Church it was customary for children to delay making their first communion until the age of thirteen or fourteen, or even later. If Pius X was to alter the entrenched practice of centuries, however, he also needed to dislodge an ancient view about the age at which children made their first confession. And to do this, he needed to alter an entrenched conviction about the 'age of discretion': the age at which children acquired the capacity to tell right from wrong.

It took another five years for him to deliver, on 8 August 1910, the encyclical *Quam Singulari*, where he sets out his thinking and teaching in detail. He starts by claiming that the Eucharist had been administered in the early Church 'even to nursing infants'. He acknowledges, however, that the practice had died out in the Latin Church, and goes on to cite the Fourth Lateran Council and the Council of Trent on the rule that the faithful should receive communion, in conjunction with confession, once a year after reaching the 'years of discretion'. But what are the years of discretion? And here he acknowledges the widespread and historic actual practice throughout the Church: 'On the age of reason or discretion', he writes, 'not a few errors and deplorable abuses have crept in during the course of time.' The first deplorable error, he avers, is that there should be a different age for confession from that for Holy Communion. In consequence, 'the age determined for the reception of First Communion was placed at ten years or twelve, and in places fourteen years or even more were required; and until that age children and youth were prohibited from Eucharistic Communion.' The age of 'discretion for confession', he goes on, 'is the time when one can distinguish between right and wrong, that is, when one arrives at a certain use of reason'. Aquinas, he claims, states that children who have 'some use of reason' should be allowed to go to communion. He then quotes Saint Antoninus as saying, 'But when a child is capable of doing wrong, this is of committing a mortal sin, then he is bound by the precept of confession', although, again, this 'authority' has nothing to say on the matter of age. Finally, he conflates a child's understanding of the nature of the Eucharist with knowledge of the difference between right and wrong. Quoting the Roman Catechism of Trent, he asserts that a confessor will judge the age of discretion as the point at which children 'have an understanding of this admirable Sacrament [Holy Communion] and if they have any desire for it.' From all this it is clear, he goes on, 'that the age of discretion for receiving Holy Communion is that at which the child knows the difference between the Eucharistic Bread and ordinary, material bread, and can therefore approach the altar with proper devotion.' He concludes the encyclical with the following decree: 'The custom of not admitting children to Confession or of not giving them absolution when they have already attained the use of reason must be entirely abandoned. The Ordinary [local bishop] shall see to it that this condition ceases absolutely, and he may, if necessary, use legal measures accordingly.'

THE MESSAGE NOW WENT OUT TO the universal Church—
bishops, congregations of religious, parish priests, missionaries, and schools. From 1910 onwards it became a matter of
Catholic belief that discretion means the ability to tell the
difference between right and wrong, and to tell the difference
between bread and wine consecrated and unconsecrated. Yet,
in arguing that the age of seven had always, in fact, been
the Church's understanding of the norm of discretion's emergence, and therefore the norm for first confession, Pius X was
flying in the face of historical fact. He was also ignoring the
wisdom of the faithful, clergy and laity, who had recognised
down the centuries that confession should not be foisted
upon children too early, and that the age of discretion differs
between individual children. It was well recognised, moreover, that the imposition of inappropriate guilt on young
children had its psychological and moral dangers. As Henry
Charles Lea, the principal nineteenth-century historian of
the sacrament, wrote: 'It seems a sacrilege to administer to
children of tender years the awful sacrament of penitence,
with its presumed requisites of contrition and charity and
a conception of its significance as the means of averting the
wrath of an offended God.'[3]

As we have seen, there had been constant debates down
the centuries over the age at which 'discretion' emerges. An
early reference arose in a question put to Timothy of Alexan-
dria at the end of the fourth century. Under discussion was
the emergence of a sense of 'responsibility' in a child. Timothy commented that some believed that responsibility began

at the age of ten; others argued much later. Pope Gregory the Great in the sixth century noted that some believed that it was not possible to sin under the age of fourteen, yet surely, he objected, and with reason, it was possible for children to lie at that age. The *obligation* to confess under pain of excommunication did not arise, as we saw, until the Fourth Lateran Council in 1215; nevertheless, the Council fathers did not settle on a specific age for first confession. Yet the heavy penalty attendant on failure to comply meant that the starting point of the obligation to confess became a topic of intense debate.[4]

The Council of Narbonne in 1244 declared the age to be fourteen, as did various other councils, synods, and canon law rulings in the thirteenth and fourteenth centuries. In 1408, at the provincial synod of Reims, the theologian Jean Charlier de Gerson concurred. In the quarrels that raged over the theology of the sacrament through the Reformation and the Counter-Reformation, there were violent differences of opinion over the authenticity of the sacrament as well as the age and frequency at which the sacrament should be administered. Charles Borromeo was all for lowering first confession to the age of five or six, although he also advocated the view, as did other moral theologians, that a child should not be given absolution but merely a blessing. Others recommended conditional absolution.

The overall history of the disputes, moreover, is a different matter from actual practice, which is harder to ascertain. By the eighteenth century there were striking differences of opinion, including the recommendation of ages significantly higher than fourteen, based on local tradition, customs, experience, and perhaps prejudice. In some cases, evidence of practice emerges from complaints. In 1703, for example, the Provincial Council of Albania denounced the practice of making first confession as late as the age of sixteen, eighteen, and even twenty. In 1747 the bishop of Padua, Cardinal Carlo Rezzonico, professed himself astounded that many young people still had not made their first confession by the age of eighteen. In terms of averages, many sources suggest that throughout the nineteenth century girls made their first confession in groups at the age of twelve or older at the same time that they made their first communion and confirmation; for boys, the age of first confession was typically thirteen or fourteen.

THE CONSEQUENCES OF Pius X's experiment on Catholic children, spanning the second decade of the twentieth century up to the early 1960s, emerge from the published writings, fiction and non-fiction, and personal correspondence and interviews occasioned by my research for this book.

Catholic life was marked during those years by a religiosity that was both defensive and combative. The enemy—atheistic communism—loomed large and clear, presenting a serious threat to the Church's very existence during the interwar and post-war years. Much was made during that era of the presence of Satan in the world. Each person, we were taught, had been assigned a guardian angel to ward off the whispered suggestions of our personal devil. Those who lived in predominantly Protestant countries or districts were often embattled with local non-Catholic antagonists. My mother, as a child in the East End of London, was taunted on her way to school by pupils from a militantly Protestant school; mutual insults, bricks, and fists flew. The tensions of Northern Ireland were being played out on the inner-city streets of England and Scotland.

When I was in the infant class of my convent school towards the end of the Second World War, one of Hitler's rockets demolished the local Anglican church, killing fifteen members of the congregation. Miss Doonan, our pious teacher, explained that God had punished those people because they were Protestants. We were taught that it was a grave sin to enter a Protestant church or attend 'the rites of their false religion'. The contempt of some East End Catholics for Protestants was matched only by their hatred of Jews. I once heard an Irish Catholic uncle referring to my genial Jewish Grandma Cornwell as 'that Yid their father's mother'.

The pope was the living symbol of Catholic unity and continuity. Loyalty to the papacy was fierce and unflinching. As the hymn went, 'God bless our Pope, the Great the Good.' Catholicism was confrontational, visible, and public. In the United States, Catholic evangelism, first by radio and then by television, achieved large audiences. By the 1950s the Rosary was being said daily to combat the Russian nuclear threat. The world over, Catholics went on processions in the streets outside their churches. Pilgrimages to Marian shrines were popular throughout Europe, especially Lourdes, Fatima, and Knock in Ireland. Devotional objects dominated the walls of Catholic homes, prosperous or poor: a crucifix in every room, a picture of the Sacred Heart in the living room, a statue of the Virgin Mary in the parental bedroom. Catholics wore the Miraculous Medal, celebrating the Immaculate Conception of the Virgin, and scapulas—items of cloth, not much bigger than postage stamps, that would hang on one's breast and back like a double-sided necklace, attached by silk strings. Scapulas had tiny pictures of Jesus or Mary on them, or perhaps a saint; some included a phrase from a prayer or a promise of spiritual protection for the wearer. It was believed that if one died wearing the scapula, one escaped Purgatory on the first Friday after one's death. Possession of a Rosary was essential. The Catholic ambiance was festooned with 'sacramentals' and devotions: holy water, holy pictures, votive candles, incense, litanies, novenas.

At the heart of Catholicism was the practice of frequent confession and communion. Preparation for these sacraments now began typically at the age of five or six, aided by vivid depictions of religious truths on roll-down oleographs—the Garden of Eden, Heaven, Hell, Purgatory, the Crucifixion, and the Resurrection. Children were introduced to the notion of sin as the breaking of God's rules. And the rules made by the Church were equivalent to God's rules.

The official catechism, taught from the age of five, was composed of questions and answers which we learnt by rote:

QUESTION: What is sin?

ANSWER: Sin is an offence against God, by any thought, word, deed, or omission against the law of God.[5]

We were taught that there were two kinds of sin. First, there was original sin, which was 'committed by Adam . . . when he ate the forbidden fruit', the stain and guilt of which had been contracted by all mankind, 'except the Blessed Virgin'. Then there were 'actual sins . . . which we ourselves commit', which in turn were of two kinds: 'mortal sin and venial sin', meaning serious sin and less serious sin. And here we came to the nub of the matter:

QUESTION: Why is it called mortal sin?

ANSWER: It is called mortal sin because it is so serious that it kills the soul and deserves hell.

QUESTION: How does mortal sin kill the soul?

ANSWER: Mortal sin kills the soul by depriving it of sanctifying grace, which is the supernatural life of the soul.

QUESTION: Is it a great evil to fall into mortal sin?

ANSWER: It is the greatest of all evils to fall into mortal sin.[6]

There was little or no mention of sin as an action that harmed others, individually or communally. It was claimed, moreover, that harm to our souls was greater than any harm to our bodies—thus giving the impression that the harm one might inflict on the body of another was not so serious a matter. The catechism asked: 'Why is the soul more important than the body?' Answer: 'Because it is a spirit and immortal.'

Meanwhile, the focus on God as one who is prone to take offence depicted Him from the outset as essentially vengeful and wrathful. It was not that the Judeo-Christian story was fundamentally pernicious so much as inadequately imparted by our teachers and the catechism text. Serious, or mortal, sin, according to orthodox Christian theology, involves deliberate rejection of the unconditional love of an all-merciful God. Instead, children of that half-century were being taught that God's love was conditional on our behaviour; that he could change his mind about us; that he withdrew his love and punished us in eternal fire if we died unconfessed. This notion was reinforced by the formal words of contrition we learned by heart and recited in confession. We begged pardon for our sins and said that we detested them 'above all things' because 'they offend your infinite goodness'.

The leading imagery of sin for Catholic children throughout much of the twentieth century suggested a trivial, petulant God obsessed with cleanliness. Sins were described as discrete dirty marks on the robe of the soul. For a child, this robe was literal, despite the soul being a spirit and immortal. You were handed a clean, white robe on the day of baptism. If you told a lie, or hit your sister, or were disobedient to your mother, black marks appeared. If you did something seriously wrong, it became entirely black and that person was destined for Hell.

Goodness, or 'holiness', was not a practice of virtue in the whole of one's daily life and relations with others, but rather, the feeling you experienced on leaving the confessional box with your robe nicely laundered.

IN THE SECOND HALF of the twentieth century, many Catholic writers recalled the trauma of confession in childhood. The American journalist Christopher Buckley wrote about his own anxiety as a child at the prospect of going to confession. You were told, he said, to 'go into a dark booth with a man dressed in black and tell [him] . . . things that you haven't even told your mother.' The experience was like bereavement of the worst kind for a child: 'It's really the most sobering thing I can imagine happening . . . short of losing your mother or father'.[7]

In Frank O'Connor's short story 'First Confession', the box's dark geography exemplifies a subtext of acute anxiety. Jackie, the authorial voice, reminiscing on the experience from the vantage of adulthood, writes: 'I was scared to death . . .' He goes on: 'It was pitch-dark, and I couldn't see priest or anything else. Then I really began to be frightened.' Jackie begins by making his confession to the panelled wall, before realising his mistake. Baffled by the arrangement of the pitch dark interior, he clambers onto the elbow rest of the penitent's kneeler (he would not have been the first or the last to do so). When the priest slams back the hatch, he can see only the boy's knees, level with the grille.[8]

First confession and communion, which had acquired the status of an infant rite of Catholic initiation, were surrounded by rules and regulations, which, to break deliberately, meant falling into mortal sin. Children, like adults, for example, were obliged to fast from midnight the night before receiving communion. In *Memories of a Catholic Girlhood*, the author Mary McCarthy reveals that on the very day of her first communion, she believed that she had committed a sacrilege. 'I took a drink of water. Unthinkingly, of course, for had it not been drilled into me that the Host must be received fasting, on penalty of mortal sin?' With the expensive dress, the veil, and the prayer book, she had not the courage to drop out. She received communion. It had only been a sip of water, she acknowledges, 'but it made no difference'. She remembers that she felt 'despair' that summer morning, adding, with pitiful understatement, 'It is quite common for children making their first communion to have just such a mishap as mine'.[9]

Another writer, the late Anthony Burgess, told how he believed he had broken the fast on his first communion day walking to the church in the rain by opening his mouth with joy to taste the shower. 'Wasn't that liquid nourishment?' it dawned on him, as he made his way to the communion rail. Mortal sins lay in wait for the growing child like a heavily infested minefield. 'It was all too easy to sin', Burgess commented. 'Life, indeed, seemed all sin. I bought a twopenny sausage roll at Price's and then remembered it was Friday. I ate it nevertheless. Still chewing, I ran to evening confession. Swallowing the last flake, I began to whimper.'[10]

For many children, the mental torture of confession began with the difficulty of finding 'sins' to tell. Many children

invented sins only to regret it, realising that they had committed a sacrilege by telling a lie in confession. In his memoir
This Boy's Life, Tobias Wolff recalls that he could not think of
a single sin to confess. Having failed to come up with anything, he was sternly dismissed from the confessional box and
told to return when he had something to tell. In the end he
appropriated a list of sins verbally suggested to him, merely
as examples, by his nun catechist. He had continued to find
it impossible to isolate a single sin from his memory: 'It felt
like fishing a swamp, where you feel the tug of something
that at first seems promising and then resistant and finally
hopeless as you realize that you've snagged the bottom, that
you have the whole planet on the other end of your line.'[11]
The problem was production of the 'list': the labelled, numbered items, detached from relationships, isolated from the
narrative flow of life as experienced and imagined.

The injustice of the punishments of Hell was baffling
to the child. Through to the 1960s, Hell—mostly taught
by classroom nuns, and preached by Franciscans, Redemp-
torists, and Passionists on parish missions—meant eternal
punishment for anyone who died with their sins unconfessed,
whether that sinner was a mass murderer or a child who had
merely missed Mass. For the generation of Catholic children
who were raised under the threat of imminent nuclear attack,
there was the additional fear of sudden death in a state of
unconfessed mortal sin.

Then there was Purgatory, where time was measured, as
on earth, in days, weeks, months, and years. The novelist

Roddy Doyle, pondering Purgatory, stoically exemplifies through his boy hero in *Paddy Clarke Ha Ha Ha* the cruel insanity of that place. It was like Hell, but not forever: 'It was about a million years for every venial sin[.] . . . Telling lies to your parents, cursing, taking the Lord's name in vain—they were all a million years. . . . If you made a good confession right before you died you didn't have to go to Purgatory at all; you went straight up to heaven'—which raised a question: 'Even if the fella killed loads of people?' The answer: 'Even.'[12]

And there was more than just fire and brimstone to the infernal torments. For Christopher Durang, author of the bitingly satirical play *Sister Mary Ignatius Explains It All for You*, instruction on Hell in preparation for confession involved another added extra: 'I picked up the understanding that mortal sin not only sends you to hell, they also pound the nails into Christ's body—sort of working in retrospect. And you know you're causing our all-loving Lord his infinite agony by something you've done.'[13]

Antonia White's convent school girl, in her novel *Frost in May*, writes up her thoughts after the annual retreat, at which the visiting priest has spoken luridly of death, judgement, and Hell. She notes that the cruel physical tortures suffered by the damned are enhanced by an added psychological factor: 'The damned suffered always from appalling thirst, their swollen tongues were parched and cracked.' But they suffered still more, she goes on, 'from agony of mind, from the separation of God, after Whom they now so bitterly longed.' They would gladly endure 'ten thousand years of torment for the sake of one second of earthly life in which they might repent and be reconciled to Him.'[14]

Catechists worked hard to get across the concept of eternity to their small charges. In his memoir *The Inside Story*, Neil McKenty (for whom the confessional was 'an up-ended coffin') remembers the description conjured up for him, when he was just seven, by a visiting Redemptorist priest at his hometown parish in Ontario, Canada: 'Now imagine a bird flying over a sand beach a thousand miles long, a hundred miles wide and fifty feet deep. This bird flies over the beach just once a year. And each year the bird picks up just one grain of sand. By the time the sand will all be gone, eternity in the ovens of hell will be just beginning.'[15]

Frank O'Connor's version of Hell's eternal punishment, as explained by a nun, was typical of the comparisons drawn by generations of catechists. The teaching sister produces a candle, takes out a half-crown, and offers it to the first boy who can hold one finger in the flame for five minutes by the school clock. No one volunteers. Then she says, 'Are you afraid of holding one finger—only one finger!—in a little candle flame for five minutes and not afraid of burning all over in roasting hot furnaces for all eternity?' Then she expatiates: 'All eternity! Just think of that! A whole life time goes by and it's nothing, not even a drop in the ocean of our sufferings.'[16]

And then, as children advanced towards puberty, there were the sins and the language of 'impurity' to deal with. The philosopher Michel Foucault argues in his *History of Sexuality* that confession shaped the modern language and perception of sexuality and the body. A bitter-sweet example is Molly Bloom's dramatic monologue in James Joyce's *Ulysses*, where she reminisces about reporting a bit of adolescent groping in confession: 'I hate that confession when I used to go to Father Corrigan he touched me father and what harm if he did where and I said on the canal bank like a fool but whereabouts on your person my child on the leg behind high up was it yes rather high up was it where you sit down yes O Lord couldnt he say bottom right out and have done with it . . .'[17]

For the writer Margaret Hebblethwaite, the difficulty of managing the language of sex and the body made confession-going baffling: 'How should we go to confession, if we did not know how to name our sins? Supposing they were sins to do with sex, and we did not know how to find words for them?'[18]

The technical language of contrition, involving such principles as 'occasions of sin' and 'firm purpose of amendment', was easily grasped, but not so easily applied to situations in real life. There could be life-changing misunderstandings. Edna O'Brien had been taught that a mere kiss was 'an occasion of sin', and therefore a mortal sin, and that her inability to make 'a firm purpose of amendment' never to do it again made her confession invalid. Her account evokes an entire era of neurotic scrupulosity inflicted on generations of young Catholics.[19]

MANY INFORMANTS, responding to my article on confession in *The Tablet* on 18 August 2012, had childhood memories of confession as an oppressive and disturbing experience.[20]

There were confessors whose oppressive intimacy was verbal rather than physical. An anonymous female correspondent wrote from the United States of her experience, at the age of ten, at the hands of a 'troubled and alcoholic' curate who 'began questioning girls in explicit and obscene detail about their sex lives during confession, suggesting things—masturbation, oral sex, even incest.' These were actions, she commented, that they had not even read about. Her reason for not complaining about this priest sheds light on a curious aspect of the 'seal of confession' from a child's point of view. 'Individually sickened, but terrified of violating the seal of the confessional and believing our word would not be trusted, we endured the lewd catechizing for weeks, not even telling one another.'

Another correspondent, a 'Ms M', told of her traumatic first confession at the age of seven: 'When it came to making my act of contrition, the priest suddenly shouted at me: "Stand up! Say the prayer again and say it as if you are truly sorry!" He made me say it three times on my feet, shaking from head to toe. I came out of that confessional box a nervous wreck.'

A woman wrote from Australia of 'so much fear on entering the dark box' when she was an inmate in a Catholic orphanage. 'My feet', she remembered, 'were soaked in my own urine from fear.' On exiting from the confessional, a nun dragged her 'by the ear to get the bucket and mop in front of everyone to clean it up.'

There are many accounts of incongruous reactions on the part of confessors. 'Ms B' in the United States wrote that she told a confessor that she was being sexually abused by her father. 'I agonised for weeks until I finally made the decision. . . . I wasn't expecting a miracle but just some words of encouragement I could hang on to.' The priest listened carefully, then responded: 'Try to avoid that occasion of sin.' She went on: 'With those words he dumped all the responsibility of what was happening on my shoulders. *I was nine years old.* I was devastated.'

Encounters with bullying confessors led to life-long disillusion. 'Mr F', in his eighty-sixth year, wrote: 'I gradually realised that loyalty and obedience could easily become words hiding a submissiveness and an unwillingness to assume responsibility for one's actions and encouraged those in authority to become unreasoning bullies.'

Many of the male respondents recalled the oppressive obligation to confess masturbation. A sixty-eight-year-old man wrote that the unseemly curiosity on the part of his parish priest started before he even had the language to understand the 'sin', let alone the experience of it. '"Have you been touching yourself?" he'd say. I knew nothing about sex, had no language to talk about it.'

Many wrote of the way in which confessors would probe for indications of sexual sin. A fifty-three-year-old gay man wrote: 'I found confessing, at best, a sterile experience; at worst, it was profoundly uncomfortable, with most of the confessors taking too keen an interest in my impure thoughts and acts.' 'Miss MG' wrote: 'I was even refused absolution and made to go to see a doctor because of my masturbation "sin." . . . It ruined my adolescence.'

The majority of correspondents recalled instructions on sin and confession that prompted guilt anxieties, commonly known as 'scruples'—a form of obsessive conscience underpinned by terrors of mortal sin and eternal Hell. A 'Dr. S' wrote: 'The catechesis of the time was just incredibly damaging, and left many children marinated in guilt and scruple, myself included.'

Another correspondent, 'Ms JN', wrote of the shock she received, at the age of twelve, on learning from the nuns that 'touching anyone else's private parts was very sinful'. Ms JN added: 'Just at the time when we were fizzing with hormones and curiosity . . . I developed scruples[,] and they made my life a misery for countless years even after I married and had children. I never discussed them with anyone.'

Nuns were given to prompting guilt feelings with outlandish suggestions. A 'Ms I', in her eighties, wrote: 'My children were told by a lovely Servite nun that if the [communion wafer] touched their teeth (during Holy Communion) they had committed a mortal sin.' Another woman, Diana, said that scruples induced in her adolescent years by confession almost led to her committing suicide. 'My scruples began to worsen. Had I swallowed toothpaste when cleaning my teeth before mass, had I fasted for long enough before communion?

I would wake in the morning and look out at the beautiful, cloudless sky, only suddenly to remember these unbearable thoughts which I could not avoid.'

Correspondents had an array of stories of inappropriate behaviour on the part of confessors. Many remember being placed on a priest's lap to make their confessions. One recalled being caned by a priest for alleged misbehaviour. 'He then sat down and took me standing between his knees to receive my confession. I was too small to kneel.'

An anonymous writer recounted his experience as the son of a Catholic prison officer. The prison chaplain acted as their parish priest, and their Sunday devotions, including confession, were held in the prison chapel: 'There was no private space in which to hear confession, except that is for the Ladies and Gents cubicle style toilets at the front door. So that is where we went for Confession. . . . Father would be seated on the toilet bowl seat, and I would kneel down in front of him.'

Of all the bizarre stories of peculiar confessional circumstances, one especially stands out. A correspondent wrote that as a little girl her first confession was heard 'in the corridor of the church, with the priest's two big dogs on either side' of him as he stood before her.

Although it is the sobering argument of this book that countless children were oppressed, and many traumatised, by the practice of early confession, there are no reliable statistics, only the memories and testimonies of those surviving generations who endured it. Less widespread, and yet profound and lasting in its consequences for victims, was the exploitation of the confessional for sexual child abuse. To understand the systemic connection between confession, the confessional oppression of children, and clerical sexual abuse of children, it is necessary to explore the seminary formation and the culture of clericalism that flourished after the pontificate of Pius X.

Eight

The Making of a Confessor

Total institutions disrupt or defile precisely those actions that in civil society have the role of attesting to the actor and those in his presence that he has some command over his world—that he is a person with 'adult' self-determination, autonomy, and freedom of action.

—Erving Goffman *Asylums*

It is not surprising that men kept in short trousers for years should be incapable of authority and responsibility when thrust upon them as parish priests in middle age.

—Charles Davis, *A Question of Conscience*

S EMINARY LIFE FROM THE 1920S TO THE 1960S WAS largely a product of Pius X's 'restorations' of the Church in the first decade of the century. The seminary training for Catholic priests, regulated centrally from the Vatican department known as Discipline of the Clergy, involved six years of full-time cloistered residence. Many seminarians had already spent between five and seven years in junior seminaries, which were similarly monastic. The aim was to create a 'cleric' whose characteristics included prompt obedience to authority in the vertical hierarchical structure, along with doctrinal acquiescence to Rome's teaching, both in content and interpretation, especially on sexual and 'life' matters. As we have seen, Pius X's seminary reforms emphasised segregation from the laity and especially from women. In theory, this was meant to produce dedication to celibacy and the disciplines of sexual continence. But the consequences also included a guarded, patriarchal attitude towards women; an expectation of deference from the lay faithful; and a tendency to close protective ranks against outsiders, involving instinctive secrecy.

The seminary prepared its ordinands to be judges and healers of souls: the arbiters and exemplars of what constituted sin and virtue. The newly ordained priest was endowed with sacramental 'faculties' bestowing powers, sanctioned by his bishop, to administer or suspend absolution of sins.

———————

ARRIVING AT THE SENIOR SEMINARY for the Catholic archdiocese of Birmingham at the age of eighteen in 1958, I entered a red-brick neo-Gothic edifice with gables, turrets, and a cloister wide enough to drive two buses abreast. Situated north of the city of Birmingham, and bordered by two highways and a cemetery, Oscott College was screened by groves of trees. There were bars on all the ground-floor windows. The building resembled, as did many Catholic seminaries at that time, a Victorian mental asylum; and it was indeed a 'total institution' as defined by sociologist Erving Goffman: 'a place of residence and work where a large number of like-situated individuals, cut off from the wider society for an appreciable period of time, together lead an enclosed, formally administered round of life.'[1]

I entered the seminary several weeks before the death of Pius XII, who had been pope for nearly twenty years, and the election of the stout and cheerful John XXIII. The ambiance of the clerical culture was patrician; legalistic in language and perspective. Attitudes towards other Christian faith groups were aloof; towards non-Christian faiths, dismissive. Seminary formation, the Church, and the priesthood appeared to us as unchanged and unchanging—*semper eadem*.

The seminaries were booming and turning out ever more ordained priests. There were 21 seminarians in my year, known as First Year Philosophy, and similar numbers in each of the years ahead of us, comprising Second Year Philosophy, followed by four years of Theology, making 120 students in all, with a dozen professors or lecturers.

There were at that time five senior seminaries in England with a similar student intake as well as four exclusively English seminaries abroad—one each in Lisbon and Valladolid, and two in Rome—all full. In the early 1960s, when I was due to be ordained, England was routinely turning out 200 ordained priests each year, about 120 diocesan and 80 from the religious orders. Elsewhere during that period ordinations amongst sizeable Catholic populations were at an all-time high, especially in Ireland, Western Europe, and the United States. Yet many of us had an impression of staleness and aridity even during those apparently halcyon years.

Only in retrospect would it be obvious that there had been something dysfunctional in the state of Catholic clericalism during our era. Given Pope John's age—he was seventy-six—nobody could have guessed that he would initiate an epoch-making council that would shake the Church to its foundations, promoting the idea of the faithful as a pilgrim people of God, engaging with the world. The shock would expose the deep-seated problems of priestly formation. The mass exodus of ordained priests worldwide from the 1960s to the 1970s, and the collapse in vocations, would speak for themselves. Locally, in England and Wales, since the year 2000 the number of newly ordained priests, diocesan and religious, has averaged just above 20 each year; compared with the early 1960s, that is a decline of 90 per cent. In the United States the ordinations collapsed from 1,575 in 1965 to 450 in 2002. The decline of potential confessors would have been critical for the fate of the sacrament of confession even had the faithful not rejected the practice: which they did.

———————

WHEN I ENTERED THE SEMINARY there were more than enough priests to confess the long lines of penitents waiting to enter the dark boxes every week. Few of us could imagine the collapse in numbers that lay ahead. In the United States, about 3 per cent of parishes, 549, were without a resident priest in 1965. In 2002, there were 2,928 priestless parishes, about 15 per cent of US parishes, and rising. By 2020, it is estimated that a quarter of all parishes, 4,656, will lack a priest. Between 1965 and 2002, the number of seminarians in the United States dropped from 49,000 to 4,700, a 90 per cent decrease. Seminaries have closed in their hundreds across America: there were 596 seminaries in 1965, and only 200 in 2000.[2]

There were many fine, decent men of generous temperament at Oscott. A small group of ex–national service men, and late vocations, exerted a modicum of common sense, knowledge of the world, and even at times ribald good humour. Yet the younger majority, fresh from junior seminaries, dominated the tone and were only too willing to be moulded by their superiors. The majority of our intake were born Catholics who had been catechized for confession from the age of six and younger. Many were from large and relatively poor families, many originally of Irish extraction.

In common with my companions who had been in the junior seminary, I had no notion of what a celibate life would in time entail. Apart from brief vacations, we had been segregated from girls and women, including mothers, aunts, sisters, and cousins. We were emotionally and socially immature, certainly not prepared to make long-term commitments about our future emotional and sexual lives and relationships. We did not know, most of us, what an intimate marital relationship was, let alone what it would mean to abstain from it for a lifetime. While final ordination would take place at the age of twenty-four, six or seven years off, the commitment was not a one-off decision to be left to the day of ordination. We had already committed ourselves to something that we did not understand.

And yet, we were not even preparing for lives as bachelors. We lived like schoolboys. Each student had his own small, sparse, identically furnished room. We were obliged to wear a cassock, Roman collar, and black shoes at all times. On rare trips outside the college, we wore black suits, black raincoats, and Roman collars. We were called at 6 A.M. for meditation in chapel before Mass at 7 A.M. A student would rap on the door and call out: '*Laus Deo*' (Praise be to God), to which one replied '*Deo Gratias*' (Thanks be to God). Breakfast, consisting of cold toast made the night before, cornflakes, and All-Bran, with anaemic coffee or tea, followed thanksgiving after Mass. There was usually time for a cigarette after breakfast. Most students and lecturers were addicted to smoking, which was seen as an aid to the celibate life.

The mornings were spent in classes (punctuated by breaks for a quick smoke), followed by prayers in church before lunch at 1 P.M. We were free between lunch and supper, which was at 7:30 P.M., when we would eat in silence while listening to stories from the lives of the saints, excerpts from the Code of Canon Law, and an improving Catholic book, read from a pulpit in the refectory. Through the long afternoons and evenings, which were meant to be taken up with private study, spiritual reading, or perhaps praying, students would spend a lot of time sitting around in each other's rooms, talking, drinking instant coffee, and, of course, smoking. If we took a walk outside the college grounds we were obliged to go in threes (having sought permission, and given a good reason), and it was laid down that there should be one in front and two behind so as not to inconvenience others on the pavements by walking three abreast. Rosary followed supper, and the Greater Silence was observed from 9 P.M., when we gathered in church for night prayers. The silence continued until breakfast the next day. 'Lights out' was at 10:15 P.M., with no exceptions.

The regime was remarkable for its restrictions. We did no voluntary social work, even though the city of Birmingham had more than its fair share of poverty, the sick, the hospitalised, the homeless, and the unemployed. Women, apart from the hidden domestic servants, never entered. No visiting speakers came. Nor were we allowed to attend lectures, concerts, movies, or the theatre on the outside. There was only one ancient radio, which was situated in the billiard room. I only got to listen to it once, when there was a repeat broadcast of the Jesuit philosopher Father Frederick Copleston's debate on the existence of God with Bertrand Russell. A single copy of *The Times* was delivered to the common room, to be somehow shared among the 120 of us. We visited no parishes, no offices, no factories. We never entered a school, and would learn nothing of child education or child psychology—although we were destined, as priests, to spend much time with children in catechism classes and confession. There was no gymnasium; there were no visits to public swimming pools. We were allowed brief holidays, but not at Christmas or Easter, when we might have come in contact with our wider families. Relatives and friends never visited. Despite much potential talent, there were no musical groups, and we had no record players. There was one out-of-tune piano. There was no television.

Seminary life in its diurnal routine essentially enabled a young man to avoid the responsibilities that are shouldered by most adults of that age. For six years we were fed and sheltered gratis. We never cooked a meal, washed a dish, or laundered a shirt; nor did we sweep the floor or change the linen on our beds. The most we did for ourselves was to polish the shiny toe caps of our black shoes. We did not serve others, even our *confrères*: we lived to ourselves alone; yet we would have been astonished had anyone suggested that we were acquiring a warped sense of entitlement.

Individualism was eradicated by routines of conformity, starting with our dress. Our hair was cut to a conformed shortness by visiting barbers. Being 'singular', or 'ostenta-tious', were the buzzwords for transgressing conformity (a contemporary in another seminary, a non-smoker, told me that his spiritual director ordered him to smoke in order to avoid being 'singular' among the majority smokers). Our lives, ruled by bells, meant that we made few choices about our day; the big decision about our future, to the end of our lives, had already been made. Even the decision to leave the seminary, we had been told, must be made by our superiors, lest we departed in bad faith. There was little scope for mak-ing committed friendships at just that time in life when the forging of significant relationships is crucial for growth in character, personality, generosity, and human empathy. We were encouraged to treat our fellow seminarians with an equal measure of detachment. 'Special' or 'particular' friendships, as they were known, could lead to occasions of sin. We were conscious, in any case, that committed relationships, apart from being a spiritual imperfection, would be pointless, as we would all be scattered geographically after ordination.

The most popular, and constantly recommended, work of spiritual guidance was the *Imitation of Christ* by Thomas à Kempis, which counselled 'custody of the eyes', avoidance of idle gossip, 'recollection' (a sense of constant, serious aware-ness), repeated examination of conscience, and avoidance of 'curiosity' about secular matters—the 'world'. We were hardly capable of sensible discussions about current affairs, as we had little knowledge of what was current on the outside. The political tendency was reactionary. The models constantly put before us were those of St. Jean-Marie Vianney—the *Curé d'Ars*, and the tragic *petite fleurette*, St. Thérèse of Lisieux, the simple young French Carmelite nun of the previous century who had achieved heroic sanctity in 'little things'.

Our conversations were trivial, schoolboyish, repetitive, and anecdotal; some even had stocks of edifying stories and preachy conversational gambits which even the averagely pious found cringe-making. Given the hothouse atmosphere, and suppressed youthful and sexual energies, there were occasional subterranean infatuations, jealousies, sulks, and periodic tears. On more than one occasion a student stood poised to throw himself off the crenelated central tower, to be talked down by the long-suffering spiritual director. Those with more self-control, or less labile emotions, would manifest a prim exterior of reproach in the face of such dramatics. For some, being priggish was a full-time job.

Every so often a student would disappear without warning from his place at table and chapel. The 'defection', which might well have been expulsion, was never discussed or explained. Following an intense on-off 'special friendship', one of our number left the seminary without warning and later threw himself under a train near Oxford.

THE WORD 'SEMINARY' derives from the Latin for 'seed': the image is of a protective environment, a greenhouse, where the seedbeds are being protected from the damaging environment of the world outside. The seeds are being specially grown, forced artificially into clerical plants. The problem for those responsible for clerical training was that the world outside had been increasingly inimical to Catholic ideals of chastity and celibacy. Pius X knew this all too well when he tightened up the disciplines of clerical formation at the beginning of the century against the background of 'Modernist' thought, which included psychoanalysis alongside a host of other 'heresies'. By the late 1950s and early 1960s, however, a tide of influence, carried through the media and known as the 'sexual revolution', was threatening traditional standards of Catholic chastity, not least within the clerical and religious estate.

Despite the attempts of our superiors to make the seminary a media-free environment, and to control our reading and our egress into the world, the impact of the new sexual freedoms seeped into our world through every nook and cranny. We did, after all, go home for several weeks a year, where we were exposed to television and magazines, and went to the cinema. Most of us had brothers and sisters in their teens and twenties whose music and dress brought the new youth culture home to us.

———————

IN THE MEANTIME, and in stark contrast, our minds were being shaped and narrowed through the educational curriculum. The first two years involved the study of Scholastic philosophy, which was unrelentingly abstract and dogmatic.

It was taught through dictated notes from the lecturer's rostrum. There was a single textbook in Latin with numbered paragraphs, like a car maintenance manual. There was a campaign within the Church to maintain Latin as the required language of our lectures, which was to impel the new Pope John XXIII, even as he planned the reforming Second Vatican Council, to order the exclusive use of Latin in seminary courses.[3] There was variety in the study of the history of philosophy, but we were obliged to endure the dictated notes of the lecturer rather than be exposed to original texts. There were no classroom discussions, or even opportunities for discussions among ourselves. We had a well-stocked library, where the dust gathered on the rarely consulted volumes. The consequence, for those of us who digested the diet of spoon-fed information, was the development of a didactic tone of voice: a dry, one-way, finger-wagging certitude. Despite the acquiescence, obedience, and humility required of us (or perhaps because of it), seminary was a school for authoritarians.

There were occasional surprise events, which only served to demonstrate the institutional tedium. There was the student who appeared in chapel for night prayers on his first evening in the college wearing pyjamas and dressing gown instead of the cassock and collar. What was he thinking! That we were a relaxed, home-spun domestic fellowship? There were gales of nervous giggles, as if a wave of insanity had gripped the entire student body. Then there was the intensely devout student, older than the rest of us, who set his room on fire with the votive candles he kept blazing all night before a statue of the Virgin by his bed. More nervous tittering ensued in the choir stalls whenever he took his place in the days that followed. On another occasion, a small, intellectually rebellious group invited a Jesuit philosopher to meet and talk with them—he had not reckoned on being smuggled into the college clandestinely through a barred window, where he got stuck for twenty minutes. Such were our small diversions and rebellions.

The courses in pastoral and moral theology, which sourced our training to be confessors, were based on treatises that went back to the original work of the paragon of moral theology—Alphonsus Liguori. There were two sets of manuals: the three-volume Latin textbook *Summa Theologiae Moralis* by H. Noldin and A. Schmitt, and the four-volume English textbook *Moral and Pastoral Theology* by H. Davis. The Noldin and Schmitt, whose first edition appeared in 1926, effectively set the direction of Catholic clerical thinking on morals up to the end of the Second Vatican Council in 1965 and somewhat beyond. For the English-speaking seminaries, Davis, first published in 1935, was essential, although sections of it, mostly dealing with sexual morals, were in Latin in order to bar the laity from acquainting themselves with material that might have put bad ideas into their heads. Davis was considered to be impressively up to date. He expounded perspectives from the latest neurophysiology in the 'morbid sexuality' sections. For example, he cited neurologist Santiago Ramón y Cajal's 'law of avalanche', from around the turn of the century, to explain how in the nerves 'a disturbance, at first localized, is diffused over a great many of the cells of the brain if attention is focused upon it.'[4] He thereby explained 'how sex feelings get beyond control if the original stimulus is fostered rather than suppressed.' He had in mind, naturally, masturbation, the single, unrelieved obsession of Catholic moral theology and daily, it sometimes seemed, preoccupation of Catholic clerics in those days.

A review of these texts tells us much about the Catholic moral mentality that shaped generations of clerical notions of virtue and sin, and hence the influence exerted via confession over generations of the Catholic young through two-thirds of the twentieth century. One is struck, first of all, by the dysfunctional casuistry. Take fasting before Holy Communion. It was taught that to break the fast and receive the Blessed Sacrament, as we have seen, was a mortal sin. The textbooks enlarged on the circumstances in which the fast might or might not be broken. The rule admitted, it was pointed out, of no exception, and it extended 'to the smallest quantity of food or drink taken as such'.

So what does it mean to 'eat' or 'drink'? The thing consumed must be 'taken exteriorly'. So it is not a violation of the fast, for example, 'to swallow blood from the gums, or teeth, or tongue, or nasal cavities', although it would be a violation of the fast 'to swallow blood flowing externally from the exterior parts of the lips, or from a cut finger, or from the nose, or to swallow tears, unless in each case only a few drops entered the mouth and were mingled with the saliva.' To violate the fast, moreover, requires that a substance 'must pass from the mouth into the stomach, so that the fast is not broken if liquid is taken into the mouth, as an antiseptic or for gargling, and is not swallowed.' A third condition insists that violation of the fast occurs 'by the action of eating and drinking', and inadvertence 'has no bearing on the matter' even if it is a 'drink given to a patient during sleep'. Davis declares that the 'divines' are still disagreeing whether a 'nutritive injection' is food, but certainly the introduction of soup or milk through a stomach pump is not allowed, 'whether the injected liquid be intended to nourish or merely to flush.' Turning to the vexed question of nail-biting, Davis reports that he believes that this does not affect the fast, 'but biting off and swallowing pieces of finger skin might do so, if the particles were more than the smallest and not mixed with saliva.'[5]

In the section on what constitutes 'food' as opposed to 'non food', the fingernails appear again. In a final wrap-up, Davis writes:

Metallic substances in specie (gold, silver, iron, lead, etc.) do not violate the fast, but if taken as powder and chemically treated, as iron jelloids, bismuth, charcoal tabloids and powder, sulphur, they do certainly violate the fast. The same is true of stone, and glass, probably of earth and chalk. Straw and green branches are nutritive, but not dry wood; human hair is not digestible, nor, probably, human nails. Wax is digestible and also linen and cotton, but neither silk nor wool. Paper is not certainly food, nor are dried fruit stones cleansed of all fruit, though the kernel is food.[6]

As we sat digesting this information, the proposition that anyone would actually consume iron jelloids, fingernails, and sulphur never struck us as absurd.

A similar approach was applied to other potential mortal sins within the ambit of obedience to ecclesiastical rules, such as late arrival at Mass (meaning that the Sunday obligation to attend Mass had not been fulfilled), and rules for days of fasting and abstinence. The law of fast days during this era, and going back centuries, prescribed that only one full meal be taken, but that a smaller 'collation' might be consumed at two points during the twenty-four hours. Lengthy casuistic argumentations followed in Noldin-Schmitt and Davis on what constituted a 'full meal': how many ounces; how long it could take (longer than two hours?); whether one could take a break in the middle, or several breaks, and so forth. Liquids were also a subject of arcane hair-splitting. 'Wine, beer, tea, cocoa, coffee, do not violate the fast, but soup, oil, thick chocolate, fruit and whole milk, are foodstuffs and violate the fast.' To complicate matters, it was allowed that while one was taking a drink, a small item of food might also be consumed '*ne potus noceat*', as Noldin had it in Latin: 'lest the drink by itself should do harm'. But there was much written on how much, and how often, these morsels accompanying drink could be consumed. Abstinence from meat on Fridays (a mortal sin to break) also had its complex reservations and ordinances. We learned, for example, that 'fish', in the view of the moralists, included 'frogs, snails, tortoises, oysters, lobsters, otters, beavers, crabs'—also, by the peculiar ancient tradition of certain dioceses, 'gulls, ducks, teals, and coot'.[7]

What we were drawing from this approach to 'moral theology' was the importance of discovering, and being conversant with, myriad distinctions and hair-splitting rules in preparation for our lives as confessors in the dark box, until common sense, individual moral agency, and exercise of conscience became redundant.

Nine

Seminary Sexology

> Immodest acts, however slight they may
> be, that are done from the motive of
> exciting lust, even though it do not ensue
> [*sic*], are grievous sins.
>
> —H. Davis, SJ, *Moral and Pastoral Theology*

SEXUAL SIN WAS THE DOMINANT TOPIC OF THE MORAL textbooks we were obliged to study in preparation for future ministry. The sections on 'Chastity and Modesty' directly invoked the sixth and ninth commandments (in the Catholic Decalogue numerology) as the ultimate source of authority: 'Thou shalt not commit adultery' and 'Thou shalt not covet thy neighbour's wife.' According to our moralists, the sixth commandment not only forbade adultery, 'but all actions which are intended to lead or which naturally lead to it, and all actions contrary to the orderly propagation of the race.' Meanwhile, the ninth commandment forbade 'all lustful thoughts and desires'. Hence it was a mortal sin to derive the slightest wilful pleasure not only from words, thoughts, or deeds involving the illicit exercise of the sexual act, but also from wilful words, thoughts, or deeds that might *lead* to such 'pleasures'.[1]

The point of the sixth and ninth commandments, then, was to inculcate in all members of the faithful the virtues of chastity and modesty, which virtues 'exclude in the unmarried all voluntary expression of the sensitive appetite for venereal pleasure.' This 'pleasure is normally associated as well with the full exercise of the generative function as with the movement of the generative organs as they are preparing to function.' All were called upon to be chaste, according to our moralists—both married and unmarried: 'the rational motive of the virtue of chastity is the reasonableness of controlling sexual appetite in the married and of excluding it in the unmarried.' At the same time, life-long virginity bestows 'a special aureole'. Marriage was instituted by God for the 'allaying of concupiscence as for the procreation of children', but 'the state of virginity is the higher and nobler state and absolutely more pleasing to God.' Then, again: 'All sexual pleasure, outside wedlock, that is directly voluntary is grievously sinful.'[2]

Homosexuality merited a mere six lines in our four-volume treatise by H. Davis, less than necrophilia. And yet the moralists established their abhorrence of homosexuality by placing it sixth in a catalogue of 'perversions of the sexual appetites, beyond the order of nature', right after sadism, masochism, fetishism, voyeurism, and exhibitionism (which, writes Davis, is often a perversion found in old men!: '*Invenitur haec perversionem in senibus*'). Homosexuality, which he termed 'contrary sexuality' ('*contraria sexualitas*'), could be between men and men or between women and women. He adds what he calls the vice of the Greeks, namely 'paederastia', meaning the love of boys.

Catholic priests could look forward to responsible roles in the running of parish schools soon after ordination. Most parish priests would be *ex officio* chairmen of the school management boards. Yet what we were taught about moral and emotional development in childhood was outlandishly misguided. 'Moral education' for children, according to Davis, should involve 'the curbing of curiosity'; 'the immediate expulsion of impure phantasies'; 'avoidance of what are called soft and sentimental friendships with those of the opposite sex at a comparatively early age, since such friendships induce precocious sexuality'; 'disapproval of mixed dances between small boys and girls, and much more, the co-education of the sexes close to the age of puberty if not earlier'; and prohibition of 'promiscuous and general friendships between the sexes.' Matched with these environmental considerations were peculiar notions of sexual physiology and psychology. 'The so called sexual necessity of young people is often produced artificially through the nervous system under constant stimulation of an erotic nature.' The principal strategy to attain chastity in children, therefore, is to inculcate control of the senses: 'Modesty in act is expressed . . . by reasonable concealment of those parts of the body whose exposure might be an occasion of lustful desire, as by abstaining from all unnecessary touching of those parts and the parts adjoining them.' Modesty of the eyes requires abstaining from 'all prurient and dangerous curiosity.' Modesty of speech involves avoidance of 'suggestive expressions'. Modesty of 'gait in man' is the avoidance of 'effeminate behaviour', and in women of 'attitudes that are bold and daring'.[3]

Impurity, too, has its distinctions. First comes 'complete venereal pleasure' that is directly voluntary outside legitimate sexual intercourse, the purpose of the latter being 'the propagation of the race, whether or not the effect ensue.' Then 'incomplete venereal pleasure', even in the 'smallest degree', is grievously sinful, since it 'has reference by its very nature to legitimate sexual intercourse'. It follows that 'it is a perversion of nature that man or woman should procure even this incomplete pleasure for their solitary gratification.'

The moralists inveighed against an array of occasions of sins of impurity, including kissing, dancing, unbridled music, and gazing on pictures ('protracted gazing [on nudes] without any just reason will usually be a grievous sin'). Sun-bathing can be an occasion of sin, also gymnastic exercise, 'even where uniforms are worn'. Special care is to be taken 'of Christian modesty in young women and girls, which is so gravely impaired by any such kind of exhibition', writes Davis, quoting the encyclical letter of Pope Pius XI on 'The Christian Education of Youth'. It was Pius XI, moreover, who in 1936 wrote an encyclical on films which was cited by Davis:

'Everyone knows what damage is done to the soul by bad motion pictures.' Pius XI might well have had a point, even in his day. But equally significant are the closed attitudes and mindset absorbed by generations of ordinands at a time when Western culture was increasingly sexually explicit and permissive.[4]

The moralists taught that even small children harboured sexual desires. Father Davis explains: 'Even the youngest children have a tendency to venereal excitation, and it would be both disgraceful and a grievous sin against chastity and justice to provoke them to it. . . . It is a delusion to suppose that a child below the age of puberty is a sexless being.' Children, 'even tiny children', must not be herded together without close supervision, since 'their animal instincts lead them into indecent play. . . . In the case of most prostitutes, the mischief is really done before the age of twelve.'[5]

For these reasons, Davis continues, Pius X had advocated frequent Holy Communion 'from their tender years', and 'daily if possible', so that 'they might thence derive strength to resist their sensual passions, to cleanse themselves from the stains of daily faults, and to avoid those graver sins to which human frailty is liable'.

Linked to frequent communion, as we have seen, was the importance of frequent confession for small children, which within a decade or so revealed problems, of which Noldin and Schmitt, as well as Davis, appear well aware. Davis advocates 'conditional absolution' in confessions when priests come across 'a child that does not appear to have come to

the use of reason'. He notes that 'many children are apt to
be perfunctory' in confessing, especially young boys. Even in
childhood, confession has become 'routine'. 'The haste with
which boys confess is a fault that must be corrected.' He is
aware, moreover, of the danger of scrupulosity in the young,
although he appears to advocate the source of the problem
while drawing attention to its consequences: 'Children should
be particularly exhorted to tell every sin they remember, not
to conceal any sin at all, even if a venial sin, for the habit of
concealing sins may grow on them, and some children suffer
mental anguish of a real sort intermittently for years owing
to an imagined sacrilegious confession.'[6] As my informants in
earlier chapters demonstrate, the exhortation to 'tell every sin'
had been the cause of the 'mental anguish' and not the cure.

———————————

MASTURBATION IS DEALT WITH at length in the moral manuals, and here, again, the 'mental anguish' of penitents is all
too evident. The topic, dealt with in Latin under the heading
'*Pollutio*', is prefaced by a preliminary introduction in English by Davis in a remarkable display of casuistry. Under
the subheading 'The duty of resisting sexual pleasure', Davis
writes of 'sexual movements', by which he means involuntary
erection in the case of men. But this must be resisted 'with
vigorous disregard and displeasure'. What he means here,
and the topic is expanded in a section written in Latin, is
the importance of resisting even a sense of enjoyment while

experiencing 'wet dreams', or nocturnal emissions (already, as we have seen, a topic of intense anxiety for the authors of confessional manuals in the early Middle Ages).

In a section headed 'Morbid Sexuality', Davis offers a recipe for dealing with the anguish of nocturnal emissions while in the same breath advocating tactics designed to provoke such anguish in the first place. In subsequent sections he goes on to claim that nocturnal emissions could arise as a result of actions that, performed in the cold light of day, are not in themselves sinful, but might, through experience, be seen to be the cause of the emissions at night—a recipe for agonising scruples over every kind of innocent activity. Again, some fashionable ideas on neurophysiology are invoked: 'As soon as sex ideas, and preoccupation with sex, find their way into consciousness, certain nerve centres are excited, and more blood finds its way to the sex centres of the spinal cord, thus highly sensitizing them. These produce physical effects on the external sex apparatus.'[7]

It is noteworthy that the masturbation section in Davis runs to five whole pages, whereas rape gets barely a third of a page. Cruelty to children and sexual molestation of minors merit no coverage whatsoever in the entire corpus of four volumes. Yet it is clear from a later section on 'solicitation' in the confessional that abuse of the young was widely known at the time of publication.

In cases of rape, Davis declares that it is a sin against chastity and justice. From foregoing discussions on chastity, it is clear that the offence is principally against God and against the soul of the perpetrator. As for justice, the nature of the injustice is not explained, it is simply posited as an abstract principle; although the moralists declare that in the case of a virgin the injustice is chiefly against the father—because his daughter's marriage prospects have been affected. On reparation, Davis asserts that a rapist should agree to marry his victim in order to put right his sin. Davis also expends space in the meagre section on rape to warn that a woman should resist the attack with all her might. (In 1950 Pius XII would canonize a girl called Maria Goretti who had died rather than surrender her virginity—a vivid example of the point made in the moral manuals.) If, however, the victim of rape enjoys the experience, she colludes in the sin. Davis does not consider that the victim might be an underage boy, or that the rape might have nothing to do with hymens and virgins.

———————

OVER 60 PER CENT of the more than three hundred lay male respondents who wrote to me in the course of my research for this book spoke of mental anguish prompted in childhood and youth because of the Church's moral teaching on masturbation, and their anxieties—even into their eighties—because of the catechetical and confessional insistence that it is a mortal sin. Priests who wrote or spoke were reticent about their own personal behaviour, moral attitudes, and mental anguish on the subject. Yet one spiritual director, a clinical psychologist who is also a priest, told me bluntly:

'Look, the diocesan priests all get by on what I call the three excesses: excessive whisky, excessive golf, and excessive *masturbation*.' In other conversations and interviews with priests, I was informed that the practice was widespread among clerics, and that there were even reports of priests either masturbating or achieving 'involuntary' orgasm in the confessional box.

Of all the sins associated with the sixth commandment, and what the moralists termed 'morbid sexuality', masturbation is the subject of the most keen, obsessive, and extensive discussion and analysis in the manuals. The point is stressed and reiterated that enjoyment of orgasm in both men women—whether the orgasm was voluntary or not, alone or aided by another, by the married or the unmarried—is deemed to be 'against Nature', in that the pleasure of the sex act being procured is detached from its true purpose—legitimate procreation. The coverage in the manuals spans an extraordinary variety of combinations and possibilities, as if a penitent might present in confession any of the following: orgasms achieved by eunuchs; males who reach orgasm but without ejaculation; coitus interruptus; orgasm while horse riding or on a bicycle; orgasm while dancing; spontaneous orgasm while viewing erotic pictures. All such actions, and many more, performed in the knowledge that orgasm might occur, are condemned as mortal sins even if the action does not result in orgasm. There is not even allowance for men who need to give specimens of their sperm for medical reasons, such as for sperm count. Davis writes: 'If for a just cause, for example, to test for sterility of disease, the doctor wishes to examine the sperm of a married man (it would not be possible for the obvious reasons, in view of what follows, to test that of an unmarried man), it is suggested to pour into a test-tube the remains of sperm which remain in the urethra after sexual intercourse.'[8]

At the same time, the manuals declare a catch-all definition: that the sin of masturbation 'consists in the use of any sexual act for the wrong purpose':

> Therefore masturbation is possible for women as well as men; in young men and in old men . . . despite the fact that the ejaculations of the latter might be slight; in men who have had vasectomies, even if they eventually cannot produce semen, and adult castrati if they are capable of erections and reaching orgasm; in prepubescent children, even though they cannot produce semen, so long as they can achieve an erection and reach orgasm; yet not infants who are incapable of producing a full erection, or orgasm, even though they are capable of emitting a prostatic liquid from the urethra.[9]

The obsession with masturbation and other forms of auto-eroticism in the moral and pastoral manuals reflects the acute anxiety that it evidently occasioned for many seminarians and priests, including moral theologians, canon lawyers, and prelates right up to the pope, through much of the twentieth century. No wonder if, as claimed by the psychotherapist and former priest A. W. Richard Sipe, who conducted an investigation in the 1990s, '80 percent of the clergy masturbate'. Richard Sipe's estimate may well have been conservative, both for today and in the past. In 1969, when Dr. William Masters of the archdiocese of St. Paul conducted a survey of 200 celibate Catholic clerics, 198 reported having masturbated that year. The remaining two, according to Masters, did not understand the question. Richard Sipe also drew attention to those clerical non-masturbators who suffer from hypogonadism, known as Kallmann syndrome—the virtual absence of sexual libido—who typically have penises no larger than three centimetres, and small testicles to match.[10]

If Alfred Kinsey's figures on masturbation are modest for the twentieth century, it seems fair to assume that the rate of practice was also similar among celibate seminarians and priests in the nineteenth century. The difference was that harsh prohibitions in the ecclesial sphere in the nineteenth century were matched by equally harsh prohibitions for psychological and medical reasons in the secular sphere.

PIUS X WAS ELECTED POPE IN 1903, the same year as the publication in Germany of Judge Daniel Paul Schreber's *Memoirs of My Nervous Illness*, which strongly influenced Freud on the topic of masturbation. In 1905, the year that Pius X advocated frequent communion, and at least by inference confession, for children aged seven and up, Freud published his *Three Essays on the Theory of Sexuality*. In his memoir of mental illness Schreber first employed the term 'soul murder', cited earlier, commenting that it was invoked because of an 'idea widespread in folk-lore and poetry of all peoples that it is somehow possible to take possession of another person's soul'. 'Soul murder', within Catholic theology, is a precise description of mortal sin—a sin that 'kills' the soul.

Schreber suffered from phases of schizophrenia, featuring delusional states that were often God-centred, religiose, and sexual. He thought that God was attempting to emasculate him. The value of his memoir is the insight it gives into the effect of a morally tyrannical father who is obsessed with combatting, above all, the destructive evil of masturbation in his children. Daniel Paul Schreber's father was Dr. Daniel Gottlieb Moritz Schreber, a famous German physician and pedagogue who published a number of best-selling books on child development, discipline, and child-rearing in the mid-nineteenth century, with a profound and widespread effect on parenting, and hence, it is widely believed, on generations of German children. Son Daniel Paul ended his life in a mental asylum, and another son committed suicide.[11]

Dr. Schreber's peer specialists on child-rearing and theories of reproduction—along with parallel 'experts' in Britain, the United States, and other parts of Europe—put masturbation highest on the list of mental, moral, and spiritual dangers for the growing child. Unchecked, it was widely believed, the individual child was headed for insanity; worse still, such behaviour could lead to the deterioration of the purity of the race. An example of this was Dr. John Laws Milton's theory, originally reported in *The Lancet* in 1854, and appearing as a book in 1857 entitled *On the Pathology and Treatment of Gonorrhoea and Spermatorrhoea*. The book eventually was published in many editions. His thesis, in brief, was that seminal emission, whether from voluntary masturbation or nocturnal emissions, would damage the sperm, leading to 'epilepsy, phthisis, insanity, paralysis, and death.' One of his recommendations for avoiding such emissions was to sleep on the floor. Yet, as the psychoanalyst Morton Schatzman suggests in his book *Soul Murder*, the obsession with masturbation by doctors, teachers, and parents, and their determination to cure it, were principally symptomatic of their own adult sexual and moral anxieties. What we are seeing in the mania for treatments and prohibition, he concludes, is adult anxiety projected onto the child. The 'clinical' measures, going well beyond Milton (who incidentally also recommended a bottle of claret a day—as 'it is useless to expect any medical action from less than a bottle a day'), included such tortures as castration, application of electricity (known as 'faradisation'), cautery of the spine and genitals, and tying bags of pebbles to the back to keep a boy from lying on his back. For the girls, the physicians applied such measures as ovariotomy (excision of an ovary), clitoridectomy (removal of the clitoris), surgical separation of the prepuce hood from the clitoris; and the use of splints.[12]

Pius X's initiatives to impose early confessions, with its strict prohibitions on impure behaviour for children barely out of infancy, and concomitant warnings of the fires of Hell, correspond in the spiritual sphere with the adult anxieties that underpinned Schreber's child psychology. Pius X's acute anxiety about priestly chastity is patently evident in his exhortation to priests published in 1908 on the golden jubilee of his own priesthood. He likens the priesthood to a boy in danger, for whom he is the fretful father—reminiscent of Schreber Senior. He writes of his anxieties in the third person as of a 'father's loving heart which beats anxiously as he looks upon an ailing child.' The priest, he goes on, 'must fear the insidious attacks of the infernal serpent. Is it not all too easy even for religious souls to be tarnished by contact with the world?' The priest who is 'corrupt and contaminated is utterly incapable of preserving [others] from corruption'. The fear of 'pollution' in the priesthood runs through the document: 'Woe to the priest who fails to respect his high dignity, and defiles by his infidelities the name of the holy God for whom he is bound to be holy. Corruptio optimi pessima.'[13]

And yet, in the sentences that follow he displays a classic instance of reaction formation—the defence mechanism invoked by psychoanalysis whereby the origins of acute anxiety are challenged, in order to be eliminated, by assuming possession of an opposite impulse. He reminds his priests of their status—they are higher than the angels—as if defilement and pollution were unthinkable in a priest. 'May chastity, the choicest ornament of our priesthood, flourish undimmed amongst you; through the splendour of this virtue, by which the priest is made like the angels, the priest wins greater veneration among the Christian flock . . .'

There is a clear connection between the Catholic moralists' condemnations and the physicians' dire warnings of masturbation's threat to the integrity of soul and body. Just as the physicians insist that the decay of adult society must be checked by salutary disciplining of the child, so Pius X's sacramental initiatives for children betray a parallel antidote for the moral pollution that, unchecked, will corrupt the priesthood. The clinical anti-masturbation antidotes inflicted on children by Dr. Schreber's methods thus connect with the Catholic moralists' insistence on the spiritual antidotes: exclusion from the Eucharist, and hence a form of self-excommunication from the Church, and fear of the 'death of the soul' and the eternal fires of Hell.

If Pius X was intent on purifying the priesthood of 'graver sins' by inculcating children with guilt and fear, the project was bound to have repercussions for those Catholic boys who would carry such guilt into their lives as priests. For clerics, the vows of permanent celibacy and chastity raise the stakes of repression and anxiety. Constant repression by psychological, moral, and physical methods is not without consequences. As the influential psychoanalyst Otto Fenichel pointed out: 'If masturbation is performed with a bad conscience and anxiety which prevent its running its natural course, this circumstance has . . . pathological consequences.'[14]

Richard Sipe's interviews with priests revealed that attempts to master masturbation were leading 'to all sorts of compromises in order to control it.' He reports on priests who 'masturbate only under great internal pressure, with no fantasy and with little pleasure. Afterwards they feel compelled to go to confession immediately, sometimes at great disruption to their lives and reality', sometimes seeking out a fellow priest in the middle of the night.[15]

Sipe found instances of anxiety so severe that some priests suffered breakdowns and other illnesses. In certain extreme cases, he found strategies that resembled, and perhaps shed light upon, the self-mortifications of Jean-Marie Vianney (who slept every night on the bare flagstones), the man held up as an exemplar by Pius X. Along with priests who self-flagellated and starved themselves, Sipe had treated priests with masturbation anxieties who had considered castration. 'One priest did in fact castrate himself, precipitating his admission to a psychiatric hospital', he reported.[16]

I HAVE KNOWN PERSONALLY three sexually abusing priests, starting with Father Leslie McCallum, who attempted to abuse me during confession in the late 1950s, and who was educated for the priesthood at Oscott, my own seminary. I have written extensively about that encounter in *Seminary Boy*, published in 2006, and will describe it more fully in Chapter 10 of this book. Father Joe Jordan, sentenced in 2002 to seven years for offences against boys just two years after leaving the Venerable English College in Rome, was the second. And the third, Father Bede Walsh, was also educated at Oscott College; he was sentenced in August 2012 to twenty-two years in prison for sexual molestation spanning twenty-two years of his ministry. Another priest confessed to me and my wife that he had decided to 'seduce' a teenage student. This man was educated at the Beda College in Rome and was the chaplain of a college, but, as far as I know, he never carried out the decision. He died in 2005.

My personal acquaintance with these priests—in addition to the interviews conducted by Marie Keenan of University College, Dublin; the work of Richard Sipe; and my further interviews and correspondence with priests and nuns over a span of two years—has shown me the importance of the so-called sexual revolution and its effect on potential and actual clerical abusers. While the term 'sexual revolution' normally applies to the late 1960s, and to student action and unrest in France and the United States, it had a longer, gradual flourishing. Among its early discussants was the Austrian psychoanalyst Wilhelm Reich, who wrote in his 1936 book *The Sexual Revolution* of the psychological dangers of sexual repression. The era of sexual permissiveness and 'sexual liberation' occurred at a time when many were noticing spasmodic recourse within seminaries and the priesthood, but mostly within the confessional, to the principle known as *epieikeia*.[17] The principle was ancient, but it was resurrected amongst the Catholic clergy, it is arguable, to resolve the rising problems of sexual liberation in the twentieth century.

I first heard the word 'epieikeia' at Oscott in 1960 when a fellow student, whom I will call 'Rev S', raised it one night when he and I were alone, breaking the rules of the house. We were drinking wine and smoking together in his room long after lights out, during the Greater Silence when speaking was forbidden. Rev S was a warm and friendly man, several years above me, who had been to Cambridge and had done National Service in the British Army. He managed to be 'singular' and even 'ostentatious' at times because of his decidedly camp exterior, which he managed to blend with his clericalism. He walked in a mincing manner, and unlike most of us, affected a clerical sash and cummerbund. He had an effeminate manner of speech that lent a tone of affection and intimacy to those admitted to his inner circle. Rev S made overtures to me because he was trying to ingratiate himself with a friend of mine in my year who had primly rejected all of Rev S's advances to take walks in the grounds or have coffee alone with him after lunch. The circumstance provides an impression of the quality of our lives. I knew what the Rev S was up to, and I felt guilty about what we were doing, and told him so. Pouring another glass of wine (he murmured as he did so: 'Drink up, it's sacramental!'), he informed me that our activity came under the heading of 'epieikeia'. It was a Greek word, he explained, applied by Aristotle to the notion of 'equity' in jurisprudence, and developed by Thomas Aquinas and later moral theologians. It meant that one could interpret a rule in a particular case against the 'letter of the law' so long as one kept reasonably within the spirit of what one assumed the legislator intended. Later, epieikeia came up in our morals classes, although we were strongly advised that the notion did not allow us to simply dispense with any law we happened not to like.[18]

By the 1960s, epieikeia was becoming an instrument of enormous power and latitude for releasing penitents in confession from burdensome situations of conscience relating to sex and difficult marital situations, such as divorce and remarriage without annulment. Just as we were being informed that it was natural to express oneself sexually (which most of us were probably managing to do anyway), here was a principle—epieikeia—that could be invoked to resolve a multiplicity of moral scruples.

In the whirlpool of cross-currents that occurred at the time of the Second Vatican Council, many Catholics expected that Rome would sanction the use of birth control pills within marriage. Ahead of that expectation (which was dashed in 1968 with Pope Paul VI's encyclical confirming the ban), many Catholics were already practising contraception. Those who had qualms took them to their confessors. There were those confessors who kept strictly within the Church's teaching; but there were others who were taking the troubled scruples of penitents onto their own consciences. The epieikeia principle was useful if such a confessor was to sleep soundly at night. There was even Thomas Aquinas to appeal to. Aquinas wrote, in defence of the principle, 'Since the lawgiver cannot have in view every single case, he shapes the law according to what happens most frequently, by directing his attention to the common good. Wherefore, if a case arise wherein the observance of that law would be hurtful to the general welfare, it should not be observed.'[19]

The principle, also referred to as 'internal forum' in the confessional, became widely used by confessors when dealing with penitents who wanted to go on the pill (with sound reasons, in the view of the confessor), and couples who wanted to remarry after divorce in good conscience and remain communicant members of the Church. But the pastoral use of epieikeia, not surprisingly, coincided with the use of the principle to resolve the private consciences of priests in their personal sexual lives. It was in fact a clerical form of 'liberation' at just the time when 'sexual liberation' was gathering strength.

Not every seminarian would study the principle of epieikeia, or even knew the term, but once the genie of the general principle was out of the bottle, through confession, spiritual direction, discussion between seminarians, and the workings of individual consciences, it was available to square any number of moral circles. Confessors and sexual abusers have admitted that the new spirit of clerical permissiveness was being applied to masturbation. Hence Father McCallum attempted to reassure me that it was not only okay, but 'normal'—everybody did it, including all the priests in the junior seminary.

Dr. Marie Keenan's interviews in Ireland with priests charged with sexual abuse reveal that these offenders used the same exculpations for masturbation as they would apply to their molestation of children. Their sexual activities with children, being largely masturbatory, never broke the oath of celibacy, in their own minds, nor could those actions be

described as fornication. Convinced, according to their studies in moral and pastoral theology, that children were eager
and apt for sexual experience (and if it was okay for a cleric,
then why not for a child), who better than a priest to intro-
duce them to some innocent, harmless, perhaps beneficial,
sexual expression, for the sake of mutual comfort? Although,
from our interviews, few, if any, priests saw their molestations
as 'beneficial' for their victims—they were mostly relieving
their own repressions.

Among the professionals in clinical psychology and
psychoanalysis whom I have consulted is the distinguished
London psychoanalyst Dr. Josephine Klein. She wanted me
to consider the following idea:

> Here you have a group of men who have been told from
> early childhood that autoerotic play is not just bad for your
> health, and not just morally wrong, or naughty (which is
> how a child would think), but deserving of an eternity
> of punishment. So most of them tried very hard, even if
> occasionally they gave in, to repress the urge. Now they
> become priests and they are constantly, frequently, in a cir-
> cumstance of extraordinary intimacy with children, often,
> to begin with, in strict privacy and darkness. Some of these
> children may be confessing to touching themselves and en-
> gaging in autoerotic play. The prospect now presents itself
> to project onto the child their own repressed desires. They
> do to the child what they would have liked to do to them-
> selves, without anxiety, in their own childhood.[20]

Exploring the circumstance further, Klein explained that
the priest's chosen victim serves as an 'object relation'—an
extension of himself—someone on whom he has transferred
his own childhood emotions. Just as the child is in danger
of bonding with the priest, the priest bonds with his victim.
The child becomes an object of childhood desires that he
subconsciously seeks to recapture. The child becomes a means
to act out, relieve, and come to terms with the suppressed
emotions and fantasies of his own childhood.

THE EVIDENCE FROM the huge circuit of depositions, police
and official diocesan reports, court accounts, interviews with
victims and perpetrators, journalists' investigations, and academic sociological research is that the clerical sexual abuser
of children, as portrayed in the media, ill accords with clinical
and criminal definitions of paedophile behaviour in men who
are not members of the clergy—which is usually restricted to
infants and even babies. The mismatch has been extensively
demonstrated by Philip Jenkins in his *Pedophiles and Priests:
Anatomy of a Contemporary Crisis*. Based on the widest and
most recent statistics, the age range of clerical sexual victims
typically spans seven to fourteen years old (the same span
to which Pius X extended first confession). It is no exagger-
ation, nor is it to treat the topic lightly, to say that, based
on the stories in previous chapters, priest-confessors have
shown themselves to be equal-opportunity abusers in every

sense within that age range: boys and girls pre-pubescent and post-pubescent. At the same time, the contention, widely held, that the number of priest 'paedophiles' is no greater than the number of paedophiles in the general population is both questionable and unhelpful. Research conducted by Professor Gerry Kearns at the National University of Ireland, Maynooth, reveals spikes in sexual abuse rising to 10 per cent of priests in certain dioceses, more than three times the calculated average percentage of paedophiles in Western countries. Professor Kearns's researches, yet to be published, may yield interesting reasons for these spikes. What we know about the phenomenon in the United States, for example, is to be found in the report of the John Jay College of Criminal Justice of the City University of New York—'The Nature and Scope of Sexual Abuse of Minors by Catholic Priests and Deacons in the United States, 1950–2002', commonly known as the John Jay Report. Published in 2004, the report had been commissioned by the US Conference of Catholic Bishops based on surveys completed by Roman Catholic dioceses in the United States. The report revealed that in the years covered by the report, some 10,667 individuals had made allegations of clerical child sexual abuse. The dioceses had been able to substantiate 6,700 accusations against 4,392 priests, about 4 per cent of all 109,694 priests who served during the time covered by the study. The number of alleged abuses increased in the 1960s, peaked in the 1970s, declined in the 1980s, and returned to the levels of the 1950s by 2005. The discoveries have been slow in coming, but similar figures are to be found in other countries around the world, not least the Republic of Ireland and Australia, the Netherlands, Belgium, Germany, Austria, France, Chile, and Brazil. It is also claimed that beyond those figures are large numbers of unreported incidents.[21]

It was originally suggested by the Vatican that the problem was one primarily of English-speaking countries, and was further sensationalised by the media in those countries. It soon became obvious, however, that the reason for the higher numbers in these countries had to do with the more assiduous legal discovery processes in the British and American traditions of law, as well as the more active practice of tort law. In other words, the phenomenon was worldwide, but remained unreported in many places.

The danger of shrugging off the abuse crisis within the priesthood as merely typical of the population as a whole is that the nature of priestly abuse of the young in the twentieth century comprises not only forms of sexual molestation, but the wider phenomenon of psychological oppression. The two forms of confessional terrorism are inextricably related, and the boundaries between the two are often indistinct. At the same time, failure to appreciate the link between abuse and the practice of confession makes it likely that Rome will not learn from the mistakes of the past.

Some thirty national reports on clergy sexual abuse were published between 1989 and 2013, as well as reports of individual court cases. The culpability of bishops is usually cited, but the reports are weak on systemic causes. There is a failure in all the reports to recognise the problems inherent in clericalism, clerical formation, and the practice of confession as crucial causes of the phenomenon of clerical sexual abuse.

Pope Benedict XVI and many bishops urged that Catholics return to frequent reception of confession with no hint of revising the age at which children are catechised and receive the sacrament. In the Vatican document 'The Priest, Minister of Divine Mercy: An Aid for Confessors and Spiritual Directors', issued in 2011, Pope Benedict XVI wrote: 'It is necessary to return to the confessional as a place in which to celebrate the Sacrament of Reconciliation, but also as a place in which "to dwell" more often.' The sacrament of confession must be 'rediscovered', states the directive. And this must be part of the 'new evangelization and the ongoing renewal of the Church'. In the entire scope of the document, the oppression of generations of children in confession goes unrecognised. Nor is there even a passing acknowledgement of the exploitation of confession by clerical abusers over decades of the last century.

In the next chapter we will explore the emerging links between confession and criminal attacks on children, the use of confession by the priests to square the circle of their pastoral and offending lives, and the far-reaching consequences for victims and their families.

PART THREE

———————

'SOUL MURDER'

Ten

Sexual Abuse in the Confessional

The Church was showing a quite new
aspect of itself, devouring its own children.

—Carlo Falconi, *The Popes in the Twentieth Century*

WHEN PRIESTS SEXUALLY ABUSE CHILDREN THEY VIOLATE
a trust between spiritual innocence and sacred father-
hood. Specialists in childhood trauma have used the term
'soul murder' to describe the profound damage that can ensue
when a priest abuses a young member of the faithful. Psychotherapist Richard Sipe, a former priest who specialises in
treatment of clerical child-abuse survivors, writes: 'A person
who has been grounded since childhood in one faith, where
their self-worth, acceptance, spiritual identity, and salvation
were vested, cannot simply forget, put it behind them or join
another faith. They can go on with their lives, but the part

that is missing cannot be restored. Something is dead; something has been truly killed.' The spiritual empowerment that might have aided recovery has been profoundly undermined. For children, it is especially difficult to separate the abusing priest from the auspices of the Church, with all its comforting and healing associations.[1]

The consequences of clerical abuse of minors have been emerging in reports of contemplated suicide, attempted suicide, and actual suicide of victims. In Melbourne, Australia, five men who claimed to have been abused while serving as altar boys in the church of the priest Ronald Pickering committed suicide. These deaths, uncovered by lawyer Judy Courtin, add to the forty other suicides in the state of Victoria by victims who had been abused by priests, according to documented police reports. Courtin is conducting investigatory research into clerical sexual abuse for Monash University's law faculty.[2]

When the original grooming, or sexual attack, occurs in the circumstance of confession, the auspices of the sacrament aggravate the harm. Sexual abuse of children linked to the confessional has not only been widespread, but is known to be especially destructive to the children involved. A priest in England, ordained thirty years ago, and for twenty years a psychotherapist treating clerical sex offenders within his diocese, wrote to me that 'in all those cases [of clerical abuse of minors], the sacrament of confession was used [by the molester] to discover vulnerability and groom candidates for abuse.'[3]

In March 2010, when the Catholic Church in Germany set up a hotline and invited victims and their families to report instances of clerical abuse in parishes and schools, more than 8,500 people responded. Andreas Zimmermann, the expert responsible for analysing the results, told the German Catholic news agency KNA that the abusing 'priests had used their moral authority and psychological effect of *rites like confession*' [my italics] to gain power over children, 'even to the point of telling them that the assaults were an expression of "God's special love" for them.'[4]

CRIMINAL JUSTICE SYSTEMS and Church authorities have failed to identify the link between confession and the access, opportunity, and special trauma of clerical abuse. When I was in my early teens I experienced the connection at first hand. In the course of interviews and extensive correspondence, I would come across many similar instances.

In my Catholic junior seminary in the late 1950s I was sexually propositioned during confession by a priest who, I discovered, had used the sacrament as a seduction tactic with other boys. I had chosen him initially as my confessor, as had other pupils in the college, because he made a point of merging his priesthood with the role of counsellor and mentor. He combined an exterior sense of piety and devotion with an extroverted, fun-loving personality. Confessions, held in his private quarters, became a treat and a privilege, the religious auspices nevertheless creating an atmosphere of unquestioning trust.[5]

Although I told him that I preferred to kneel to make my confession, this priest, Father Leslie McCallum of the archdiocese of Birmingham in England, insisted that I sit in an armchair and accept a glass of Madeira. How different from the more traditionalist priests on the staff, who avoided familiarity and sociability. Father McCallum's priest colleagues seemed, in contrast, cold and austere; they continued to conduct confessions impersonally, behind a screen in the college sacristy. Father McCallum was a picture of devotion when robed and in the sanctuary, where I had often served his Mass. His manner of making his thanksgiving at the back of the church was a model of recollection, as if communing directly with the divine. Outside of the church he offered warmth, humour, and friendship: he seemed to understand our adolescent ways of thinking. He was up to date with the latest novels and films. He had a record player on which he played Elvis Presley numbers, music we would only otherwise hear on our vacations back at home.

On the occasion in question, having imbibed the usual glass of Madeira, and before I could finish my laundry list of peccadillos, he interrupted to ask: 'Have you had problems with sexual sins?' Then he said that I shouldn't feel any guilt about masturbation because not to masturbate was abnormal. The American Kinsey report on sexual behaviour, he said, stated that 99.9 per cent of all males masturbated.

Then he asked if he could see my penis so that he could manipulate it to discover whether I had any of the 'well-known deformities that led to excessive erections'. Nothing wrong with masturbation, he was saying: just not good for the health to do it too much. Five years earlier I had been abused in a public toilet in London by a man who started his overtures with similar blandishments. Now, I stood up and left the room. I said nothing about the incident to anyone in authority in the college because I felt that it would be my word against Father McCallum's. In any case, even penitents in those days believed that the seal of confession applied to them. Thereafter, whenever we passed, he would smile and greet me as if nothing had happened.

The following year, Father McCallum was removed from the junior seminary and appointed chaplain to a boy's preparatory boarding school, to care for the souls of an even younger age group of boys than ours. He had clearly been trying his seductions on other students, and his superiors had got wind of it. The decision of the archbishop of Birmingham to move him to a place where he might continue his grooming activities was typical of Catholic hierarchies at that time. Another feature of this experience was his mention of the Kinsey report, indicating the view, acceptable among some clerics by the 1950s, that despite the vow of celibacy, sexual expression in the form of auto-eroticism was not merely okay, but essential: here was permissiveness revealing a despotic streak. The beginnings of the sexually permissive society were affecting elements, restricted but significant, within the long repressed Catholic clerical caste for whom confession now became an opportunity for grooming potential victims.[6]

ALTHOUGH EXTENSIVE STUDIES of Catholic clerical sexual abuse have been conducted in the United States and Ireland, there have been less detailed reports in other countries where it is known nevertheless that abuse has been widespread, including Germany, Italy, Austria, Belgium, the Netherlands, Brazil, and Australia. Obstacles to rigorous research continue to arise, a result of clerical secrecy and reluctance on the part of Church authorities to cooperate. For example, on 9 January 2013, the German bishops' conference cancelled a research project it had agreed to undertake in 2011 in combination with the Criminological Research Institute of Lower Saxony, headed by Professor Christian Pfeiffer. Pfeiffer accused the bishops of trying to censor abuse investigations. A Forsa Institute poll published in *Christ & Welt*, a supplement of the Germany weekly newspaper *Die Zeit*, claimed that the closure of the enquiry had done further damage to the reputation of the Catholic clergy in Germany. According to the poll, 75 per cent of the German respondents believed that the Catholic Church was trying to prevent a comprehensive investigation.[7]

Yet even where reports of clerical abuse have been open and extensive, statistics have failed to show the connection between abuse and the practice of confession. As we saw earlier, the principal American report on sexual abuse in the Catholic

Church, commissioned by the US bishops and conducted by John Jay College of Criminal Justice at the City University of New York, found that, from 1950 to 2002, 10,667 individuals had made allegations of child sexual abuse. Of these, 6,700 accusations of abuse had been substantiated against 4,329 priests. The John Jay Report cited the locations of attacks, separating, for example, the confessional box from the sacristy, where the priest vests in liturgical robes (or other private places within the church building); the priests' living quarters; and locations outside of the parish. The numbers were misleading, however, since the methodology suggested that confession as a context of abuse occurs only within a traditional confessional box. By the late 1950s, not only was the practice of confession moving out of the box, but the boundaries of the sacrament were also being blurred—as with Father McCallum's socializing-counselling mode as confessor. By the 1960s confession was routinely taking place at different locations within the church precincts and beyond. As it happens, the John Jay figures for boys showed that 29.6 per cent of abusive encounters took place in the confessional box, elsewhere within the church building (such as the sacristy), or in the priest's house, where children's confessions were frequently taking place by the late 1950s; for girls, the figure was an accumulated 27.8 per cent. Trips and social events as locations of abuse accounted for almost 40 per cent of incidents for both sexes.[8]

According to my interviews and the letters I received from respondents, as well as official reports in many countries, abusive relationships between cleric and child have almost invariably begun as a continuation of the sacrament of confession. Although the statistics about the locations of abuse cited in the John Jay Report are an important feature of the evidence, it is only in the stories of abuse that we see the repeated connection between the initial trust accorded the priest as sacramental minister—confessor—and his multidimensional status as trusted spiritual 'father', counsellor, mentor, and friend that continues in other contexts and places. That status, with the unequal power relationship it implies, the access the priest has to the child, and the child's unquestioning trust, once in place, continues to govern the relationship on trips, retreats, country walks, social occasions (often in a priest's private room), sporting activities, hikes, campfire parties, and journeys alone or in groups by car.

In a typical case cited in the report on clerical abuse in the Diocese of Cloyne in Ireland, for example, a boy victim told the police of scattered locations of abuse originally linked with confession. The complainant, Patrick, had told police that in 1983 he was on retreat at a convent in Mallow. He went to confession, he claimed, with a priest in a private room, where the priest asked him to take off his clothes. The priest, he alleged, touched his genitals and kissed his lips. The priest admitted that abuse took place in a variety of locations, including the sacristy of the church in Shanballymore in North Cork and when they were walking together on a quiet country road. The priest pleaded guilty to three counts of indecency against a sixteen-year-old youth during 1982 and 1983 and was given an eighteen-month suspended sentence.[9]

A report contained in a child welfare document published by the Diocese of Cloyne revealed how confession, and accompanying abuse, could take place far distant from the church. A female complainant wrote to her bishop alleging that a certain priest 'sexually abused her during a young people's retreat'. She further alleged that 'the abuse took place during the hearing of her confession which was conducted in a bedroom at the retreat house. She was instructed to lie on the bed for her confession to be heard. [The priest] then abused her.'[10]

At the same time, narratives of abuse show how the attitudes of priests towards sexuality and their familiarity with the young were beginning to change during the late 1950s and into the 1960s. The black suit and Roman collar were coming off, and priests were often indistinguishable from the laity in all but their special status. According to one witness, Ansgar Hocke, reporting to the Round Table Group in Germany on clerical sexual abuse at his school in 1960s, a new spirit of permissiveness had arisen among priests: 'The days of the priests in cassocks, who shouted at their students, were deeply conservative and who saw the catechism as their only guideline, were coming to an end.' Priests now seemed to be breathing new life into the schools, Hocke noted. 'But we didn't see how sick and unstable they were.' The pupils seemed to feel that the priests had a right to sexual happiness. 'We knew that the young priests were excluded from this happiness, and we often saw how helpless they were.' The pupils who belonged to a Father R.'s inner circle were constantly subjected, he said, to 'one-on-one talks', suggesting a continuity between the privileged access of confession and intimate counselling beyond. The sessions sometimes took place in a basement, which quickly acquired a notorious reputation among students, who referred to it as the 'masturbation basement' or the 'interrogation room'. A former student said: 'He wanted to watch me masturbate, and he touched me while I was doing it.'[11]

The tendency for priests to fraternise socially with young boys coincided with the easing of the physical boundaries established by the old-style confessional booths: hence Father McCallum's practice of hearing confession in his room from the comfort of armchairs. Yet, as the boys in the German case indicate, the priests had not undergone a corresponding development in maturity to cope with the new climate of 'liberation'. Moreover, a slippage was occurring between confession as the strict performance of the ritual, on the one hand, and, on the other, modes of counselling and hospitality that included plying even prepubescent boys and girls with cigarettes and alcohol during or after confession. In one Irish report, a Father Calder was alleged to have heard confessions in his study before repairing to his private quarters, where he offered boys alcoholic 'concoctions'.[12] In another report, a Father Drust was said to have routinely seduced a girl named Ulla by offering her sherry in his private room:

> Ulla is the younger of two daughters of a family with whom Fr Drust appears to have formed a close relationship [he would also abuse Ulla's sister]. She first met Fr Drust

when she was aged seven or eight in 1964/65. She said that the sexual abuse began a few months later. Initially the abuse occurred in his car when he put her in his lap. Some time afterwards she started to visit his house at weekends. In her statement to the Gardaí in 2002 she stated that Fr Drust would give her three or four glasses of sherry and she would wake up in bed the following morning. He would then abuse her. Sometimes he would bring her toast in bed. When she was nine he taught her to shave him. She said that Fr Drust referred to her as his 'Lolita'.[13]

Privileged access and the availability of opportunities for intimate encounters were invariably preceded by chance, or contrived, 'pious' overtures. A priest responsible for rehabilitating abusing clerics in his diocese in England described how one abuser, popular in his diocese as confessor and spiritual director, would begin his grooming tactics by saying: 'I have been praying about you and I feel you have sexual problems you need to talk about.'[14] The potential of the penitent for abuse could thus be safely probed within the boundaries of a 'religious' context.

An example of the warped 'religiose' nature of grooming and sexual activity within the confessional situation is told by the American writer Paul Hendrickson (a former *Washington Post* journalist, later director of the non-fiction writing program at Pennsylvania State University). He describes a confession ritual in a priest's room in the 1960s which he endured once or twice a week for more than five years, starting at the age of eleven: 'I would go in, sit in a chair beside his desk, talk for a short while, await his nod, unzipper my trousers, take out my penis, rub it while I allowed impure thoughts to flow through my brain, and, at the point where I felt myself fully large and close to emission, say "Father, I'm ready now."' The priest would then reach over and hand him a black wooden crucifix. 'I would then begin reciting the various reasons why I wished to conquer this temptation. . . . The power of the crucified Savior in my left hand as overpowering the evil of impurity and the world in my right.'[15]

The sexual exploitation of the confessional could be stealthy, devious, and long-term in the planning. A 'Mrs. GC' wrote to me of the sexual abuse inflicted on her sister after a long process of grooming that involved the priest seeking friendship with her parents and siblings. Mrs. GC was seven at the time, several years younger than the sister who was being groomed. The priest, a Father Brown, was a former missionary and popular in his South London parish. After Mrs. GC started going to confession, the priest would press her into service to make assignations for him with the elder sister. 'I was the go-between. "Where is your sister?" he would whisper through the grille. "Tell her to come up to my room." It all came to an abrupt end, although I didn't know why for many years. He had taken my sister to the races one day and sexually abused her in an extremely gross manner in an empty compartment on the train coming back. She became a depressive; I'm convinced it was because of this experience that she eventually committed suicide.'[16]

While some abusers were careful to cover their tracks, others were quite blatant and would take extraordinary risks in public. One Father Grennan of Monageer in Ireland even flagrantly attacked an entire class of twelve-year-old girls, one by one, on the high altar of his Church in 1984. Other attacks took place within enclosed institutions where children had no parents to whom they could report. There were even examples of deaf children being abused by priests, the perpetrators confident that they would not be reported verbally. Some sixty former students of the Montreal Institute for the Deaf are currently bringing a class action lawsuit against the religious order of priests that runs the institution, citing sexual abuse over a number of years going back to 1980. Abuse within the confessional situation was an important feature of the allegations. A similar circumstance has been revealed in the case of Father Lawrence Murphy, director of an institution for the deaf in Milwaukee, Wisconsin, and subject of the documentary film *Mea Culpa, Mea Culpa*. Father Murphy routinely began his seductions, carried out over thirty years, in the confessional.[17]

In a much publicised institutional case in Northern Ireland, Kate Walmsley was initially abused by a priest in the confessional box while being cared for by the Sisters of Nazareth in Derry. It appears that one of the nuns who helped run the institution had colluded with the abuse. 'Every Saturday a nun used to hand me over to a priest', Kate reported to the media. 'Even if I was in the middle of a group of children I used to be taken out of the queue and kept to last. The first time this happened, when I was eight, he was putting his hands down my top and down my pants. He then started bringing me to a room behind the altar and he would abuse me there.'[18]

Confession is a ritual in which the penitents tell their own sins, not the sins of others; hence, it has never been a situation in which victims have felt encouraged to report occasions of abuse against themselves. But some attempts by victims to report a sexual attack by a priest to a confessor have resulted in further abuse. An example is described in the Ryan Report, which focused on abuse in Irish industrial, orphanage, and reform institutions. A victim alleged that when, in confession, he disclosed abuse by a priest, he was assaulted and raped by that confessor. According to the Cloyne Report, when priests were told of allegations against other priests outside of the confessional, they had neglected to share these charges with their bishop on the grounds that the allegations had the 'character of a confession', and were under the 'seal'.[19]

———————

THE 'DATABASE OF Publicly Accused Roman Catholic Priests, Nuns, Brothers, Deacons, and Seminarians in the US' and the US 'Special Reports: Catholic Bishops and Sex Abuse' comprise allegations of many offences committed by priests in a confessional situation who subsequently confessed or were found guilty in the courts of the United States. These databases, detailed and yet hardly comprehensive, show similarities with offences committed in many other countries. Attacks occurring during confession included kissing, digital penetration of girls, and sodomy of boys; the use of confession 'to scout for victims'; 'the asking of very intimate questions during confession and of using the confessional to learn people's weaknesses'; the practice of masturbating young penitents who were 'seated on the confessor's lap'; encouraging children to drink alcohol before, during, and after confession; and showing children pornographic pictures in confession.[20]

The failure of bishops to act forms an important dimension of the abuse phenomenon in many reports. For example, in the diocese of St. Louis, Missouri, Archbishop Justin Rigali delayed dismissing priests until after the clerical abuse scandals broke in the archdiocese of Boston. One of these priests, Father Joseph Ross, had sexually abused an eleven-year-old boy during confession in 1988.

The failure of bishops and superiors of religious orders to act has been evident worldwide. Father Brendan Smyth, who joined the Norbertine Order in the Republic of Ireland in 1945, was credibly guilty of several hundred crimes of sexual abuse, many involving a confessional situation, spread over forty years in the Republic, in Northern Ireland, and in the United States. Neither the superiors of his order nor the bishops of the dioceses in which he worked reported him to the police. His first conviction followed a report to the police of his molestation of four siblings in Belfast. He fled to the Republic after his arrest in 1991 and hid out in Kilnacrott

Abbey. The failure of the Fianna Fail Labour Party coalition to cooperate with his extradition led to the resignation of the government. In 2010 Cardinal Cahal Daly's successor as Roman Catholic archbishop of Armagh, Cardinal Sean Brady, faced criticism after he admitted that he was the notary in 1975 when two teenage boys testified against Smyth in a canon law tribunal. The boys had taken an oath under threat of excommunication never to speak of their allegations again. Their submissions had been endowed, by the ecclesiastical authorities, with the secrecy of the seal of sacramental confession.

In other cases, bishops attempting to defrock priests for the offence recognised in canon law as solicitation of sex in the confessional found it difficult to prompt Rome into action. Laicisation was deemed to be the exclusive responsibility of the Vatican. For example, Bishop Manuel D. Moreno of Tucson, Arizona, failed to persuade Cardinal Joseph Ratzinger, who was then head of the Congregation for the Doctrine of the Faith, to laicise a priest, despite a series of credible allegations made in 1997. The priest had been accused of five crimes, including sexual solicitation in the confessional. It took another seven years for the Vatican to defrock the individual. In the meantime, it was Bishop Moreno who took the blame publicly for the delay.

Cases of confessional abusers have also involved high-ranking prelates, such as Cardinal Hans Hermann Groër of Vienna, who sexually attacked as many as twelve boys at the monastic school where he taught in the 1960s. In 2011, one

of Chile's most senior priests, Monsignor Fernando Karadima, was accused of committing sexual abuse while hearing
confessions dating back to the 1990s.[21]

In a class all his own as 'confessional' abuser, and yet indic-
ative of Rome's lax handling of the phenomenon, is a prominent cleric, the late Father Marcial Maciel, Mexican founder
of the Legion of Christ—still one of the fastest-growing
orders in the Church, with more than 500 priests and 2,500
seminarians in 15 countries. Through much of his ministry,
Maciel, who died in 2008 at the age of eighty-four, enjoyed
the reputation of a saint and worldwide builder of churches
and schools. But he led a secret, depraved life, aided by the
fact that every new member of the order was obliged to swear
an oath never to divulge information about him under any
circumstances.

Over several decades, Maciel ordered boys of twelve and
younger to masturbate him, persuading them that they were
helping him with a 'medical' condition. He also asserted, in
an attempt to assuage their sense of guilt, that Pope Pius XII
had given him permission to have assisted orgasms to release
the painful build-up of semen. Of the many witnesses, the
testimony of Juan Vaca will suffice. The first attack, one of
many that persisted for several years, occurred in the junior
seminary that Maciel had founded in Tlalpan, a borough of
Mexico City.

One evening, Vaca, aged twelve, was called to Maciel's
bedroom, where he found the priest ostensibly ill in bed complaining of intestinal pains. Maciel asked the boy to rub his

stomach, then encouraged him to masturbate him. 'I was in shock', Vaca testified. 'He was a holy man . . . a very loving man. He was my father.' On a subsequent evening he abused Vaca together with a second boy.

Vaca said, 'I told him I didn't feel right. I wanted to go to confession. Maciel said, "There is nothing wrong. You don't have to go to confession."' When Vaca insisted, he recalled, 'Maciel said, "Here, I will give you absolution."' The priest then proceeded with the bestowal of a blessing. With that act Maciel crossed a boundary that the Catholic Church regards as reprehensible in the extreme. The offence, according to canon law, is known as 'complicit absolution'. Other accusers would in time declare that Maciel gave them absolution as well for the sexual acts they had performed with him.[22]

For more than a decade beginning in 1995, victims of Maciel's religiose debauchery denounced him to the Vatican, yet, under Pope John Paul II, they received no acknowledgement, let alone satisfaction. There was a perception on the part of Maciel's victims and their lawyers that an official conspiracy of silence had been established by the Vatican. They cited documents issued by the Holy Office (guardian of Catholic orthodoxy), first in 1922 and again in 1962, entitled *Crimen Solliciationis* (The Crime of [Sexual] Solicitation). The document, on the face of it, called for secrecy in cases involving a priest's abuse of the confessional to sexually abuse a child. The history of the documents, however, and their effects on the clerical abuse phenomenon are complex.[23]

Only after the death of John Paul II did his successor, Benedict XVI, move rapidly to deprive Maciel of his priestly privileges (known as 'faculties'), ordering him into a permanent retreat where he was to 'do penance'. He was never arrested and never charged by a criminal justice system in any jurisdiction. A measure of the protection accorded Maciel, despite evidence of his abuses dating back to the 1950s, was the systematic exoneration accorded him by a conservative Catholic media. An example of this involved a prominent American priest, the late Father Richard John Neuhaus, editor-in-chief of the journal *First Things* and close friend of John Paul II. Neuhaus continued to support Maciel in the pages of his influential Washington, DC–based periodical despite the mounting evidence against him. Neuhaus wrote, with a stylish flourish: 'Stories about Catholic priests have a certain *cachet*—and for trial lawyers, a promise of cash— that is usually lacking in other cases.' He went on to tell his readers that he had sought the opinion of an unnamed cardinal 'in whom I have unbounded confidence and who has been involved in the case who tells me that the charges are "pure invention, without the slightest foundation."' In consequence, he said, 'I have arrived at a *moral certainty* that the charges are false and malicious.' In conclusion, he wrote, 'It counts as evidence that Pope John Paul II, who almost certainly is aware of the charges, has strongly, consistently, and publicly praised Fr. Maciel and the Legion.'[24]

John Paul II had praised Maciel as an 'efficacious guide to youth' and had favoured the Legion with praise on many occasions. John Paul's verdict on the clerical abuse crisis, delivered in 2002, reveals much about the moral and cultural gulf between the realities of abuse for the victims and the rarefied, out-of-touch perspective of John Paul's papacy: 'We are personally and profoundly afflicted by the sins of some of our brothers who have betrayed the grace of Ordination in succumbing even to the most grievous forms of the *mysterium iniquitatis* at work in the world. . . . A dark shadow of suspicion is cast over all the other fine priests who perform their ministry with honesty and integrity.'[25]

His first thought, then, was of his own sense of affliction rather than that of the victims, and next for the image of the Catholic priesthood. When it came to the nature of the crime, he characterised it as 'the mystery of iniquity', taken from 2 Thessalonians 7, which speaks of the end of the world and the coming of the 'wicked one'. Clerical abuse is not therefore the work of men, it is the work of Satan.

IF THERE IS A 'MYSTERY' about clerical sexual abuse, however, it is how so many abusing priests have squared the circle of their offences against the young and have managed to continue in their ministries, appearing 'holy' to their congregations. How does an individual priest preach and administer the sacraments in one part of his life, and yet knowingly attack and debauch the youngest of his charges in another, even within the sacramental act of confession itself?

Up to a point, the answer appears to lie within the priest's own upbringing as a Catholic child in the era, including his early catechesis and practice of confession, as well as in aspects of his seminary formation. The abuser's own use of the sacrament of confession for himself, moreover, connects with those explanations. A priest in Queensland, Australia, went to confession some 1,500 times to admit sexually abusing boys. In a 2003 affidavit, the then sixty-eight-year-old Michael Joseph McArdle, who was jailed for six years beginning in October of that year, claimed to have made confession about his paedophile activities to about thirty different priests over a twenty-five-year period. He noted: 'As the children would leave after each respective assault, I would feel an overwhelming sense of sadness for them and remorse, so much so it would almost be physical. I was devastated after the assaults, every one of them. So distressed would I become that I would attend confessionals weekly and on other occasions fortnightly and would confess that I had been sexually assaulting young boys.' He said the only assistance or advice he was given was to undertake penance in the form of prayer. He claimed that after each confession, 'it was like a magic wand had been waved over me'. McArdle's affidavit would appear to contradict a widespread view in Ireland that child sex abusers are unlikely to admit their abuse to a priest in the confessional.[26]

The sociologist and psychotherapist Dr. Marie Keenan, of University College, Dublin, conducted a series of remarkable interviews with offending priests who had served their jail sentences in Ireland. Her findings offer a unique resource for understanding the doublethink of priests who abuse children, and who not only remain active in their ministries but also appear to their congregations to be men of piety and devotion.

Most of the priests whom she interviewed for the project said they had routinely confessed their 'sins' to a fellow priest, confident that their crimes would be protected by the seal of the confessional. 'Father A', for example, spoke of the mechanical process of confession, whereby the slate was 'wiped clean', as he put it, and he could begin to feel good about himself again. 'After each abuse occurrence I felt full of guilt and at the earliest opportunity I sought to confess and receive absolution', he said. He admitted that although his confessions were 'well-intentioned', there was a sense in which he was going through a 'mechanical process'. Absolution effected a degree of 'relief and a feeling of a new beginning'. Father A was well aware that the efficacy of the sacrament depended on a 'firm purpose of amendment' and future avoidance of 'occasions of sin'—'there was always a resolution' not to sin again. Uppermost in his mind, however, was the importance of *feeling* virtuous again—'It effected a degree of relief', he said. The discomfort to be endured in confessing his sins did not lay in confronting his guilt. Nor was it the prospect of altering his behaviour. Rather, it was the embarrassment of telling those 'sins' to the priest. And here the interview with Father A reinforced confession's scope for avoiding moral realities: 'It seemed to ease my conscience that I was truly making an effort to change and to stop . . . and going to confession and being able to couch it in such a way that, you know, I didn't have to give the full story.'[27]

In saying that he didn't have to 'give the full story', Father A was admitting that he found a form of words that enabled him to secure absolution without being totally frank with the priest who was hearing his confession. The penitent could keep, with casuistic smartness, within the rules of the conditions of a valid confession in order to obtain absolution, and yet save himself embarrassment by a process of deliberate 'amphibology', as the morality textbooks put it—the art of saying something without actually saying it. Thus, instead of saying 'I sexually abused a boy of nine years of age in an act of sodomy, and I am a priest', he might say: 'I performed an impure act with another person', keeping his priesthood, and the age of his victim, to himself. Some priests might ask whether the 'person' was male or female, married or unmarried; yet, as confessors have told me in interviews, they would probably not ask whether the 'person' was a child, and it would not occur to them to ask if the penitent was a priest. Hence the penitent priest would tell the sin, and yet *not* tell the sin, an Orwellesque species of 'doublethink' of the kind we saw developing within the priesthood under Pius X in Chapter 4.

Even as Father A described the manner of his confession to Dr. Keenan, he was engaging in doublethink: 'Perhaps I minimized in my accounts, but I did not think so. I certainly agonized as to how to present the abuse, and maybe the language used probably veiled the horror of the action. It was not open denial, but maybe it was not unadulterated truth either.'

Here the priest is struggling to keep his head above moral water. A crucial key to Father A's strategy, shared by other priests interviewed for Dr. Keenan's project, was the admission that his confessors were 'carefully selected' by him. In other words, he avoided confessors who might ask uncomfortable questions, or respond harshly to what they had heard. Only once, Father A stated, was he caught out. 'I went to confession and this man absolutely just went for me . . . he just said to me, "you know what you are doing is not alone morally wrong but it is a criminal act."'

The incident prompts consideration of the role of the confessors who either knew or guessed what their priestly penitents were confessing to, and who then neglected to react appropriately. At one point in his interview, Father A admitted his surprise that he had not been severely reproached more often. ('In all the times I confessed to abusing a minor I can only remember one occasion when I got a reprimand or advice not to do this thing.') Yet he had already explained that on most occasions he had not admitted to the confessor the true nature of his sin, or reported his status.[28]

What was in the minds of those confessors who failed to issue a reprimand? My attempts at eliciting the confessor's perspective have not prospered. Out of the dozens of priests whom I approached, only one former confessor, now laicised, whose ministry ceased some thirty years ago, admitted that a priest had come to him on more than one occasion to confess child sexual abuse. 'What did you say to him?' I asked. 'I didn't say anything', he replied. 'I gave him three Hail Marys or something like that. . . . We didn't think such things were all that terrible years ago.'

Many of the priests I interviewed told me they would not necessarily have known for certain what was being confessed, and if they had suspected, they would not have wished to probe. A former Jesuit priest had this to say: 'It was laid down in our moral and pastoral textbooks that we should not show too much curiosity. . . . Mostly you just wanted to get through the penitents as efficiently as you could. Possibly we suspected, but did not want to go there.'

Another of my interviewees, who was a young priest in the early 1960s, but had been laicised for some fifty years, refused to answer the question. Despite the fact that we were discussing a ministry he left half a century ago, he had serious scruples about doing violence to the seal of confession. He wished the interview to be anonymous and withheld even basic circumstantial information, saying:

Let me put it this way: you might know where I practised as a priest in those days. You might know of a priest in that area who was charged with child sexual abuse and eventually sent to prison. You could then put two and two together, and guess that this person came to me to confess that sin. I have to tell you that it would be wrong of me, in my opinion, to let you know either way—that I did, or that I didn't have such a priest come to me. Because I wouldn't want you to think, that if I did, I would tell you. All I will say is this: when people came to me confessing impurity or sexual intercourse with another, I would want to know the marital status of the person I was speaking to, although I was unlikely to ask whether he was a priest, and the status of the sexual partner, whether married or not; and whether the sex was consensual or not. I don't think that I would automatically ask if it was a child, or non-consensual: that would have been up to the penitent to confess such a thing. Some priests would want to know whether contraception had been used; I tended not to want to know that, or to discuss contraception unless the penitent raised it.

What was lacking among the priestly penitent abusers, and evidently among many of their confessors, too, was a mature sense of the nature of clerical abuse as having grievous consequences for another person. In attempting to describe why he thought his behaviour was wrong, Father A spoke initially of 'guilt, shame, and fear that I would get caught'. His consciousness of what he had done was entirely self-centred. He regretted that he was 'not taking steps to deal with the compulsion which was causing me to sin'. There were times, he went on, 'when I was quite upset with myself and the way I was going.' He dwelt on his 'weaknesses', yet took comfort that God 'was the father of the Prodigal Son and I saw myself as fitting into the parable.'[29]

He granted in his interview with Dr. Keenan that his 'behaviour was not okay'. He knew that it was 'contrary to the system of morality' he had been taught. He had 'breached the moral code', yet 'the intention to hurt was not in my mind', he said. He expanded on his reference to a 'moral code' by saying, 'I persuaded myself that while there was a moral breach, the harm to the young person was minimal. The fact that the other person did not object was a factor in my "justification" of the behaviour in that there was a sort of tacit assent to the "intrusion."' And yet, this was not entirely true, he conceded: 'This was dishonest and distorted thinking because the fact is that I had already ensured submission by targeting only those whom I believed would be compliant. I knew in my heart that the fact that the person showed no enthusiasm whatever was sufficient sign of unwillingness. So there was much double-thinking going on.'

One reads through the nine interviews provided by Dr. Keenan hoping for one small indication of awareness of the consequences of the abuse on the young victims on the part of these former priests, but to no avail. Reading between the lines, it seems likely that Dr. Keenan had suggested that there was a question of 'justice' to be considered. One interviewee responded: 'I did not think about justice to the individual . . . it was about how far did you go with yourself in the process before committing a sin. The individual was not considered.'[30]

The moral mindset is that of a person who habitually neglects to consider the otherness of people—a failure to consider consequences in the real world in which people live and have their being; a rule-bound ethic with no developed sense of individual, authentic conscience; a person trapped in a moral stage of infancy. At the same time the mindset is typical of a view of human nature that is essentially dualistic—recognising a split between body and soul—with the body being held of less value than the soul. The predicament is reminiscent of the unfeeling personality of the psychopath, although in the case of the priest, we are dealing with years of learnt behaviour in the institutionalised environment of the seminary.

What we are witnessing is a distorted religious imagination that has been shaped by narratives and metaphors of confessional experience. And these narratives and metaphors were first inculcated in childhood and adolescence and further reinforced during years of seminary formation. It is to the imaginative force of confessional experience that we must now turn to understand the impact of confession on generations of the faithful starting in the first half of the twentieth century.

Eleven

Confession Imagined

> Eamon could not imagine trying to
> explain to him, even in the darkness of
> the confessional, what he and Anne had
> done together. . . . Until now, the state
> of mortal sin seemed unimaginable . . .
>
> —Colm Tóibín, *The Heather Blazing*

THE DARK BOX IS STILL TO BE SEEN IN USE IN CATHEDRALS
and large city churches, where penitents continue to
wait their turn in the pews. These are Catholics who still
find spiritual consolation whispering their sins into the ear
of the shadowy priest beyond a screen of anonymity. As we
have seen, in 2011 Pope Benedict XVI advocated a return to
confession, as of old. Yet in countless lesser churches where
the box has not been broken up for firewood, church janitors
have found the hidden space useful as a storage closet for vac-
uum cleaners, brooms, and cleaning products. The dwindling

numbers of priests could never bring back the 'old days', even if there was a renewed appetite on the part of Catholics to confess weekly. Yet the dark box continues to live in the memories of the generations born before the early 1970s.

The box also lives on, as in its heyday, in literature and film, persisting in an enduring radioactive half-life of the popular imagination. These evocations of the confessional tell us something of the robust iconography of the sacrament as it was reinstituted following the counter-reforming Council of Trent. The literary exploitation of confession occurs in the work of many Catholic writers throughout the twentieth century—cradle, convert, practising, and lapsed. Edith Wharton's short story 'Confession' portrays a jealous husband who masquerades as a confessor to catch out his adulterous wife. But he fails to discover her secrets, because she, albeit unconscious of her husband's masquerade, lies in the confessional—denying any sexual sin. Georges Bernanos, in *The Diary of a Country Priest*, enters the consciousness of a curate tantalised by the sexuality of a seven-year-old. Evelyn Waugh depicts the deathbed confession of an aristocrat, Lord Marchmain, while Graham Greene explores the 'dangerous edge' of the confessions of a whiskey priest and an ex-pat adulterer. The Italian writer Luigi Meneghello, in *Deliver Us*, explores childhood stratagems for confessing offences against 'modesty', and the heroine in Colm Tóibín's *Mothers and Sons* objects to making a confession to an Italian priest in case he fails to understand the true nature of her sins. Confessions and the dark box also make appearances in the fiction of, among many others, Heinrich Böll, Italo Svevo, Anthony Burgess, Umberto Eco, Muriel Spark, and John Banville.

By the 1950s the theme was equally popular in cinema. Alfred Hitchcock's *I Confess* deals with the pressures of the seal of the confessional on a priest who has been accused of murder. The priest knows the true identity of the murderer, who has come to him in confession, but his lips are sealed. Jean-Pierre Melville's *Léon Morin, Prêtre*, dramatizes a penitent sexual temptress. Federico Fellini reminisces about his childhood experiences with oppressive priests in *8½* and *Amarcord*, and Martin Scorsese's *Mean Streets* explores the penitential theology of the young gangster-saint Charlie. Charlie prefers to make his penance on the sidewalks and bars of Brooklyn, all too conscious of eternal suffering: 'And you don't fuck with the infinite!' he says. Confessors make cameo appearances in Francis Ford Coppola's *The Godfather*, Ulu Grosbard's *True Confessions*, Clint Eastwood's *Gran Torino*, and Martin McDonagh's *In Bruges*— which opens with an assassin shooting a paedophile priest in an old-style confessional box. Echoing Chaucer's Pardoner's Tale, in which money is seen as the root of evil (and three villains manage to kill each other), McDonagh's film proposes that the root of all evil is sexual child abuse. As Robert Stone, author of *A Flag for Sunrise*, would note half a century on from Pius X's decrees, there is 'enough material within Catholicism to keep you performing for years and years and years.'[1]

Two writers more than any others in the twentieth century have contributed to the imaginative and spiritual significance of confession as ritual and as a major theme in one's spiritual life story. The confession of James Joyce's hero Stephen Dedalus in *A Portrait of the Artist as a Young Man* marks the beginning of Stephen's spiritual and artistic journey, a journey culminating in Stephen's rejection of a priestly vocation and the blossoming of his literary calling. A spiritual metanoia, a turning towards the religious life, parallels his bid for liberation into a life in literature. The narrative evokes the confession as spiritual life story; but the sacramental ritual lies at the heart of the book.

In surely the most powerful description of a teenage confession ever written, Joyce depicts the trepidation of a young man entering the dark box, the disgust of sexual sin and fear of the terrors of hell familiar to generations of cradle Catholic youth. 'He was next. He stood up in terror and walked blindly into the box. At last it had come. . . . The slide clicked back and his heart bounded in his breast.' The sins trickled from his lips 'in shameful drops from his soul festering and oozing like a sore, a squalid stream of vice. The last sins oozed forth, sluggish, filthy'. The imagery matches the 'putrid', 'liquid' rottenness of the soul in Hell, themes fresh on Stephen's mind from the Jesuit priest's homily that had brought him to confess in the first place.[2]

As the priest says the words of absolution, Stephen experiences that moment of relief familiar to Catholics of every era: 'The old and weary voice fell like sweet rain upon his quaking parching heart. How sweet and sad!' And then he walks home, 'conscious of an invisible grace pervading and making light his limbs.'

But the confessional experience leads not so much to liberation as to the urge to regulate and regiment his life in the pursuit of holiness. In the course of this 'intricate piety and self restraint', he is often in and out of that confessional box now, relating 'doubts and scruples, some momentary inattention at prayer, a movement of trivial anger in his soul or a subtle wilfulness in speech or act'. His confession becomes 'a channel for the escape of scrupulous and unrepented imperfections.' His piety is noticed, leading to an encounter with the Jesuit director of the university, who broaches the possibility of Stephen's vocation to the priesthood.[3]

In presenting the advantages of the priesthood, the Jesuit invokes the power of the priest to absolve sin, with echoes of Satan's temptation of Christ in the desert: 'No king or emperor on this earth has the power of the priest of God. No angel or archangel in heaven, no saint, not even the Blessed Virgin herself has the power of a priest of God: the power of the keys, the power to bind and to loose from sin, the power of exorcism, the power to cast out from the creatures of God the evil spirits that have power over them'. And the Jesuit adds to this peroration: 'What an awful power, Stephen!'[4]

The priest's temptation to the power of absolution of sins meets with fantasies Stephen has already entertained of being a confessor. The preferred penitents of his imagination are 'women, and of girls'; the drama of the imagined encounters involves the secrecy of their sins and the contrast between the sins of women and his own priestly innocence: 'His soul had loved to muse in secret on this desire. He had seen himself, a young and silent-mannered priest, entering a confessional swiftly. . . . He would know obscure things, hidden from others . . . the sinful longings and sinful thoughts and sinful acts, of others, hearing them murmured into his ears in the confessional under the shame of a darkened chapel by the lips of women and of girls . . . He would hold his secret knowledge and secret power, being as sinless as the innocent . . .'[5]

The sustained fantasy that follows, as Stephen walks home, then walks out once more towards the strand and the sea, is an alternative examination of conscience, an alternative 'confession', in the sense originally employed by the early Christian fathers—confession as profession of faith, culminating in conversion of life: a vocation. 'This was the call of life to his soul not the dull gross voice of the world of duties and despair, not the inhuman voice that had called him to the pale service of the altar.' Encountering a girl on the strand, the vision of her standing bare-legged on the water's edge, 'passed into his soul for ever'. Her bosom was 'slight and soft as the breast of some dark plumaged dove', an alternative mystery to his earlier religiose vision of the soul that 'seemed to answer with the same inaudible voice, surrendering herself: *Inter ubera mea commorabitur* [He shall lie between my breasts]', and the 'the unseen Paraclete, Whose symbols were a dove and a mighty wind, to sin against Whom was a sin beyond forgiveness'. A life of freedom and writing in Europe beckoned.[6]

Contemporaneously with Joyce's novel, a very different kind of literary confession and spiritual liberation was proving a mass best-seller throughout the Catholic world in hundreds of editions and translations. St. Thérèse of Lisieux was a Carmelite nun who had entered the convent at the unusually youthful age of fifteen. Born in 1873, she was dead by 1897, wracked with tuberculosis and exhausted by the rigours of the highly ascetical, enclosed Carmelite convent she had entered while still little more than a child.

Losing her mother at the age of four, and her eldest sisters to the convent soon afterwards, Thérèse was prone to introversion, scrupulosity, psychosomatic illness, and an intense religiosity. The story of her short life, compiled and edited posthumously from three manuscripts, was published in English in 1912 as *Sœur Thérèse of Lisieux: The Little Flower*. It remains as popular to this day in the realm of Catholic piety as Joyce's *Portrait* does in that of Modernist literary novels. The autobiography of Thérèse is precisely the fulfilment of the 'pale life in service of the altar' that Stephen rejects. The book's internal commentary establishes that the narrative was composed out of a series of drafts written under obedience to her sister, her religious superior. This most Anti-Modernist of confessions, by the nun whom Pius X called the 'greatest saint of the modern period', is arguably the first *post*-Modernist 'confession' and hagiography, given the author's apologetic, self-conscious commentary on its construction. At the same time, its confessional impetus betrays an admission of profound scepticism more radical even than that of many confessed agnostics and atheists of the period. It is hard to think of a piece of Christian spiritual writing, including the *Dark Night of the Soul* of St. John of

the Cross, in which a 'saint's' trials of faith have been publicly
confessed so unremittingly—to extremes of agonised despair.
In the year before she died, Thérèse suffered for months 'in
the midst of the darkest storm'. She writes of an iron curtain
that rises up to the heavens, blotting out the stars; of crawl-
ing through a tunnel, walking in thick mists, and plunging
into a black hole where 'everything has disappeared'. She
hears the darkness speak to her mockingly, telling her that
the heavenly country is all a dream, that she is destined for a
night darker than ever, of mere non-existence.[7]

What appealed to the clergy about Thérèse's story, and
especially to Pius X, who initiated the process for her beatification in 1914, was her religious acquiescence and obedience
to her superiors in everything, whatever the temptations to
independence of spirit, whatever the doubts and temptations
to rebellion. She proved equally attractive to senior Catholic
theologians and intellectuals. The Catholic historian Henri
Daniel-Rops argued that she posed the 'irrefutable answer' to
the 'assertions of Nietzsche and Karl Marx' as well as to 'all
forms of contemporary apostasy'. She overcame her profound
doubt, he argued, with an act of love arising from sheer, in-
transigent will. In his book *Holy Daring*, John Udris noted
a strange paradox: 'Her strategy is "not to struggle against
the chimeras of the night" but to surrender oneself in the
certainty that we are being carried. She counsels a consent
not to see; a consent which confounds the "empty" fear which
she felt so unfitting for such a little child.' Thérèse's obedient confession of '*serviam*' stands at the opposite extreme to
Joyce's confession of '*non serviam*'.[8]

Joyce's handling of the sacrament of penance, in the case of Stephen's original conversion of life, exemplifies, as does Thérèse's entire life story in the convent, the Catholic confessional dilemma. The conversion of life, the metanoia, involves a radical decision to seek the face of God. Yet there is a price to be paid in self-inflicted wounds and the stifling of human emotions and instincts. Stephen has noted the first temptation: the acquisition of a power greater than that of the angels—of binding and loosing in Heaven and Hell. Later he observes the mirthless face of the early morning priest: 'eyeless and sour-favoured and devout, shot with pink tinges of suffocated anger.' The combination of temptation to power and the realities of ultimate self-denial have inevitable consequences: as Richard Crashaw put it in a poem in honour of St. Teresa of Avila, the Spanish mystic and Thérèse's spiritual model, 'the wounded is the wounding heart.'[9]

ON ANOTHER PLANE, in the mundane world of everyday Catholic realities, the dilemma proposed by the life of Thérèse was being played out in the sexual lives of countless Catholic couples throughout the twentieth century. With the availability of cheap and efficient condoms, followed in the 1960s by the birth control pill, Catholics were faced with a choice between following the Church's teaching on contraception or lowering their spiritual ideals (risking the loss of Heaven) and opting for the benefits of a planned family. The Church's awareness of this dilemma, which no devout,

yet sexually active, Catholic was spared, was evinced by Pius
XI's 1930 encyclical *Casti Connubii* (Of Chaste Marriage).
The encyclical became the Ur-text for subsequent popes,
from Pius XII (with his advocacy of the 'rhythm method')
through John Paul II's frequent animadversions on 'sexology'.
Pius XI's insistence on the sinful nature of contraception, and
the duty of priests to preach its evils, was uncompromising.
Contraception, he declared, was 'a horrible crime' (adding,
with evident approval, that in times past it was 'punished
with death'). Quoting St. Augustine, he went on: 'Intercourse
even with one's legitimate wife is unlawful and wicked where
the conception of the offspring is prevented. Onan, the son
of Juda, did this and the Lord killed him for it.'

The encounter between a sinning married person and the
priest was a time for firm instruction, reproof, and reconciliation. 'We admonish, therefore, priests, . . . in virtue of Our
supreme authority and in Our solicitude for the salvation
of souls, not to allow the faithful entrusted to them to err
regarding this most grave law of God', wrote Pius XI. He
went on: 'Much more, that they keep themselves immune
from such false opinions, in no way conniving in them.' Any
deviation from the Church's teaching within the confessional,
he warned, placed a heavy burden on the conscience of the
confessor. 'If any confessor or pastor of souls, which may God
forbid, lead the faithful entrusted to him into these errors or
should at least confirm them by approval or by guilty silence,
let him be mindful of the fact that he must render a strict
account to God, the Supreme Judge, for the betrayal of his

sacred trust, and let him take to himself the words of Christ: "They are blind and leaders of the blind: and if the blind lead the blind, both fall into the pit.'"[10]

———

As THE LIBERATIONS OF THE 1960S swept through the many worlds of the Catholic faithful, the *serviam* of married Catholics—typical of my grandmother, who had eight children, one of whom died, and who herself died at the age of fifty—was giving way to *non serviam*, at least where sexual practice and confession were concerned. There was a simultaneous decline, particularly on the part of the laity, in obedience to papal authority, as well as a plunge in the number of Catholics practising confession. The trends were revealed in two studies, one in Germany and the other in the United States. The former was reported by the moral theologian Bernard Häring in 1979, the latter by Andrew Greeley, the Chicago-based priest, novelist and sociologist of religion, in 1993. Greeley claimed that only 32 per cent of Catholics thought it was 'certainly true' that the pope was infallible in matters of faith and morals. One proposed cause was a rejection of papal teaching on contraception; another was social and political awakening on the part of women. With the invention and mass distribution of the birth control pill, women were in control of their reproductive lives in an unprecedented way. The 'liberation' of the sex act from procreative liability created scope for effective family planning, creating tensions for devout Catholics, who were constantly exposed to the clerical warnings of 'sinfulness', accompanied by the advocacy of 'abstinence', or the calendar-watching option of the 'safe period'. In the wider sexual revolution of the 1960s, moreover, the pill had made cohabitation of unmarried couples both feasible and acceptable. The link between responsible parenthood and economic security was becoming a norm. Sexually active Catholics were adopting these trends in developed countries, and their rates of divorce were beginning to equal those of non-Catholic couples.[11]

As we saw earlier, following the Second Vatican Council the faithful, lay and clerical, had expected a relaxation of the papal condemnation of artificial contraception. It was widely believed that the Church would soon allow freedom of conscience on the question for married couples. It was not to be. In 1968, Pope Paul VI made the uncollegial decision to publish his encyclical *Humanae Vitae*, which stressed the principle that 'each and every marriage act must remain open to the transmission of life.' Not only did he stress that contraception was a mortal sin within marriage, but he also said that contraception compounded the sin of sex outside of marriage. Homosexuality was also condemned. The Church's views on homosexuality would be spelled out in more detail in a declaration made by the Congregation for the Doctrine of the Faith in 1975, which ruled that homosexual practices and all masturbation were 'disordered' and constituted mortal sins.[12]

After *Humanae Vitae*, two crucial tendencies occurred with important implications for confession. Although actual figures are unknown, and probably unknowable, there is an abundance of anecdotal evidence of a massive decline of confessional practice, and of course the decline is quite obvious to anyone who has been a Catholic during these years. There were those Catholics who refused to believe, despite the Church's teaching, that their sexual behaviour was wrong, particularly when it came to the use of contraception within marriage. Confession was nevertheless difficult for them, as they balked at making a 'bad confession' by not admitting their use of contraception. Catholics brought up from childhood in the faith knew only too well that absolution depended on a 'firm purpose of amendment'. So, on their own consciences, they decided to go to communion at Mass while giving up on confession altogether. In contrast, there were those Catholics who simply abandoned their Catholicism in a process of self-exclusion, having decided that it was too difficult to live up to the Church's sexual teachings.

The position of confessors was invidious. Anthony Kenny, an Oxford philosopher, was a Catholic curate in Liverpool in the early 1960s. In his memoir *A Path from Rome*, a significant 'confessional' narrative of its time, he outlined the dilemma of confessors. 'The wrongness of contraception had been taught as explicitly and definitively by the Church as any moral doctrine. Yet, like most of the Church's critics, I could see little force in the natural law arguments against it.' He found himself constantly repeating and enforcing the Church's teaching even though he was conscious that, 'If the other doctrines I doubted turned out false, then in general no one was a loser but myself; but in a case like this it was others who were paying the penalty if the advice was wrong.' Kenny wrote that he had no alternative but to follow the Church's doctrine. This was a confessional admission of his decision for '*serviam*', despite the consequences for his penitents.[13]

Many priests, however, were beginning to rebel within the confessional, taking matters on their own conscience and telling their female penitents to go ahead and take the pill. The situation served to increase the anxiety of many priests during this period and added impetus to the mass walkout of some 100,000 priests worldwide in the following decades.

Conscious of the wide-scale collapse of confessional practice, in 1973 Pope Paul VI announced a revision of the 'Sacrament of Reconciliation', as confession was now to be known. He distinguished three legitimate rituals: First, the traditional, one-on-one, individual confession; second, a communal service of contrition with individual confession available for those who wished for it; and third, a communal service in which the congregation received 'general absolution' of their sins without recounting them individually to a confessor. It was laid down within the rubric for the third form that any grave sin should nevertheless be confessed at a subsequent individual confession. In the years that followed, many priests began to use the rite of general absolution routinely, especially in the run-up to Easter, and it proved to be popular among congregations. Priests reported that the general absolution rite was bringing many lapsed Catholics back to church.[14]

In Rome, however, the new pope, John Paul II, elected in 1978, and his new doctrinal enforcer, Cardinal Joseph Ratzinger, appointed in 1982, were unhappy. The time had come for yet another overhaul of the theology and practice of the sacrament, this time in the form of a retrenchment. In 1983 John Paul convened a synod of bishops in Rome to discuss 'Reconciliation and Penance'. On the face of it, the meeting was in continuity with the Second Vatican Council, being an attempt to resolve the evident crises collegially by consulting with the bishops. The synod had been preceded by a theological commission that had called for recognition of the social dimension of sin, and hence of such matters as a communal conscience and offences against the common good—including economic crime and pollution of the environment. The commission also advocated recognition of the variety of forms of the sacrament in pastoral practice, thereby noting the benefits of the rite of general absolution in bringing lapsed Catholics back into the fold.[15]

In the verbal and written submissions made by the bishops from all over the world, the issue of general absolution was raised repeatedly. Bishops from missionary countries, especially in Africa and Latin America, spoke of the advantage of the rite as a way of administering the sacrament to large numbers of people, many of whom may have travelled for days to hear one Mass in their region. The issue was again raised by the cardinal archbishop of Milan, Carlo Mario Martini, who was charged with collating the more than two hundred verbal and written views expressed on the matter by the bishops. But in delivering his own summary, the new head of the Congregation for the Doctrine of Faith, Cardinal Ratzinger, insisted that absolution must be administered individually and not to a group, except in situations of grave emergency, and even then, with the penitent intending to make a one-on-one individual confession later.

A year after the synod, John Paul II issued an 'apostolic exhortation' ignoring the concerns raised by many of the bishops at the synod. As with Paul VI's encyclical *Humanae Vitae*, it was the pontiff taking upon himself the ultimate teaching role and ignoring the collegial authority of his bishops. Citing the Council of Trent, four hundred years back, rather than the recent Second Vatican Council, he spoke in his apostolic exhortation of confession as having a 'juridical' and a 'medicinal' character. In its final section, individual, as opposed to general, absolution was advocated as the only means of healing the soul in mortal sin. In a ruling that many priests saw as a bid to exert clerical control over individual souls and consciences, the ritual of general absolution was banned.[16]

John Paul II, as a priest in his youth, had been in the habit of spending an entire hour delivering spiritual direction to each individual penitent who came to him. He saw confession as a 'drama', an act of intense religious imagination in which a person's ideal self and real self were contrasted and compared in the presence of the confessor. This approach (he spoke elsewhere of typically taking more than an hour over each confession when he was a parish priest) hardly helped to solve the predicament of priests serving thousands of souls across vast terrains of the third world. Nor did it address the clear evidence that there were fewer priests every year in the developed world. Nor was he listening to the lay faithful any more than he had heeded his bishops at the synod.[17]

John Paul II acknowledged the notion of 'social sin' that had been put forward by the Latin American bishops, but he remained wedded to that imaginative 'drama' of the individual soul in its 'vertical' relationship with his or her better self, and with God, in the presence of the confessor, who acted as a kind of theatrical director.

The question of the age for first confession was not addressed, but the exhortation confirmed that, without exception, first communion must be preceded by first confession. Yet concerns about the inappropriateness of confession from the age of seven had been voiced by parents who retained memories of oppression in the confessional. In 1973, responding to parental anxieties, the German bishops had allowed that the rule of first confession before first communion might be waived, allowing parents to make the decision on the ideal age for their children to receive the sacrament. By 1977, under pressure from Rome, the proviso was withdrawn. Lay Catholics and pastors nevertheless continued to be anxious about children being forced to make their confessions at a tender age, when the majority of the faithful had ceased going to confession at all.[18]

The moral theologian Professor John Mahoney, SJ, writing to me about the problem of early confession, argued:

What I find hard to accept is not the passing of regular confession, like many other devotions, but the way in which the passing is officially deplored, and we are still apparently trying to drill into children making their 'first confession' and the need to make their confession weekly, in spite of the fact that their teachers and parents (and priests) have given up this regular practice. It smacks of inconsistency and even intellectual dishonesty, which is particularly reprehensible with regard to young children. The Church needs courageously in this, as in so many other practices, to review its approach and teaching.

———————————

MEANWHILE, THERE WAS an impression throughout the 1980s that the split between teaching and practice on sexual matters was widening. Was there any hope of a resolution to problems that were driving Catholics from the Church in ever growing numbers? In 1993 I interviewed Cardinal Carlo Mario Martini, who was considered until his death in 2012 to be a leading progressive voice in the Church and even a likely candidate someday to be pope. As it turned out, he would be the chief rival to Joseph Ratzinger in the 2005 conclave following the death of John Paul II. In our conversation, which took place in the cardinal's palace in Milan, he revealed himself to be remote from the simplistic liberal image promoted by many of his supporters and detractors. On contraception, however, the 'sin' that had driven so many sexually active Catholics from confession, and indeed the Church, he made a bold statement: 'Contraception is something special, to do with special points of moral teaching. There is a contrast in attitude between northern countries and Latin countries on moral questions. In Italy we believe the ideal is set high so as to attain something. In other countries they think that they must actually achieve the ideal, and they are anxious if they fail.' The perspective admitted a measure of relativism, and the language was interesting: the Church's teaching on contraception was a 'special point' rather than an infallible doctrine. He elaborated:

> I don't know what the development will be as regards contraception. But I believe that the Church's teaching has not been expressed so well. The fact is that the problem of contraception is relatively new; it was only really possible with new techniques in the past forty or so years. The Church, on the other hand, thinks very slowly, so I'm confident we will find some formula to state things better, so that the problem is better understood and more adapted to reality. I admit that there is a gap and that bothers me, but I am confident it can be overcome.

Cardinal Martini went on to give an example of how a similar problem was resolved in the past: 'Usury', he said, 'was an almost insurmountable impediment in the fourteenth century, but little by little we began to see the problem in a different light, although it took centuries to resolve it.'

Talking of the antagonisms and divisions within the Church, he said: 'We are not all contemporaries in a biographical sense. We are in the 1990s, but some Catholics are still mentally in the 1960s and some in the 1940s, and some even in the last century; it's inevitable that there will be clashes of mentalities.'[19]

Twelve

Varieties of
Confessional Experience

> Nothing could be more impossible than
> that God should be wrath. For wrath
> and friendship are two contraries. He
> that layeth and destroyeth our wrath,
> and maketh us meek and mild—we
> must believe that he is ever, in the same
> love, meek and mild; which is contrary
> to wrath.
>
> —Julian of Norwich, *Revelations of Divine Love*

THE GENERATIONAL DIFFERENCES BETWEEN CATHOLICS
are amply illustrated in the correspondence generated
in the course of my research.[1] In addition to the many people
responding to my article in *The Tablet* who still carried memories of torment and abuse, I heard from some who had never
found confession to be a negative experience personally, yet

still voiced positive criticisms. The correspondence as a whole presented a variety of perspectives based on respondents' personal experiences and the contrasts between quotations I heard from the young and the old, married people and single people, cradle Catholics and converts, laypeople, priests, and one bishop. All in all, the material provides a wide-ranging overview of current attitudes and practices, suggesting that the sacrament continues to evolve.

The current generation of young Catholics, aged fourteen to twenty-four in my sample, are now largely free of the oppressive confessional practices of the past that prompted unwarranted guilt and fear. First confession is still part of the celebration of first communion for young children. However, pastors and parents are now complicit in imparting to them the idea that confession is a brief and insignificant threshold to the more important celebration of the Eucharist. Pastors, catechists, and parents do their best to make light of the ritual. Confessor and child-penitent sit side by side, or facing each other, in full sight of the congregation. There is a tendency to eliminate sin language and to emphasise a God who loves and forgives.[2]

A fourteen-year-old correspondent wrote that on the occasion of her first confession when she was eight, the priest greeted her with a smile, and she talked to him 'about things I had done wrong.' She remembers 'we spoke freely and I relaxed. . . . I told him about not cleaning my bedroom, or not obeying my mother, all of which made him chuckle jovially.' Since her first confession this correspondent has attended the sacrament on only one other occasion, this time in preparation for her confirmation four years later. Her account is typical of today's experience. Like others in her age group, she receives the Eucharist whenever she goes to Mass.

Young Catholics attending Catholic schools are encouraged, perhaps before Easter, to attend a single communal ritual of contrition, followed by the opportunity to make individual confession to one of several attending priests. I was told of experiments whereby schoolchildren will confess in small groups: admitting, for example, that they have been guilty of belonging to a bullying clique.

Not every priest is a chuckling jovial pastor, but young people appear to be decisive in rejecting traditionalist, hard-line approaches. One young single Catholic, twenty-three and recently graduated from college, noted the contrast between two priests she had known. 'When I made my first holy communion I was used to the loving, creative, forgiving God which both my parents educated me in and our local priest', she wrote. When the family moved, she came up against a new priest who expressed a Christianity that was 'cruel and unforgiving'. This priest, she said, 'quite changed my ideas about my faith.' She remembers sitting in the pews on Sundays, covering her ears as the priest described 'the shocking lengths women will go to for an abortion', and how her 'ever forgiving God would never forgive their sin.' She had never suffered oppression or abuse in confession, but feels no compulsion to confess, and believes that censorious priests turn away more and more Catholics 'who struggle in the modern world to find a happy balance between their lives and their faith.'

A recent convert to Catholicism in her sixties acknowledged that she approaches confession without the hang-ups of cradle Catholics of her generation. She had never been instructed on how to make her confession. She, too, spoke of 'wrongs she has done to God, to society, to friends and neighbours, to my family, to myself', rather than of 'sins'. It is more challenging, she believes, 'saying these wrongs out loud to the priest than simply acknowledging them to myself. . . . And I must be pre-pared to make amends for my wrongdoings.' She wrote that she does not come out of confession feeling forgiven. 'After all, what is "being forgiven"? I don't feel that the priest saying the absolution is the same as being truly forgiven.'

Some correspondents wrote of valuing the anonymity of old-style confession. An eighty-three-year-old nun who had entered the religious life in the 1950s wrote that she goes to confession at Westminster Cathedral so that she cannot be recognised by the confessor: 'I go to confession about five times a year. I have to wait a long time in a long queue which gives me time to prepare. I find the priests ready to spend time in discussing the issues which I confess and which I could not describe as sins but rather as imperfections which can hinder the spiritual life.'

Many more, however, wrote of preferring to confess to a sympathetic priest that they knew. For them, the ritual of the sacrament was less important than the relationship. Some of these correspondents stressed that spiritual direction was more important than feeling forgiven. Indeed, many seeking spiritual direction preferred a woman counsellor to a priest. One correspondent wrote, 'I have a spiritual director, a lovely Carmelite sister who gives me direction in my prayer life.' She added, 'The deepening of my relationship with God occurs most strongly through contemplative prayer, through which I receive his grace. In this fast moving and noisy world, the return to the old Christian practices of quiet prayer times and praying the Scriptures would seem a most healthy way forward to gain reconciliation with God. In the words of the little catechism "Why did God make me? To know him, to love him and to serve him . . ." We do need to get to know him—the other two follow on.'

A Franciscan priest wrote, in a similar mode, that 'confession as a regular practice can now feel infantile and misdirected. Catholic life is no longer compliance with a catalogue of precepts governing every detail of behaviour.' The life of the spirit grows more, he said, 'by aspiring to ideals than [by] avoiding failures. What we need is a practice to take us deeper in understanding God's action in us, our motivation, and growing self-knowledge, in that order.' For this reason he questions the 'focus on absolution', which can be 'misleading'. He advocated the function of 'the Celtic Soul Friend', a figure that other correspondents also invoked. 'He or she . . . is someone sympathetic, wise and spiritual acting as a catalyst on our personal journey', he wrote.[3]

Many of the correspondents attempted to tell a story of their developing relationships with confession over a lifetime.

One woman who had been brought up outside the Church converted to Catholicism following her university years. She began to confess weekly, but saw it merely as a chore, a discipline. After several years she decided to confess only once a year, during Lent, and always to a strange confessor. This practice came to an end in 1983, when a priest gave her, as she put it, 'inappropriate' advice. She gave up confession on principle. 'The Church's emphasis on one-on-one confession now seems to me misguided, with the potential to encourage a power complex in the clergy and infantilism in the laity. It does not allow for communal sin (e.g., my totally unwilling but unavoidable involvement in the Iraq war because I contributed to its cost through taxation).' As with so many correspondents, she found the services of general absolution uplifting. 'If the Church wants more people to go to confession, bring back general absolution.'

Divorce and remarriage without an annulment has separated many Catholics not only from confession but from the Church. Yet some nevertheless find their way back with an understanding priest. An American woman who has been three times married and twice divorced wrote that she gave up confession when she went on the birth control pill. 'My Catholic upbringing couldn't balance this with me being true to my faith, so I left the Church—angry at God', she wrote. It was the experience of being at her mother's deathbed that brought her back to the Church: 'It was difficult, I was divorced, married, divorced, married. Approaching my local church, the parish priest was very supportive, a 70-year-old worldly priest. He helped me prepare an application for an annulment for my first marriage, the other two were only register type.' She wrote, "I am full of the joys of my faith.'

Some correspondents raised the phenomenon of counselling and psychotherapy, which continue to flourish while confession declines. A 'consultant analyst' speculated that the need to unburden has shifted from the confessional to the therapist's couch. 'Counselling and psychotherapy', he wrote, 'have become more widespread because they not only make sense to many people but are also ways of effecting change.' He argued that 'talk' therapies have been characterised as spiritual technologies—ways of helping people to change and find healing for their brokenness. He believes that loss and pain are central themes in most therapies, and that adjustment to change in human beings takes time. 'For me, psychotherapy means "soul healing." I wonder if part of the current problem is the language of sin rather than that of change and growth. The former is currently deeply unpopular while the latter is understandable to more people.'

A woman in her late forties wrote that she had enjoyed spiritual direction since her twenties and finds that this, along with daily quiet time, keeping a journal, and the like, is usually enough to allow her to 'reflect on my journey and see what is going astray, where I am drawn and where I feel driven.' About once or twice a year she seeks something 'more formal', although not necessarily in a Catholic church. 'I last went to a reconciliation service in Holy Week in an Anglican setting', she said. She values going on retreats, where she gets 'a great sense of clearing out and a new start.' This woman was not alone in declaring her belief that 'forgiveness is there always. The sacrament is more about my recognition that I've been forgiven, my acceptance of that forgiveness.'

There were many correspondents who were critical of Catholic confessional practice even though they had not personally been victims of abuse. Their experiences in youth, however, measured the distance between the pre–Vatican II Church and the Church today. An ex-priest wrote that there is great satisfaction to be gained from confession, since it is only natural to offload the burdens on one's mind. He takes this to be 'a fundamental human experience and need.' Yet, now in his sixties, he recalls the unnecessary, negative impact on children. 'Our models for purity in adolescence were Dominic Savio an Italian youth of the mid-nineteenth century who died of pleurisy at the age of fifteen. As a child he put stones in his bed to be uncomfortable and wore a hair shirt. Then there was Maria Goretti, murdered during a rape attack by the family's lodger . . . We fought impure thoughts as energetically and wearily as our father fought the Germans.' Only today, half a century on, can he see the funny side of it. 'I can chuckle at our local curate who used to ask us as *children*—"Are you married or single?"—when we confessed in unbroken voices to having dirty thoughts.'

A former seminarian, now a professed Buddhist, commented on his years in junior seminary. He never experienced abuse, yet his story reveals the constructive potential of one former Catholic's negative experiences. 'For an adolescent with a little imagination, the idea that sexual transgressions *killed* the soul was horrifying', he wrote. 'You had to see yourself as having deliberately cut yourself off from God's grace, the most important thing in life, and it made the need for the confessional even stronger: one had to get absolution if one was to restore life to one's own soul, a restoration that depended absolutely upon the power of the church.' But, even worse, he wrote, 'was the hatred of the body that this ideology of mortal sin brought about, a hatred of a body whose impulses led to this constant death of the soul, and a self-loathing at the weakness that led to the succumbing to these evil impulses.' It was not until he was in his early thirties, he went on, that he overcame the negative feelings this training generated. He wondered whether the process of seminary formation did not lead to a kind of erosion of a future priest's moral integrity. 'One either repressed the horror of mortal sin and separation from God and acted almost as an automaton; or one was cynical about the whole story of mortal sin and sexual transgression and got on with it under the cover of priestly prestige.' He concluded by saying, 'Thank God I never became a priest.'

Only one bishop wrote in response to my invitation in *The Tablet*. Like Anthony Kenny, author of *The Path from Rome* (discussed in Chapter 11), the bishop turned the tables by writing about the burdens of a confessor. 'We ask about the effect on the penitent of the "shopping list" confession, but what about its effect on the priest? I found that the daily round of almost entirely predictable minor infringements of what was perceived of as "Church rules" quite frustrating and dispiriting. Only once did I experience a satisfactory encounter when one individual actually said that he was not ready for absolution at the end of the meeting, and was not ready for some time after that.' The bishop believes that the 'shopping list' confessions were an attempt to engage with the guilt that many felt and still feel as Catholics. 'On the one hand', he said, 'I think this is a pity that Catholics were made to feel guilty by an over-emphasis on sin and the threat of hell, but on the other hand it is a recognition that none of us is responding sufficiently to the call of the gospel.' The laundry list and the brief penance gave people temporary relief, he went on, but 'often (in my own experience) more akin to coming out of the dentist, glad the experience is over and pleased to have been strong enough to do it.' He asserted that:

> the people in our churches are not good or less good because they come to confession or not. They are going to be 'better Catholics' (whatever that might mean) if they are trying to deepen their understanding of what faith might mean to them. *Deus Caritas Est* [God Is Love] reminds us that faith is an encounter with a person, and that the basic message of the gospel is that 'God loved the world so much . . .' If the Sacrament of Reconciliation can help us to be more loveable, then all the better; if it reinforces my belief that I am not loveable, then so much the worse.

Epilogue

It is very odd that the view of God as
seen from the Church should ever be
simply the view of God as seen from
Hell. For damnation must be just being
fixed in this illusion, stuck forever with
the God of the Law, stuck forever with
the God provided by our sin.

—Herbert McCabe, OP, *The Tablet*, 5 March 2011

PSYCHOANALYST AND PHILOSOPHER JULIA KRISTEVA
has written of the residents of 'steel city'—her metaphor
for the collective maladies of the psyche that blight much
of Western life. Its denizens, she declares, have nothing to do
except 'buy and sell goods and images, which amounts to the
same thing, since they both are dull, shallow symbols . . . while
in the next street, heaps of filth abound and drugs accompany
the sleep or the fury of the social outcasts.' There are those
who attempt to 'create a space for an "inner zone"—a secret

garden, an intimate quarter, or more simply and ambitiously, a psychic life.' For the most part, however, the majority remain just 'as anxious, depressed, neurotic, and psychotic as the Freudian unconscious would wish them to be.' In view of this state of affairs, she says, psychoanalysis has much work to do, since 'Freud's doctrine seeks precisely to free us from this suppressed space of psychological ill-being.' The problem, though, is that the benefits of psychoanalysis have been thwarted by pharmacological fixes, superficial talk therapy, and 'plain ignorance'. What chance is there in these circumstances, she asks, for psychoanalysis to ease our dislocations and perplexities?[1]

In the same way, it could be argued that the scope and benefits of the sacrament of penance to ease the ills of the soul have been relativized and obscured, not only by the myriad 'fess-up', 'guilt-trip' alternatives of the late twentieth century, but by the long-term trivialisation of the sacrament itself. The routine, frequent, 'devotional' guilt-fix confessions imposed on my generation—and those of my parents and grandparents— were a travesty of the true potential of the sacrament, as many of my correspondents, lay and clerical, men and women, have argued from personal experience. In the case of children, the practice was inappropriate, harmful, and in many cases lastingly so.

Just as psychoanalysis offers narrative depth, a willingness to explore backwards and forwards, and a drive to know oneself and to transform oneself and grow, so sacramental confession has the potential capacity to administer knowledge of the whole of one's spiritual life, past, present, and future, in relation to one's faith community and in relation to God.

Connected with the recent decline of confession, moreover, are significant shifts in Christian perceptions of sin. The word for 'sin' in many languages derives from the idea of 'missing the mark'—in Greek, *hamartia*. For Catholics under traditionalist disciplines and catechesis of confession, this 'missing the mark' traditionally meant a failure to live up to God's laws. Catholic children growing up in the first half of the twentieth century were taught that their sins were offenses against God's infinite goodness. God was the all-powerful, big 'I AM' who stood in readiness to be offended, and even to punish for all eternity.

The capital sins worthy of God's anger and punishment were the Ten Commandments of the Bible, or the Seven Deadly Sins of the Desert Fathers. But from the Middle Ages on, moralists increasingly encouraged preoccupation with those subtle sins of interiority and the fine gradations of motives and intentions. The least 'impure thought' was a mortal sin, an offence against God and one's soul. Human failings were categorised into checklists of imperfections disconnected from circumstances and relationships.

The era of the Enlightenment tended to revive and reinforce the separation of the conscious inward soul from the world. Moral and ascetical theology emphasised those 'virtues' proper to a medieval cloister—as advocated, for example, by Thomas à Kempis's early fifteenth-century *The Imitation of*

Christ. Here is a typical passage from *Imitation* illustrating this intense preoccupation with self:

> Rest from inordinate desire of knowledge, for therein is found much distraction and deceit. Those who have knowledge desire to appear learned, and to be called wise. Many things there are to know which profiteth little or nothing to the soul. And foolish out of measure is he who attendeth upon other things rather than those which serve to his soul's health. Many words satisfy not the soul, but a good life refresheth the mind, and a pure conscience giveth great confidence towards God.[2]

The highest virtue consisted in the individual soul's union with God, involving aspirations to perfect recollection, detachment, poverty of spirit, purity of heart, humility, and obedience to spiritual authority.

The idea of virtue as the pursuit of the common good, however, had also been active in Christianity. Its intellectual origins date back to ancient Greece and the ethics of Aristotle. Humans, according to his philosophy, are communal animals. Virtue, wholeness, is the nurturing of one's true purpose or goal in everyday life, whether in trade, husbandry, manual skills, education, or medicine—that is, to be of service to one's community. Aristotle's ethics, adopted and adapted by the Christian philosopher Thomas Aquinas, have been a feature, albeit subterranean, of Catholic moral philosophy to this day. Its revival in recent decades has been a central dynamic for groups that seek to express Catholicism's social dimension. The philosophical foundations for this restoration have been provided by moral philosophers such as Alasdair MacIntyre, the Aristotelian and Thomist scholar. In parallel, the idea of sin as 'social' rather than interior finds expression alongside the liberation theologies developed and practised in the third world—for example, by Leonardo Boff in Latin America.[3]

The tensions within the Catholic Church between inwardly preoccupied virtue, on the one hand, and liberation virtue, on the other, are well known. Borrowing from the history of science, some liberal theologians have described their distance from 'traditionalist' theology as being comparable to the so-called paradigm shift in the natural sciences. In other words, Catholic teaching is no longer seen as immutable, patriarchal, exclusive, defensive, and militant, but as open to historical, cultural, and social factors, willing to engage society and the non-Catholic world. This perspective has been given practical impetus by younger generations of lay Catholics who find in Christianity a duty to combat social, economic, and political injustice. Their moral concerns focus not on the exquisite state of their souls, but on the alleviation of poverty, homelessness, hunger, and disease; care for the environment; and peace building. They seek to combat the 'sins' of racism, sexism, child abuse, and the oppression of minorities.[4]

In the meantime, an ancient and enduring idea of sin, unfamiliar to the catechists of my childhood, but widely accepted today, declares that if there is a Hell it consists not

in a physical place of torture but in a person's deliberate
abandonment of God's love through the sin of self-idolatry.
It is not God who rejects and punishes the 'sinner', but the
self-adulator who turns away from God's unconditional love.

The notion finds expression in the Book of Genesis. In
Hebrew, the word *yetzer* is often employed to denote sin. It
is related, however, to the word for 'creation', *yetzirah*, and to
the word for 'imagine' (which is another form of creation—
making something out of nothing). In Genesis the power of
imagination is synonymous with the sin of Adam and Eve in
the Garden of Eden. Satan tempts our first parents to acquire
'the Knowledge of Good and Evil', which sets them on the
path to rivalling God. 'For God knows that when you eat
of it your eyes will be opened, and you will be like God,
knowing good and evil', Satan tells Eve. But it is the power
of imagination that makes a moral life possible. It makes
possible the recollection of past actions, options taken or rejected. Imagination is the capacity to envision future choices
and weigh their comparative consequences. The power of
imagination thus becomes both the source of freedom and
a potential curse. For at the heart of the Genesis myth is a
powerful metaphor for the human capacity to supplant God
in a life of self-love.[5]

Self-adulation has been explored down the centuries in
works of religious and artistic imagination: from Narcissus
in Greek mythology, to Sophocles' Electra, to the sins of avarice, pride, and envy in Dante's *Divine Comedy*. Two kinds of
narcissism are portrayed in Shakespeare's *Othello*—that of the

Moor and the diabolical Iago. Christopher Marlowe's Dr. Faustus barters earthly self-aggrandisement for an eternity of punishment. John Milton's Satan is the archetype of supreme pride and God-envy. And in Oscar Wilde's *Picture of Dorian Gray*, Gray's vanity is matched by his selfishness in everyday life.

A powerful example of the predicament of grotesque self-centredness in mid-twentieth-century literature is to be found in William Golding's novel *Pincher Martin*. Martin is shipwrecked in the Atlantic. The action of the novel takes place, one eventually understands, at the moment of Martin's death. Martin cannot accept death, however, because he cannot surrender his voracious ego. We are given to believe that he is stranded on a rock. In fact, as he drowns, he is exploring a missing jagged tooth in his mouth, to which he clings as his final vestige of ownership, colonising it and subjecting it to his will. If there is a Hell, according to Golding, it is in the inability to accept one's creatureliness, one's finitude—one's consciousness of a creator on the horizon of existence. In the course of the novel we are told of Martin's legendary lifelong selfishness: 'This painted bastard here takes anything he can lay his hands on. Not food . . . that's far too simple. He takes the best part, the best seat, the most money, the best notice, the best woman. He was born with his mouth and his flies open and both hands out to grab. He's a cosmic case of the bugger who gets his penny and someone else's bun.' In Martin's life, self-idolatry manifests itself in acquisitiveness, possessing, and having.[6]

There are flashes of a mysterious black lightning, suggestive of divine influence, seeking to distract Martin from his inward egotistic insistence on being the very centre and meaning of life and the universe. The play of the lightning is reminiscent of the water snakes in Coleridge's *Ancient Mariner*: it seeks to find a chink in the carapace of Martin's egotism, even as he draws his self-protective claws in ever tighter: 'There was nothing but the centre and the claws. They were huge and strong and inflamed to red. They closed on each other. They contracted.'[7]

We never know whether Martin finally yields his inexorable narcissism to the divinity of black lightning. Some commentators suggest that Martin finally submits, and that the novel is a portrait of Purgatory rather than Hell.[8]

THE POINT OF CHRISTIANITY, according to a constituency of theologians of the 'new paradigm', is to teach by example the virtues of spiritual community in contrast to the sin of self-adulation. Christianity is essentially, therefore, a community, a 'school of prayer and friendship', rather than a hierarchical reformatory of top-down dogma. The Catholic Church, however, has been a community in conflict with itself on this issue, with far-reaching implications for the sacrament of confession.[9]

During the recent celebrations for the half-century that has elapsed since the beginning of the Second Vatican Council, that momentous event for the world's Catholics has been explained in several different ways. Whatever else its goals, the Council attempted to overturn much of the legalistic, centralising, Anti-Modernist tendencies of the Church of the Piuses (Pius X, XI, and XII). The Council was not entirely successful in achieving that aim, however, and where it succeeded there have been gradual, inexorable processes of retrenchment by recent popes. The society that invokes Pius X's name—the Society of Pius X—demonstrates the discontent of those who regret the loss of that former, patriarchal, citadel Church of immutable truths, dictatorial rulings, and a punitive God.

The Second Vatican Council declared in two key documents that confession, or the sacrament of penance, was a reconciliation that took place not only between God and the individual soul, but between the fellowship of the people of God and each individual Christian as a member of the congregation and the community at large. The decision of Council Fathers to emphasise the long-neglected social nature of the sacrament, and the social nature of sin, had much to do with their determination to recover aspects of practice and doctrine that had been lost down the centuries. Exploring the communal rather than the purely private and devotional aspect of confession's past traditions, the French theologian Henri de Lubac offered this insight: 'The reconciliation of the sinner is in the first place a reconciliation with the Church, this latter constituting an efficacious sign of reconciliation with God.' The Council, in turn, stressed the need for the

Church to engage with society and with other Christians, other religions, and the world. Its final decree, which found much resistance from conservatives, proclaimed freedom of religion and conscience. The Council, finally, acknowledged that salvation is not a monopoly of Catholics, and that the moral life of religion is communitarian, rather than private and interior.[10]

It has been argued by Church historians that, in its conflict with the Protestant reformers John Wycliffe, John Hus, and Martin Luther, Catholicism came to emphasise its controlling, legal, and juridical structures over its communitarian fellowship. As the Catholic theologian Karl Rahner put it: 'The individualism of modern times, the origin of which can already be found in the late Middle Ages', meant that 'grace became more and more something which is worked out between God and the individual alone and taken in isolation.' The Second Vatican Council sought to rectify this emphasis by recovering the idea of communal reconciliation practised in the early Church.[11]

This background explains in part why the rite of congregational or general confession and absolution was so popular through the 1970s, and why it brought so many people back to the faith who had been lapsed for years. It appeared to strike a chord in many Catholics, consistent with the spirit of renewal of the times. The majority of my respondents lamented the banning of this rite, and pastors had reasons to lament it, too.

The Second Vatican Council prompted a re-examination, moreover, of that essential Greek term *metanoia*—meaning transformation, or change of heart and mind—which had created such fierce divisions over the understanding of the sacrament of confession at the time of the Reformation. *Metanoia* is neither the doing of penance nor the judgement and sacramental operation of the minister, conciliar theologians concluded, but a person's rejection of self-centredness, and an inclination of the heart towards God. Thus the Council sought to advocate both individual and communal virtues in the subordination of self to God and to the community. Does a 'sinner' require the absolution of a priest to return to God? The view of many theologians and lay Catholics today is that a penitent is reconciled with God *before* going to confession, not as a result of it. Were the Church officially and clearly to expound this teaching, many Catholics would be released from lingering guilt that keeps them from practice. It should also reduce the dangerous clerical assumption of unearthly power so aptly encapsulated in James Joyce's portrayal of the temptation of Stephen Dedalus in *A Portrait of the Artist as a Young Man*: 'He would hold his secret knowledge and secret power, being as sinless as the innocent . . .' Stephen's temptation to priestly supremacy involved, as well, the masculine power of the confessor over the submissive female penitent, and the unequal power relationship of a confessor over a child. Stephen fantasises that he would know the 'sinful longings and sinful thoughts and sinful acts . . . murmured into his ears . . . by the lips of women and girls: but rendered immune mysteriously at his ordination by the imposition of hands his soul would pass again uncontaminated to the white peace of the altar.'[12]

The late Father Herbert McCabe, a Dominican theologian, gave a homily on confession not long before he died: 'You are not forgiven because you confess your sin', he said. 'You confess your sin, recognise yourself for what you are, *because* you are forgiven.' The theologian Karl Rahner, citing Augustine, made the same point, invoking the image of Lazarus rising from the tomb. When a Christian stands outside the confessional ready to tell his sins to a priest, 'he has already been raised by the word of grace of Christ from the tomb of sin like a Lazarus[;] . . . he has already begun to live.'[13]

ACKNOWLEDGEMENTS

THIS BOOK OWES ITS EXISTENCE TO the late Peter Carson, my publisher for forty years at Allen Lane, Viking-Penguin, and Profile Books. Peter midwifed the text of this book until his death in January 2013. He is sorely missed by colleagues and the rest of the publishing world. Being above all an 'authors' publisher', he is especially missed by the many writers he discovered, nurtured, and inspired. My personal debt to him is incalculable.

My research has drawn on a wide circuit of recent scholarly work on the role of confession in the Middle Ages and the early modern period, especially in the archives of the Spanish Inquisition and canon law tribunals in Italy. Counter-Reformation studies continue to attract scholars, and their work provides new perspectives and overviews of a period and subject that, from a Catholic view, had become closer to apologetics than authentic history. A critical overview of modern manuals of moral and pastoral theology, from Alphonsus Liguori to Henry Davis, has enabled me to form an impression of a confessor's formation in the seminaries through the first two-thirds of the past century. For the link between sexual abuse and confession in the second half of the twentieth century, official reports from the United States, Canada, Ireland, Germany, and Australia have been crucial. Information continues to come in piecemeal via the media and the courts.

I was part of a seminar at University College, Dublin, in the spring of 2012 run by Dr. Marie Keenan, whose interviews with offending priests (on leaving jail) have proved essential to my research. I am grateful to Dr. Keenan for permission to quote from interviews with priests who had served jail sentences as a result of convictions relating to clerical sexual abuse. Research on the local incidence of abuse conducted by Professor Gerry Kearns (who also participated in the seminar) of Maynooth University College, Dublin, has also proved invaluable. Understanding the psychological dimensions of confession, and stages of moral development, took me to the works of Sigmund Freud, Carl Jung, Jean Piaget, Lawrence Kohlberg, and others as well as to the ideas of Michel Foucault. At the same time, I have derived considerable benefit from my conversations with the psychoanalyst and sociologist Professor Juliet Mitchell of the University of Cambridge and with the London psychoanalyst Josephine Klein.

In the summer of 2012 I was invited by the international Catholic weekly *The Tablet* to publish an article on the neglect of confession. In consequence I received more than three hundred responses from readers around the world. This correspondence, together with interviews with penitents and confessors, has provided ample source material for the views expressed by the lay and clerical Catholic faithful that I have discussed in Part Three. I am indebted to Catherine

Pepinster, editor of *The Tablet*, for publishing my article. In addition, I thank all the respondents for their contributions. Their views have been essential even if they are not cited in the text. Charles Lysaght; Professor Bryan Fanning of University College, Dublin; and the late Dr. Pádraic Conway of the Newman Centre, Dublin, also helped to expedite my research and discussions in Ireland.

I have also benefited from my correspondence with Father Desmond O'Donnell, OMI. Dr. David Bernard McLoughlin of Newman University College enlightened me on the topic of penitentials. The moral theologian Father Jim McManus advised me on questions relating to Alphonsus Liguori.

I would also like to thank Professor Nicholas Lash, Dr. Mary Laven, Nathan Brooker, and Roger Labrie for reading the book, or parts of it, in manuscript form, and for their valued comments; and I must thank Father Alban McCoy, Canon John Koenig, Janet Lash, John Wilkins, Professor John Mahoney, Dr. Christopher Burlinson and Dr. Michael McGhee for their insights on specific matters.

In addition, I thank my friend and agent Clare Alexander in London, Zoë Pagnamenta in New York, and my publishers Andrew Franklin, Lara Heimert, and Jens Dehning.

This book was written under the hospitable auspices of Jesus College, Cambridge, for which I thank its Master and Fellows. Finally, I am especially grateful to my friend and 'reader' Professor Stephen Heath of Jesus College, Cambridge, for his encouragement and advice, and for scrutinising the manuscript and proofs. Any remaining infelicities are my responsibility.

SELECT BIBLIOGRAPHY

Alvarez, David. *Spies in the Vatican: Espionage and Intrigue from Napoleon to the Holocaust*. Lawrence, KS, 2002.

Augustine. *The Confessions of Saint Augustine*. Translated by E. M. Blaiklock. London, 1987.

Bamji, Alexandra, Geert H. Janssen, and Mary Laven, eds. *The Ashgate Research Companion to the Counter-Reformation*. Surrey, UK, 2013.

Beattie Jung, Patricia, and Joseph Andrew Coray, eds. *Sexual Diversity and Catholicism: Toward the Development of Moral Theology*. Collegeville, MN, 2001.

Bell, Rudolph M. *Holy Anorexia*. Chicago, 1985.

Berry, Jason, and Gerald Renner. *Vows of Silence: The Abuse of Power in the Papacy of John Paul II*. New York, 2004.

Bieler, Ludwig, ed., with an Appendix by D. A. Binchy. *The Irish Penitentials*. Dublin, 1975.

Biller, Peter, and A. J. Minnis, eds. *Handling Sin: Confession in the Middle Ages*. Woodbridge, UK, 1998.

Bossy, John. *Christianity in the West, 1400–1700*. Oxford, 1985.

Brooks, Peter. *Troubling Confessions: Speaking Guilt in Law and Literature*. Chicago, 2000.

Brown, Judith C. *Immodest Acts: The Life of a Lesbian Nun in Renaissance Italy*. Oxford, 1986.

Brown, Peter. *Augustine of Hippo*. London, 1969.

———. *The Body and Society: Men, Women and Sexual Renunciation in Early Christianity*. London, 1988.

———. *The Cult of the Saints: Its Rise and Function in Latin Christianity*. Chicago, 1981.

Cabrol, Fernand, OSB. *Liturgical Prayer: Its History and Spirit.* Translated by a Benedictine of Stanbrook [Dame Agatha Scott Elliott, OSB]. London, 1922.

Catholic Church, Congregation for the Clergy. *The Priest, Minister of Mercy: An Aid for Confessors and Spiritual Directors,* www.clerus.org/clerus/dati/2011-05/20-13/Sussidio_per_Confessori_en.pdf. Vatican City, 2011.

Chadwick, Owen. *A History of the Popes, 1830–1914.* Oxford, 1998.

Cohn, Norman. *The Pursuit of the Millennium.* London, 1993.

Collins, Mary, and David Power, eds. *The Fate of Confession.* Concilium, vol. 190. Edinburgh, 1987.

Collins, Paul. *Papal Power: A Proposal for Change in Catholicism's Third Millennium.* London, 1997.

———, ed. *From Inquisition to Freedom: Seven Prominent Catholics and Their Struggle with the Vatican.* London, 2001.

Cornwell, John. *Breaking Faith: The Pope, the People, and the Fate of Catholicism.* New York 2001.

———. *Darwin's Angel: An Angelic Riposte to* The God Delusion. London, 2007.

———. *The Hiding Places of God: A Personal Journey into the World of Religious Visions, Holy Objects and Miracles.* New York, 1991.

———. *Hitler's Pope: The Secret History of Pius XII.* New York, 1999.

———. *The Pontiff in Winter: Triumph and Conflict in the Reign of John Paul II.* New York, 2005.

———. *Seminary Boy: A Memoir.* New York, 2006.

Cozzens, Donald B. *The Changing Face of the Priesthood.* Collegeville, MN, 2000.

Cuneo, Michael W. *The Smoke of Satan.* New York, 1999.

Dal-Gal, Hieronymo. *Pius X: The Life-Story of the Beatus.* Translated by Thomas F. Murray. Dublin, 1953.

Daly, Gabriel. *Transcendence and Immanence: A Study in Catholic Modernism and Integralism.* Oxford, 1980.

Daniel-Rops, Henri. *History of the Church of Christ.* 10 vols. London, 1959–1967.

Davis, Charles. *A Question of Conscience.* London, 1967.

Davis, H., SJ. *Moral and Pastoral Theology.* Vol. 1, *Human Acts, Law, Sin, Virtue.* London, 1943.

———. *Moral and Pastoral Theology*. Vol. 2, *Commandments of God, Precepts of the Church*. London, 1943.

———. *Moral and Pastoral Theology*. Vol. 3, *Sacraments (I)*. London, 1943.

———. *Moral and Pastoral Theology*. Vol. 4, *Sacraments (II)*. London, 1943.

De Boer, Wietse. *The Conquest of the Soul: Confession, Discipline, and Public Order in Counter-Reformation Milan*. Leiden, 2001.

De Lubac, Henri. *Catholicism, Christ and the Common Destiny of Man*. English trans. San Francisco, 1988.

———. *The Christian Faith: An Essay on the Structure of the Apostle's Creed*. Translated by Brother Richard Arnandez, FSC. San Francisco, 1986.

———. *Theological Fragments*. English trans. San Francisco, 1989.

De Vaux, Roland. *Ancient Israel: Its Life and Institutions*. Translated by John McHugh. London, 1962.

Duchesne, L. *Christian Worship: Its Origin and Evolution*. Translated by M. L. McClure. London, 1904.

Duffy, Eamon. *Faith in Our Fathers: Reflections on Catholic Tradition*. New York, 2004.

———. *Fires of Faith: Catholic England Under Mary Tudor*. New Haven, CT, 2010.

———. *Saints and Sinners: A History of the Popes*. New Haven, CT, 1997.

Durkheim, Emile. *The Elementary Forms of the Religious Life*. Translated by Joseph Ward Swain. London, 1968.

Eagleton, Terry. *On Evil*. New Haven, CT, 2010.

Elliott, Dyan. *Proving Woman: Female Spirituality and Inquisitional Culture in the Later Middle Ages*. Princeton, NJ, 2004.

Falconi, Carlo. *The Popes in the Twentieth Century, from Pius X to John XXIII*. Translated by Muriel Grindrod. London, 1967.

Fitzpatrick, P. J. *In Breaking of Bread*. Cambridge, UK, 1993.

Flannery, Austin, OP, ed. *Vatican Council II: Vatican Collection*, vol. 2. Collegeville, MN, 1982.

Foucault, Michel. *The History of Sexuality*. Vol. 1, *The Will to Knowledge*. Translated by Robert Hurley. London, 1978.

———. *Religion and Culture*. New York, 1999.

Frassetto, Michael. *Heretic Lives*. London, 2007.

Furlong, Monica, ed. *Our Childhood's Pattern: Memories of Growing Up Christian*. London, 1995.

Galanter, Marc. *Cults: Faith, Healing, and Coercion*. New York, 1989.

Goffman, Erving. *Asylums: Essays on the Social Situation of Mental Patients and Other Inmates*. London, 1982.

Golding, William. *Pincher Martin*. New York, 1956.

Hacking, Ian. *Rewriting the Soul: Multiple Personality and the Science of Memory*. Princeton, NJ, 1995.

Haile, H. G. *Luther: A Biography*. London, 1980.

Hales, E. E. Y. *Pio Nono: A Study in European Politics and Religion in the Nineteenth Century*. London, 1956.

Haliczer, Stephen. *Sexuality in the Confessional: A Sacrament Profaned*. Oxford, 1996.

Häring, Bernard. *Free and Faithful in Christ: Moral Theology for Priests and Laity*. Vol. 1, *General Moral Theology*. Slough, UK, 1978.

———. *Free and Faithful in Christ: Moral Theology for Priests and Laity*. Vol. 2, *The Truth Will Set You Free*. Slough, UK, 1979.

Hastings, Adrian, ed. *Bishops and Writers*. Cambridge, UK, 1977.

Heath, Stephen. *The Sexual Fix*. London, 1982.

Hendrickson, Paul. *Seminary: A Search*. New York, 1983.

Holland, Tom. *Millennium: The End of the World and the Forging of Christendom*. London, 2008.

Jenkins, Philip. *Pedophiles and Priests: Anatomy of a Contemporary Crisis*. Oxford, 1996.

Joyce, James. *A Portrait of the Artist as a Young Man*. London, 1992[1916].

———. *Ulysses*, ed. Hans Walter Gabler. Middlesex, UK, 1986 [1922].

Jurgens, William A. *The Faith of the Early Fathers*, vol. 1. Collegeville, MN, 1970.

Katz, Steven T., ed. *The Cambridge History of Judaism*. Vol. 4, *The Late Roman-Rabbinic Period*. Cambridge, UK, 2006.

Keenan, Marie. *Child Sexual Abuse and the Catholic Church: Gender, Power, and Organizational Culture*. Oxford, 2012.

Kelly, J. N. D. *Early Christian Doctrines*, 5th ed. London, 1985.

———. *The Oxford Dictionary of Popes*. Oxford, 1987.

Kennedy, Eugene. *Tomorrow's Catholics, Yesterday's Church: The Two Cultures of American Catholicism*. New York, 1995.

Kenny, Anthony. *A Path from Rome: An Autobiography*. Oxford, 1986.

Küng, Hans. *The Church*. London, 1976.

Lambert, Malcolm. *The Cathars*. Oxford, 1998.

————. *Medieval Heresy: Popular Movements from the Georgian Reform to the Reformation*. Oxford, 1992.

Lane Fox, Robin. *Pagans and Christians in the Mediterranean World from the Second Century AD to the Conversion of Constantine*. London, 1986.

Laven, Mary. *Virgins of Venice: Enclosed Lives and Broken Vows in the Renaissance Convent*. London, 2003.

Lawler, Rev. Ronald, Joseph Boyle Jr., and William E. May. *Catholic Sexual Ethics: A Summary, Explanation, and Defense*, 2nd ed. Huntingdon, IN, 1988.

Lea, Henry Charles. *A History of Auricular Confession and Indulgences in the Latin Church*. Vol. 1, *Confession and Absolution*. London, 1896.

————. *A History of Auricular Confession and Indulgences in the Latin Church*. Vol. 2, *Confession and Absolution*. London, 1896.

Le Goff, Jacques. *The Birth of Purgatory*. Translated by Arthur Goldhammer. London, 1984.

Levack, Brian P. *The Witch-Hunt in Early Modern Europe*, 2nd ed. New York, 1995.

Liebreich, Karen. *Fallen Order: A History*. London, 2004.

MacCulloch, Diarmaid. *A History of Christianity: The First Three Thousand Years*. London, 2010.

————. *Thomas Cranmer: A Life*. New Haven, CT, 1996.

MacIntyre, Alasdair. *After Virtue: A Study in Moral Theory*. London, 1985.

Macquarrie, John. *A Guide to the Sacraments*. London, 1997.

Mahoney, John. *The Making of Moral Theology: A Study of the Roman Catholic Tradition*. Oxford, 1989.

McCabe, Herbert. 'Self-Confessed Sinners'. *The Tablet*, 5 March 2011, 14.

Milbank, John. *Being Reconciled: Ontology and Pardon*. London, 2003.

Mooney, Bel. *Devout Sceptics: Conversations on Faith and Doubt.* London, 2003.

Morgan, Ben. *On Becoming God: Late Medieval Mysticism and the Modern Western Self.* New York, 2013.

Myers, W. David. *'Poor, Sinning Folk': Confession and Conscience in Counter-Reformation Germany.* London, 1996.

Noldin, H., SJ. *Summa Theologiae Moralis.* Vol. 1, *De Principiis, De Censuris, De Sexto.* Rome, 1940.

———. *Summa Theologiae Moralis.* Vol. 2, *De Praeceptis.* Rome, 1940.

———. *Summa Theologiae Moralis.* Vol. 3, *De Sacramentis.* Rome, 1940.

Occhiogrosso, Peter, ed. *Once a Catholic: Prominent Catholics and Ex-Catholics Reveal the Influence of the Church on Their Lives and Work.* Boston, 1987.

O'Malley, John W. *Trent: What Happened at the Council.* Cambridge, MA, 2013.

Oxenham, John. *A Saint in the Making: From the Valley of the Singing Blackbird to St. Peter's, Rome.* London, 1931.

Pantin, W. A. *The English Church in the Fourteenth Century.* Cambridge, UK, 1955.

Petre, M. D. *Von Hügel and Tyrrell: The Story of a Friendship.* London, 1937.

Plante, Thomas G., ed. *Bless Me Father for I Have Sinned: Perspectives on Sexual Abuse Committed by Roman Catholic Priests.* London, 1999.

Poschmann, B. *Penance and Anointing of the Sick.* London, 1964.

Rahner, Karl. *Theological Investigations.* Vol. 1, *God, Christ, Mary and Grace.* London, 1961.

———. *Theological Investigations.* Vol. 2, *Man in the Church.* London, 1963.

———. *Theological Investigations.* Vol. 7, *Further Theology of the Spiritual Life I.* London, 1981.

———. *Theological Investigations.* Vol. 9, *Writings of 1965–7 I.* London, 1981.

———. *Theological Investigations.* Vol. 10, *Writings of 1965–7 II.* London, 1984.

———. *Theological Investigations*. Vol. 11, *Confrontations I*. London, 1981.

———. *Theological Investigations*. Vol. 12, *Confrontations II*. London, 1987.

Ranke-Heinemann, Uta. *Eunuchs for Heaven: The Catholic Church and Sexuality*. Translated by John Brownjohn. London, 1990.

Ratté, John. *Three Modernists: Alfred Loisy, William L. Sullivan and George Tyrrel*. London, 1968.

Ratzinger, Joseph, with Vittorio Messori. *The Ratzinger Report: An Exclusive Interview on the State of the Church*. Translated by Salvator Attanasio and Graham Harrison. San Francisco, 1985.

Sackville-West, Vita. *The Eagle and the Dove: A Study in Contrasts*. London, 1947.

Schatzman, Morton. *Soul Murder: Persecution in the Family*. London, 1973.

Sipe, A. W. Richard. *A Secret World: Sexuality and the Search for Celibacy*. New York, 1990.

———. *Sex, Priests and Power: Anatomy of a Crisis*. New York, 1995.

Tanner, Norman. *Decrees of the Ecumenical Councils*, 2 vols. Georgetown, MD, 1990.

Taylor, Charles. *Sources of the Self: The Making of the Modern Identity*. Cambridge, MA, 1992.

Taylor, Chloë. *The Culture of Confession from Augustine to Foucault: A Genealogy of the 'Confessing Animal'*. New York, 2009.

Thérèse of Lisieux, *Story of a Soul: The Autobiography of St. Thérèse of Lisieux*. Translated by John Clarke. Washington, DC, 1975.

Turpin, Joanne. *Catholic Treasures New and Old: Traditions, Customs and Practices*. Cincinnati, 1994.

Udris, John. *Holy Daring: The Fearless Trust of St. Thérèse of Lisieux*. Leominster, UK, 1997.

Watts, Fraser, ed. *Spiritual Healing: Scientific and Religious Perspectives*. Cambridge, UK, 2011.

Weatherhead, Leslie D. *Psychology, Religion and Healing*. London, 1951.

Weigel, George. *Witness to Hope: The Biography of John Paul II*. New York, 1999.

NOTES

Prologue

1. See the document issued by the Catholic Church, Congregation for the Clergy, entitled *The Priest, Minister of Divine Mercy: An Aid for Confessors and Spiritual Directors* (Vatican City, 2011), www.clerus .org/clerus/dati/2011-05/20-13/Sussidio_per_Confessori_en.pdf. The document opens citing Pope Benedict XVI's allocution to the Tribunal of the Apostolic Penitentiary in 2010: 'It is necessary to return to the confessional as a place in which to celebrate the Sacrament of Reconciliation, but also as a place in which to "dwell" more often, so that the faithful may find compassion, advice and comfort, feel that they are loved and understood by God and experience the presence of Divine Mercy beside the Real Presence in the Eucharist.' See also Hans Küng and David Tracy, eds., *Paradigm Change in Theology: A Symposium for the Future* (London, 1989).

2. Corpus Christi College, Cambridge, Library, MS 148. For commentary and translation into English, see Michael Haren, 'Confession, Social Ethics and Social Discipline in the "Memoriale Presbiterorum" and "The Interrogatories for Officials, Lawyers and Secular Estates of the 'Memoriale Presbiterorum' and Secular Estates of the 'Memoriale Presbiterorum'"', in Peter Biller and A. J. Minnis, eds., *Handling Sin: Confession in the Middle Ages* (Woodbridge, UK, 1998), 123ff. See W. A. Pantin, *The English Church in the Fourteenth Century* (Cambridge, UK, 1955), Chapter 9, 'Manuals for Parish Priests', 189ff.

3. Fourth Lateran Council, 1215. See John Bossy, *Christianity in the West, 1400–1700* (Oxford, 1985), 49. Bossy finds evidence for a lowering of the age of confession from puberty to seven in the early fifteenth century, yet this practice appears to be localised and temporary,

For a wider survey of child confession, see Henry Charles Lea, *A History of Auricular Confession and Indulgences in the Latin Church*, vol. 2 (London, 1896), 400ff.

4. William Shakespeare, *The Merchant of Venice*, Act 4, scene 1.

5. William Wordsworth, 'Ode: Intimations of Immortality from Recollections of Early Childhood', 1804.

6. For a discussion of this contention, see Leslie D. Weatherhead, *Psychology, Religion and Healing* (London, 1951), 329.

7. Conversation with Paul Vallely, author of *Pope Francis: Untying the Knots* (London, 2013).

8. Marie Keenan, *Child Sexual Abuse and the Catholic Church: Gender, Power, and Organizational Culture* (Oxford, 2012), 162–169.

9. Center for Applied Research in the Apostolate (CARA), 'The Sacrament of Reconciliation', n.d., http://cara.georgetown.edu /CARAServices/FRStats/reconciliation.pdf. The testimonies quoted from my research in various chapters of this book are from correspondence I received in response to my article in *The Tablet* on 18 August 2012 entitled 'Where Are the Penitents?' at www.thetablet .co.uk/article/163100 and are in my personal files.

10. Carol Ann Duffy, 'Confession', in *Mean Time* (London, 2013), and 'Ash Wednesday 1984', in *Standing Female Nude* (London, 1998); Christopher Logue, *Prince Charming: A Memoir* (London, 1999), 33.

11. Logue, *Prince Charming*, 12.

One: Early Penitents and Their Penances

1. In the Latin rite, 'Memento homo quia pulvus es et in pulverem reverteris', deriving from God's curse on Adam after his and Eve's disobedience recounted in Genesis 3.19: 'You are dust, and to dust you shall return.'

2. Psalm 51.3, 102.9; Jonah 3.6; Steven T. Katz, ed., *Cambridge History of Judaism*, vol. 4, *The Late Roman-Rabbinic Period* (Cambridge, UK, 2006), 941; Roland de Vaux, *Ancient Israel: Its Life and Institutions*, trans. John McHugh (London, 1962), 507–510.

3. Luke 7.47; Henry Charles Lea, *A History of Auricular Confession and Indulgences in the Latin Church*, vol. 1 (London, 1896), 3–4.

4. See L. Duchesne, *Christian Worship: Its Origin and Evolution* (London, 1904), 435–443; John Mahoney, *The Making of Moral The-*

ology: A Study of the Roman Catholic Tradition (Oxford, 1989), 2–5; Robin Lane Fox, *Pagans and Christians in the Mediterranean World from the Second Century AD to the Conversion of Constantine* (London, 1986), 336. For quotations from the clergy and laity, see Duchesne, *Christian Worship*, 443. For quotation from St. Jerome, see Michel Foucault, 'Christianity and Confession' (lecture), in Foucault, *The Politics of Truth* (Los Angeles, 1997), 207; see also Chloë Taylor, *The Culture of Confession from Augustine to Foucault: A Genealogy of the 'Confessing Animal'* (New York, 2009), 18–19.

5. For Tertullian on the body, continence, and misogyny, see Peter Brown, *The Body and Society: Men, Women and Sexual Renunciation in Early Christianity* (London, 1988), 76–82. For Bishop Cyprian's conclusion, see B. Poschmann, *Penance and Anointing of the Sick* (London, 1964), 55.

6. Ludwig Bieler, ed., with an Appendix by D. A. Binchy, *The Irish Penitentials* (Dublin, 1975), 97.

7. Ibid., 107.

8. Ibid., 219.

9. Ibid., 223.

10. See Peter Brown, *The Cult of the Saints: Its Rise and Function in Latin Christianity* (Chicago, 1981).

11. Gregory VII, *The Register of Pope Gregory VII, 1073–1085*, trans. H. E. Cowdrey (Oxford, 1972), 3.10a; see also Tom Holland, *Millennium: The End of the World and the Forging of Christendom* (London, 2008), xviff.

12. For Abelard's life and writings, see Jeffrey E. Brower and Kevin Guilfoy, eds., *The Cambridge Companion to Abelard* (Cambridge, UK, 2004).

13. See Pierre J. Payer, *Book of Gomorrah: An Eleventh-Century Treatise Against Clerical Homosexual Practices* (Waterloo, Ontario, 1962).

Two: Confession into Its Own

1. II. J. Denzinger and A. Schönmetzer, *Enchiridion Symbolorum et Definitionum* (Barcelona, 1963), 813; John Mahoney, *The Making of Moral Theology: A Study of the Roman Catholic Tradition* (Oxford, 1989), 19.

2. See J. P. Migne, ed., *Patrologiae Cursus Completus*, Series Latina, vol. 187 (Paris, 1833).

3. Chloë Taylor, *The Culture of Confession from Augustine to Foucault: A Genealogy of the 'Confessing Animal'* (New York, 2009), 51.

4. Henry Charles Lea, *A History of Auricular Confession and Indulgences in the Latin Church*, vol. 1 (London, 1896), 400.

5. See Chapter 1 on confession in late medieval Germany in W. David Myers, *'Poor, Sinning Folk': Confession and Conscience in Counter-Reformation Germany* (London, 1996).

6. Taylor, *Culture of Confession*, 56.

7. Thomas Tentler, *Sin and Confession on the Eve of Reformation* (Princeton, NJ, 1977), 141ff; Thomas à Kempis, *Imitation of Christ* (London, 1952), 236.

8. Taylor, *Culture of Confession*, 55ff.

9. David Hugh Farmer, *Oxford Dictionary of the Saints* (Oxford, 1987), 139; Dyan Elliott, *Proving Woman: Female Spirituality and Inquisitional Culture in the Later Middle Ages* (Princeton, NJ, 2004), 88–111.

10. For more information on the Beguines, see Walter Simons, *Cities of Ladies: Beguine Communities in the Low Countries, 1200–1565* (Philadelphia, 2001), 35–60. James of Vitry is quoted in Elliot, *Proving Woman*, 51.

11. On the matter of Catherine's confessions, see Friedrich von Huegel, *The Mystical Element of Religion*, vol. 1 (London, 1923), 117ff.

12. For the development of the concept of Purgatory, see Jacques Le Goff, *The Birth of Purgatory*, trans. Arthur Goldhammer (London, 1984), 4–7, 12.

13. Stephen Haliczer, *Sexuality in the Confessional: A Sacrament Profaned* (Oxford, 1996), 11.

14. For transgressions of priests in Italy on the eve of the Reformation, see Mary Laven, *Virgins of Venice: Enclosed Lives and Broken Vows in the Renaissance Convent* (London, 2003). For the other examples in this paragraph, see Wietse de Boer, *The Conquest of the Soul: Confession, Discipline, and the Public Order in Counter-Reformation Milan* (Leiden, 2001), 30.

15. De Boer, *Conquest of the Soul*, 18–19.

16. Peter Ackroyd, *The History of England*, vol. 2 (London, 2012), 26.

17. See Haliczer, *Sexuality in the Confessional*, 12.

18. Taylor, *Culture of Confession*, 63ff.

19. See, for example, Diarmaid MacCulloch, *Thomas Cranmer: A Life* (New Haven, CT, 1996), 161–162.

Three: Confession and the Counter-Reformers

1. For a fresh overview of the Council of Trent and the Counter-Reformation, see Mary Laven, 'Introduction', in Alexandra Bamji, Geert H. Janssen, and Mary Laven, eds., *The Ashgate Research Companion to the Counter-Reformation* (Surrey, UK, 2013).

2. H. Daniel-Rops, *History of the Church of Christ*, vol. 5, *The Catholic Reformation*, trans. John Warrington (London, 1962), 80; Hubert Jedin, *A History of the Council of Trent*, trans. Dom Ernest Graf, vol. 2 (St. Louis, 1961), 26; John W. O'Malley, *Trent: What Happened at the Council* (Cambridge, MA, 2013), 107.

3. Wietse de Boer, *The Conquest of the Soul: Confession, Discipline, and Public Order in Counter-Reformation Milan* (Leiden, 2001), 39.

4. W. David Myers, *'Poor, Sinning Folk': Confession and Conscience in Counter Reformation Germany* (London, 1996), 117–119.

5. Eamon Duffy, *Fires of Faith: Catholic England Under Mary Tudor* (New Haven, CT, 2010), 15.

6. Ibid., 132–133.

7. P. D. Stenger, 'Treasonous Reconciliations: Robert Southwell, Religious Polemic, and the Criminalisation of Confession', *Reformation* 16 (2011): 5.35.

8. De Boer, *Conquest of the Soul*, 43.

9. David Hugh Farmer, *Oxford Dictionary of the Saints* (Oxford, 1987), 55.

10. De Boer, *Conquest of the Soul*, 5.

11. Ibid., 14.

12. *Avertenze di monsignore illustrissime cardinale Borromeo, arcivescovo di Milano, a I Confessori della citt'a, et diocese sua)*, in *Acta Ecclesiae Mediolanensis*, vol. 2 (Milan, 1890–1896), cited De Boer, *Conquest of the Soul*, xix.

13. Stephen Haliczer, *Sexuality in the Confessional: A Sacrament Profaned* (Oxford, 1996), 100.

14. Ibid., 99.

15. De Boer, *Conquest of the Soul*, 86ff.

16. See John Bossy, 'The Social History of Confession', *Transactions of the Royal Historical Society*, 5th series, 25 (1975): 30; John Bossy, *Christianity in the West, 1400–1700* (Oxford, 1985), 45–50, 127ff.

17. Swift writes of the benefits to be received 'either by eructation, or expiration, or evomition' in the 'whispering office'. Jonathan Swift, *Selected Works*, vol. 1 (London, 1823), 96–97. Cardinal Thomas Cajetan is quoted in De Boer, *Conquest of the Soul*, 101. The quotation from the provost of Santa Fedele is in De Boer, *Conquest of the Soul*, 122.

18. Mary Laven, *Virgins of Venice: Enclosed Lives and Broken Vows in the Renaissance Convent* (London, 2003), 173.

19. Alonso de Andrade, *Libro de guía de la virtud y de la imitación de Neustra Señora* (*A Guide in the Virtue and Imitation of Our Lady*), is cited in Haliczer, *Sexuality in the Confessional*, 89–90. Ippolito Capilupi is quoted in Laven, *Virgins of Venice*, 162.

20. The account of Fra Gaspar de Nájera is in Haliczer, *Sexuality in the Confessional*, 99; the account of Fra Antonio de Arvelo is in the same work on pp. 99–100.

21. Ibid., 102.

22. Ibid., 103.

23. Ibid., 169.

24. For the story of the Piarist Congregation that was responsible for educating thousands of children over four centuries, see Karen Liebreich, *Fallen Order: A History* (London, 2004). For the account of Father Stefano Cherubini, see p. 71 of the same work.

25. Judith C. Brown, *Immodest Acts: The Life of a Lesbian Nun in Renaissance Italy* (Oxford, 1986), 14.

26. Ibid., 17–18, 19.

27. For comparative estimates of regional and pan-European prosecutions and executions, see Brian P. Levack, *The Witch-Hunt in Early Modern Europe*, 2nd ed. (London, 1995), 21–26.

28. For Alonso de Salazar, see Haliczer, *Sexuality in the Confessional*, 89, 220n20. Piero Camporesi's account and the quotation by Girolamo Cardano are in *Bread of Dreams*, trans. David Gentilcore (Cambridge, 1989), 125. On Joseph of Cupertino, see John Cornwell, *Powers of Darkness, Powers of Light* (London, 1991), 292–303.

29. See Friedrich Spee, *Cautio Criminalis: Or, Book on Witch Trials*, trans. Marcus Hellyer (Charlottesville, VA, 2003). The introduction contains biographical details of Spee's life.

30. Biographies of Teresa of Avila of note include Rowan Williams, *Teresa of Avila* (London, 2004); Vita Sackville-West, *The Eagle and the Dove* (London, 1943); and Stephen Clissold, *St. Teresa of Avila* (London, 1979).

31. Clissold, *St. Teresa of Avila*, 51.

32. Ibid., 100.

33. See Rudolph M. Bell, *Holy Anorexia* (Chicago, 1985). For Urban VIII, see his p. 151; for Benedict XIV, see pp. 160–161.

Four: Fact, Fiction, and Anticlericalism

1. Alphonsus Liguori, *The Way of Salvation and of Perfection* (New York, 1926 [1767]), 451.

2. See Chapter 1, 'The Influence of Auricular Confession', in John Mahoney *The Making of Moral Theology: A Study of the Roman Catholic Tradition* (Oxford, 1987).

3. Ibid., 33–34.

4. For overviews of Jansenism in English, see Owen Chadwick, *The Popes and European Revolution* (Cambridge, 1980), 573ff; Owen Chadwick, *From Bossuet to Newman* (Cambridge, 1987), 57ff; also, in Italian, L. Vereccke, *Storia della teologia morale moderna*, vol. 3 (Rome, 1979–1980).

5. For the vexed debates between probabilism and probabiliorism, see Mahoney *Making of Moral Theology*, 134–143.

6. Ibid., 142–143; Frederick M. Jones, ed., *Alphonsus de Liguori: Selected Writings* (New York, 1999), esp. 209–214.

7. Anthony Gavin, *The Great Red Dragon, Or, The Master-Key to Popery* (Boston, 1854), 70.

8. Quoted in Meriol Trevor, *Newman: The Pillar of the Cloud* (London, 1962), 352.

9. Stephen Haliczer, *Sexuality in the Confessional: A Sacrament Profaned* (Oxford, 1996), 186.

10. Richard Hofstadter, 'Paranoid Style in American Politics', *Harper's Magazine*, November 1964.

11. Charles Stephen Dessain, et al., eds., *The Letters and Diaries of John Henry Newman* (Oxford, 1961–2008), xiv, 110.

12. John Henry Newman, *Lectures on Catholicism in England* (Birmingham, UK, 1851), 43.

13. Ibid., xv, 280.

14. Among the many hagiographical lives of Jean Vianney in English, the most informative is John Oxenham, *A Saint in the Making: From the Valley of the Singing Blackbird to St. Peter's, Rome* (London, 1931).

Five: The Pope Who 'Restored' Catholicism

1. For the life and papacy of Pius X, see Hieronymo Dal-Gal, *Pius X: The Life-Story of the Beatus*, trans. Thomas F Murray (Dublin, 1953); G. Romanato, *Pio X: La vita di papa Sarto* (Milan, 1992), based on the deposition for canonization; Carlo Falconi, *The Popes in the Twentieth Century from Pius X to John XXIII*, trans. Muriel Grindrod (London, 1967), 1ff; Eamon Duffy, *Saints and Sinners: A History of the Popes* (New Haven, CT, 1997), 245ff; Owen Chadwick, *A History of the Popes, 1830–1914* (Oxford, 1998), 332ff.

2. Dal-Gal, *Pius X*, 111.

3. Duffy, *Saints and Sinners*, 245.

4. The Society of Pius X, SSPX, was founded in 1970 by Archbishop Marcel Lefebvre of France. The group defended the right to say the Tridentine Mass and laments the loss of traditions that flourished before the Second Vatican Council.

5. Chadwick, *History of the Popes*, 344. Chadwick wrote: 'As he grew older, or more used to power, the authoritarian streak in him grew also, [and] he found it harder to bear contradiction.'

6. *E Supremi*, Encyclical of Pope Pius X on the Restoration of All Things in Christ to the Patriarchs, Primates, Archbishops, Bishops, and Other Ordinaries in Peace and Communion with the Apostolic See, 4 October 1903, www.vatican.va/holy_father/pius_x/encyclicals/documents/hf_p-x_enc_04101903_e-supremi_en.html.

7. Quoted in Falconi, *Popes in the Twentieth Century*, 14.

8. Quoted in ibid.

9. *Pieni L'Animo*, Encyclical of Pope Pius X on the Clergy in Italy to the Venerable Bretheren, the Archbishops, and Bishops of Italy, 28 July 1906, www.vatican.va/holy_father/pius_x/encyclicals/documents/hf_p-x_enc_28071906_pieni-l'animo_en.html.

10. Georges Bernanos, *Diary of a Country Priest*, trans. Pamela Morris (New York, 2002), 73.

11. On Modernism, see Nicholas Lash, 'Modernism, aggiornamento and the night battle', in Adrian Hastings, ed., *Bishops and*

Writers (Cambridge, 1977), 51ff. The Leo XIII quotations are in G. Fogarty *The Vatican and the American Hierarchy from 1870 to 1965* (Wilmington, DE, 1985), 178.

12. Falconi, *Popes in the Twentieth Century*, 54.

Six: Pius X's Spy-Net

1. For a detailed history of the Anti-Modernist campaign, see Émile Poulat, *Intégrisme et catholicisme intégral* (Paris, 1969).

2. Owen Chadwick, *A History of the Popes, 1830–1914* (Oxford, 1998).

3. For the range of Benigni's clandestine activities, see David Alvarez, *Spies in the Vatican: Espionage and Intrigue from Napoleon to the Holocaust* (Lawrence, KS, 2002), 80ff; see also Émile Poulat, *Histoire dogme et critique dans la crise moderniste: Suivi de La réflexion d'Alphonse Dupront* (Paris, 1996 [1962]).

4. Peter Hebblethwaite, John XXIII (London, 1994), 74.

5. The oath was promulgated on 1 September 1910. The full text is available on several websites, including, for example, 'The Oath Against Modernism', Papal Encyclicals Online, www.papalencyclicals .net/Pius10/p10moath.htm. The oath includes: 'I sincerely hold that the doctrine of faith was handed down to us from the apostles through the orthodox Fathers in exactly the same meaning and always in the same purport . . . , Likewise, I reject that method of judging and interpreting Sacred Scripture which, departing from the tradition of the Church, the analogy of faith, and the norms of the Apostolic See, embraces the misrepresentations of the rationalists and with no prudence or restraint adopts textual criticism as the one and supreme norm. . . . Finally, I declare that I am completely opposed to the error of the modernists who hold that there is nothing divine in sacred tradition. . . . I firmly hold, then, and shall hold to my dying breath the belief of the Fathers in the *charism* of truth, which certainly is, was, and always will be in the succession of the episcopacy from the apostles. The purpose of this is, then, not that dogma may be tailored according to what seems better and more suited to the culture of each age; rather, that the absolute and immutable truth preached by the apostles from the beginning may never be believed to be different, may never be understood in any other way. . . . I promise that I shall

keep all these articles faithfully, entirely, and sincerely, and guard them inviolate, in no way deviating from them in teaching or in any way in word or in writing. . . . Thus I promise, this I swear, so help me God. . . .' On the implications of the Anti-Modernist oath, see, for example, Paul Collins, *Papal Power: A Proposal for Change in Catholicism's Third Millennium* (London, 1997), 66–67.

6. George Orwell, *Nineteen Eighty-Four* (London, 1949), 32.

7. *Codex Juris Canonici PII X Pontificis* (Vatican City, 1917); the pocket edition runs to 890 pages.

8. U. Stutz, *Der Geist des Codex Juris Canonici* (Stuttgart, 1918), 50.

9. *Codex Juris Canonici*, canons 1323, 1324. In the standard edition of the Code of Canon Law that would remain in use until 1983, there was a clarification: 'Such are all doctrinal decrees of the Holy See, even though they be not infallibly proposed, and even though they come from the Sacred Congregations with the approval of the Holy Father, or from the Biblical Commission. . . . Such decrees do not receive the assent of faith; they are not *de fide catholica*. But they merit genuine internal and intellectual consent and loyal obedience.'

10. *Codex Juris Canonici*, canons 1325, 246, 1386.

Seven: The Great Confessional Experiment

1. Pope St. Pius X, *Sacra Tridentina* (On Frequent and Daily Reception of Holy Communion), 20 December 1905, Eternal Word Television Network (EWTN), www.ewtn.com/library/CURIA/CDWFREQ.HTM.

2. See Owen Chadwick, *A History of the Popes, 1830–1914* (Oxford, 1998), 361ff. Chadwick notes, 'Historians, in hindsight, if asked which act of which pope did most to affect the Church since 1800, would put their finger on this change of 1905–6, the encouragement of frequent, even daily communion, and receiving of it by children' (p. 362). On the *Quam Singulari*, see www.papalencyclicals.net/Piuslo/ploquam.htm

3. See Henry Charles Lea, *A History of Auricular Confession and Indulgences in the Latin Church*, vol. 1 (London, 1896), 400ff.

4. Ibid., 400.

5. Catechism of Christian Doctrine ('Penny Catechism') taught in many English-speaking countries, originally published in 1889.

6. Ibid.

7. Peter Occhiogrosso, ed., *Once a Catholic: Prominent Catholics and Ex-Catholics Reveal the Influence of the Church on Their Lives and Work* (Boston, 1987), 236.

8. Frank O'Connor, 'First Confession', in *The Cornet Player Who Betrayed Ireland* (London, 2005), 17.

9. Mary McCarthy, *Memories of a Catholic Girlhood* (New York, 1957).

10. Anthony Burgess, *Little Wilson and Big God* (London, 1987), 45.

11. Tobias Wolff, *This Boy's Life* (London, 1989), 17ff.

12. Roddy Doyle, *Paddy Clarke Ha Ha Ha* (London, 1993), 84.

13. Occhiogrosso, ed., *Once a Catholic*, 295.

14. Antonia White, *Frost in May* (London, 1978), 134.

15. Neil McKenty, *The Inside Story* (Quebec, 1997), 21.

16. O'Connor, 'First Confession', 19.

17. Michel Foucault, *History of Sexuality*, vol. 1, trans. Robert Hurley (London, 1998), 20. Foucault wrote: 'An imperative was established: Not only will you confess to acts contravening the law, but you will seek to transform your desire, your every desire, into discourse.' The quotation from Molly Bloom is in James Joyce, *Ulysses*, ed. Hans Walter Gabler (London, 1986 [1922]), 610.

18. Margaret Hebblethwaite, 'Gift of Faith', in Monica Furlong, ed., *Our Childhood's Pattern: Memories of Growing Up Christian* (London, 1995), 37.

19. Bel Mooney, ed., *Devout Sceptics: Conversations on Faith and Doubt* (London, 2003), 90.

20. See my article in *The Tablet* on 18 August 2012 entitled 'Where Are the Penitents?' at www.thetablet.co.uk/article/163100.

Eight: The Making of a Confessor

1. Erving Goffman, *Asylums: Essays on the Social Situation of Mental Patients and Other Inmates* (London, 1982), 11.

2. For a wide range of statistics in the United States and worldwide, see the publications at the Center for Applied Research in the Apostolate (CARA) at Georgetown University, http://cara.georgetown.edu /Publications/Publications.html; see also the website of UK Priest, http://ukpriest.org/resources-and-events/statistics.

3. Pope John XXIII, *Veterum Sapientia* (On the Promotion of the Study of Latin), Apostolic Constitution, 22 February 1962, Papal

Encyclicals Online, www.papalencyclicals.net/John23/j23veterum
.htm.

4. H. Davis, SJ, *Moral and Pastoral Theology*, 4 vols. (London, 1943), 2:235.

5. Ibid., 3:212ff.

6. Ibid., 3:215.

7. Ibid., 2:436.

Nine: Seminary Sexology

1. H. Davis, SJ, *Moral and Pastoral Theology*, 4 vols. (London, 1943), 2:200.

2. Ibid., 2:205.

3. Ibid., 2:204.

4. Ibid., 2:229.

5. Ibid., 2:230–231.

6. Ibid., 2:295.

7. Ibid., 2:234.

8. Ibid., 2:243.

9. Ibid., 2:24.

10. A. W. Richard Sipe, *A Secret World: Sexuality and the Search for Celibacy* (New York, 1990), 139.

11. Michael Haneke's film *White Ribbon* (2009), which depicts a rural village in Germany on the eve of the First World War, portrays a Lutheran pastor father who quizzes his son on the subject of self-abuse and compels him to sleep with his hands tied at night. Critics of the movie have commented that the pastor's treatment of his children is typical of Schreber's recommendations. Haneke appears to be suggesting that this pedagogic terrorism was a prelude to the authoritarian spirit that would sweep Germany in subsequent decades, erupting into two world wars.

12. Stephen Heath, *The Sexual Fix* (London, 1982), 22; Morton Schatzman, *Soul Murder: Persecution in the Family* (London, 1973), 105.

13. Pope Pius X, *Haerent Animo* (To the Catholic Clergy on Priestly Sanctity), Apostolic Exhortation, 4 August 1908, Papal Encyclicals Online, www.papalencyclicals.net/Pius10/p10haer.htm.

14. Sipe, *Secret World*, 142.

15. On the wide-ranging practice of masturbation in the Catholic priesthood and its consequences, see ibid., 139–158.

16. Ibid., 143.

17. The term is from the Greek. Several spellings are used in English, including 'epiky' (*Oxford English Dictionary*) and 'epicheia'.

18. Davis, *Moral and Pastoral Theology*, 1:187.

19. Thomas Aquinas, *Summa Theologica*, S 1.2, Q. 96, a.6, c.

20. Interview in London with Dr. Josephine Klein, 14 August 2012.

21. Philip Jenkins, *Pedophiles and Priests: Anatomy of a Contemporary Crisis* (Oxford, 1996), esp. Chapter 7, 'Pedophilia and Child Abuse'; John Jay College of Criminal Justice, City University of New York, 'The Nature and Scope of Sexual Abuse of Minors by Catholic Priests and Deacons in the United States, 1950–2002' (John Jay Report), commissioned by the US Conference of Catholic Bishops, based on surveys completed by the Roman Catholic dioceses in the United States. The initial version of the report was posted on the Internet on 27 February 2004, with corrections and revisions posted on 16 April. The printed version was published in June 2004. See PDF at www.usccb.org/issues-and-action/child-and-youth-protection/upload/The-Nature-and-Scope-of-Sexual-Abuse-of-Minors-by-Catholic-Priests-and-Deacons-in-the-United-States-1950-2002.pdf.

Ten: Sexual Abuse in the Confessional

1. Leonard Shengold, *Soul Murder: The Effects of Childhood Abuse and Deprivation* (New York, 1989); Morton Schatzman, *Soul Murder: Persecution in the Family* (London, 1973); A. W. Richard Sipe, 'Loss of Faith', 10 December 2002, Sipe Comments, www.awrsipe.com/Comments/2002-12-10-Loss_of_Faith.htm.

2. Father Pickering fled Australia in 1993 before he could be charged. See Nick McKenzie, Richard Baker, and Josh Gordon, "Suicides Linked to Clergy's Sex Abuse," *Sydney Morning Herald*, 14 April 2012, www.smh.com.au/national/suicides-linked-to-clergys-sex-abuse-20120413-1wzcy.html.

3. All testimonies quoted from my research ('Tablet Testimonies') are from correspondence I received in response to my article in *The Tablet* on 18 August 2012 entitled 'Where Are the Penitents?' at www.thetablet.co.uk/article/163100, in my personal files, and interviews I conducted.

4. Christa Pongratz-Lippitt, *The Tablet*, 26 January 2013. The hotline closed in January 2013.

5. The archdiocesan junior seminary, St. Wilfrid's, Cotton College, North Staffordshire, was closed in 1987. The incident is reported in my book *Seminary Boy* (London, 2006).

6. See Alfred C. Kinsey, Wardell B. Pomeroy, and Clyde E. Martin, *Sexual Behavior in the Human Male* (Philadelphia, 1948), 499 ff. The report never claimed that 99.9 per cent of males practised masturbation. Under the heading of 'Incidences and Frequencies', the report claims: 'By even the stricter definition, masturbation may be identified in the histories of a very high proportion of human males. Ultimately about 92 per cent of the total population is involved in masturbation which leads to orgasm. More individuals (96%) of the college level and 95 per cent of the high school group, are ultimately included.'

7. *Christ & Welt* (supplement to *Die Zeit*), 16 January 2013.

8. John Jay College of Criminal Justice, City University of New York, 'The Nature and Scope of Sexual Abuse of Minors by Catholic Priests and Deacons in the United States, 1950–2002' (John Jay Report), 2004, commissioned by the US Conference of Catholic Bishops, www.usccb.org/issues-and-action/child-and-youth-protection /upload/The-Nature-and-Scope-of-Sexual-Abuse-of-Minors-by -Catholic-Priests-and-Deacons-in-the-United-States-1950-2002.pdf, 78ff.

9. Dublin Archdiocese Commission of Investigation, 'Report into the Catholic Diocese of Cloyne' (Cloyne Report), December 2010, http://s3.documentcloud.org/documents/216118/cloyne-report .pdf; Barry Roche, "Only One Priest in Report Has Been Convicted in Court," *Irish Times*, 15 July 2011, www.irishtimes.com /newspaper/ireland/2011/0715/1224300763481.html, reprinted at BishopAccountability.org, www.bishop-accountability.org/news 2011/07_08/2011_07_15_Roche_OnlyOne.htm.

10. Elliott Report, June 2008, on the 'Management of Two Child Protection Cases in the Diocese of Cloyne', cited in Diocese of Cloyne, 'Safeguarding Children', Annual Report for the Year Ending 31 December 2010', www.cloynediocese.ie/safeguarding-children/.

11. According to Department of Justice and Equality, Northern Ireland, Report by Commission of Investigation into Catholic Archdiocese of Dublin (Murphy Report), Chapter 11, 'Introduction to Investigation of the 46 Priests', in Part 2, 354ff, available at www

.justice.ie/en/JELR/Pages/PB09000504, the behaviour of a parish priest, Father Gallagher, was regarded as odd but nevertheless acceptable in the light of new 'attitudes': 'In December 1984, there was "general fuss and skittishness" when one of the classes in St Mary's were going to confession. The principal investigated the cause of this fuss and was told by the girls that Fr Gallagher kissed each of them after confession. What the girls did not tell her at that time was that during confession he used to run his hands all over their bodies inside their clothing and then kissed them all on the lips at the end of confession. The principal again spoke about the matter to Fr Gallagher who said that, if the behaviour offended the girls, he would stop. The principal, incredibly, felt that perhaps Fr Gallagher's approach reflected the newer approach to the sacrament of reconciliation (confession) and took the matter no further.' The quotations from Ansgar Hocke are in *Der Spiegel*, Issue 6, 2010.

12. See 'Cloyne Report—Fr. Calder', RTE News, 13 July 2011, www.rte.ie/news/2011/0713/cloyne_calder.html, reprinted at BishopAccountability.org, www.bishop-accountability.org/news 2011/07_08/2011_07_13_RTENews_CloyneReport1.htm.

13. Cloyne Report, Chapter 15.

14. Tablet Testimonies.

15. Paul Hendrickson, *Seminary: A Search* (New York, 1983), 166–167.

16. Tablet Testimonies.

17. In 1988, ten girls complained that they had been sexually molested by a Father James Grennan when he heard their confessions in the sanctuary of the parish church of Monageer in Ireland. The girls were around twelve years old at the time and they made the complaint to the principal of Monageer National School, Mr. Pat Higgins. A social worker was sent to interview the girls, followed by a doctor, who provided a 'composite' report. Father Grennan took confessions sitting on a chair on the altar, with each child, one by one, kneeling on a cushion at his feet. 'The rest of the class remained in their seats and were told to keep their eyes closed because they were in a house of God and to show respect.' During each confession, the priest would grasp the child's hands in his hands and pull them towards his private parts. His zipper was described as 'half down'. 'He would pull the child close and rub his face and mouth around

their jaw while asking them questions about their families.' He was also described as 'putting his hands under their skirts and fondling their legs to mid-thigh level.' There were other occasions involving fondling children in their upper bodies under their clothing, or placing them on his lap. See 'The Ferns Report', a report commissioned by the Irish government in the Roman Catholic Diocese of Ferns in County Wexford, Ireland, October 2005, www.documentcloud .org/documents/243711-2-complete-ferns-report-so-ireland.html, 82. For the account from the Montreal Institute for the Deaf, see 'Quebec Catholic Priests Accused of Sexually Abusing Deaf, Mute Boys', 31 August 2010, Examiner.com, www.examiner.com/article /quebec-catholic-priests-accused-of-sexually-abusing-deaf-mute-boys.

18. 'Abuse Victim "Hurt" by Confession Stance', 31 August 2011, UTV, www.u.tv/News/Abuse-victim-%E2%80%98hurt-by-confession -stance/516683ca-2d00-48dd-b527-cacbd7f63571, reprinted at BishopAccountability.org, www.bishop-accountability.org/news 2011/07_08/2011_08_31_Utv_AbuseVictim.htm.

19. Commission to Inquire into Child Abuse (CICA), 'Investigation Committee Report' (Ryan Report), 20 May 2009, www .childabusecommission.com/rpt/. The Ryan Report is one of a range of measures introduced by the Irish Government to investigate the extent and effects of abuse on children from 1936 onwards. The CICA is commonly known in Ireland as the Ryan Commission (previously 'the Laffoy Commission'), after its chair, Justice Seán Ryan. Judge Mary Laffoy resigned on 2 September 2003, following a departmental review on costs and resources. She felt that 'the cumulative effect of those factors effectively negated the guarantee of independence conferred on the Commission and militated against it being able to perform its statutory functions.' The commission's work started in 1999.

20. For the 'Database of Publicly Accused Roman Catholic Priests, Nuns, Brothers, Deacons, and Seminarians in the US', see www.bishop -accountability.org/; for 'Special Reports: Catholic Bishops and Sex Abuse', see www.bishop-accountability.org/resources/resource-files /databases/DallasMorningNewsBishops.htm.

21. Cardinal Groër, who at an earlier stage was a Benedictine abbot, was accused of abusing boys in the confessional in Austria. Four of his fellow bishops, including his successor, Cardinal Archbishop Chris-

toph Schönborn, confirmed the credibility of the many accusations against him. At least twelve men have testified that, when they were boys at a church school, Groër would invite them to his room to hear their confessions, after which he asked them to take off their clothes and abused them sexually. A widely reported consequence of Groër's depravity is that thousands of Austrian Catholics have lapsed from Catholicism. Many more joined radical groups seeking to combat Vatican centralisation and conservatism. See Katrin Bennhold, "Future Pope's Role in Abuse Case Was Complex," *New York Times*, 26 April 2010, www.nytimes.com/2010/04/27/world/europe/27vienna.html ?pagewanted=all&_r=0. Monsignor Fernando Karadima was the subject of 'credible' accusations in 2011 of sexual abuse in confession two decades earlier. Karadima, who was well connected in government and business circles, was well known as a prelate who had trained many priests, including four bishops. The accusations involved allegations by five former minors. The Vatican ordered the priest into retirement and a life of penance. The Chilean court, while accepting the truth of the allegations, declared that the offences were outside of the statute of limitations. The case was reported in 'Chilean Priest Allegedly Abused 5 Young Men', *Huffington Post*, 22 April 2010, www.huffington post.com/2010/04/23/chilean-priest-allegedly-_n_549769.html; 'Chile Judge Rules Out Trial for Priest over Abuses', *Huffington Post*, 14 November 2011, www.huffingtonpost.com/huff-wires/20111114 /lt-chile-priest-abuse/.

22. Jason Berry and Gerald Renner, *Vows of Silence* (New York, 2004), 143.

23. The document's role, interpreted by some as proof of a Vatican conspiracy of secrecy, is a matter of dispute. See, for example, Andrew Brown's Guardian Blog of 22 July 2010 at www.guardian.co .uk/commentisfree/andrewbrown/2010/jul/22/religion-catholicism -vatican-paedophilia-secrecy, which Brown wrote in response to Nicholas P. Cafardi's article in *Commonweal* on 21 July 2010, entitled 'The Scandal of Secrecy: Canon Law & the Sexual-Abuse Crisis', archived at https://www.commonwealmagazine.org/scandal-secrecy. In response to both articles, see also Tom Doyle's blog (Voice from the Desert). The nub of the debate is that the Holy See's policy on paedophile priests was so secret that the bishops did not know about

it. The document dealt with how bishops should treat information such as allegations against a priest for abuse of pre-adolescent children in confession, acts described as *crimen pessimum* (the foulest crime). Doyle, a former canon lawyer who campaigns for victims of clerical sexual abuse, maintains that there was no centrally organised cover-up as a result of the document, but instead an entire 'culture' of secrecy.

24. Richard John Neuhaus, 'Orthodoxy and "Parallel Monologues"', *First Things*, March 2002, www.firstthings.com/article/2009/02/orthodoxy-and-8220parallel-monologues8221-22; see also John Cornwell, *Pontiff in Winter* (New York, 2004), 259.

25. Letter of the Holy Father Pope John Paul II to Priests for Holy Thursday 2002, 17 March 2002, www.vatican.va/holy_father/john_paul_ii/letters/2002/documents/hf_jp-ii_let_20020321_priests-holy-thursday_en.html.

26. 'Confessional Secrets', *Irish Times*, 31 August 2011, reprinted at BishopAccountability.org, www.bishop-accountability.org/news2011/07_08/2011_08_31_IrishTimes_ConfessionalSecrets.htm.

27. Marie Keenan, *Child Sexual Abuse and the Catholic Church: Gender, Power, and Organizational Culture* (Oxford, 2012), 163.

28. Ibid., 164.

29. Ibid., 165.

30. Ibid., 166–167.

Eleven: Confession Imagined

1. Robert Stone, 'The Way the World Is', in Peter Ochiogrosso, ed., *Once a Catholic: Prominent Catholics and Ex-Catholics Discuss the Influence of the Church and Their Lives and Work* (Boston, 1987), 49.

2. James Joyce, *A Portrait of the Artist as a Young Man* (London, 1992 [1916]), 155.

3. Ibid., 159ff.

4. Ibid., 171.

5. Ibid., 172.

6. Ibid., 185–186, 164, 161.

7. Thérèse of Lisieux, *Story of a Soul: The Autobiography of St. Thérèse of Lisieux*, trans. John Clarke (Washington, DC, 1975), 190, 213.

8. Henri Daniel-Rops, *History of the Church of Christ*, vol. 9, *A Fight for God*, trans. John Warrington (London, 1963), 425; John Udris,

Holy Daring: The Fearless Trust of St. Thérèse of Lisieux (Leominster, UK, 1997), 68.

9. Richard Crashaw, 'The Flaming Heart', l. 74, available at www .bartleby.com/236/29.html.

10. *Casti Connubii*, Encyclical of Pope Pius XI on Christian Marriage to the Venerable Brethern, Patriarchs, Primates, Archbishops, Bishops, and Other Local Ordinaries Enjoying Peace and Communion with the Apostolic See, 31 December 1930, www.vatican.va /holy_father/pius_xi/encyclicals/documents/hf_p-xi_enc_31121930 _casti-connubii_en.html.

11. Bernard Häring, *Free and Faithful in Christ*, vol. 2 (Middle Green, UK, 1979), 256. For Andrew Greeley's statistics on Catholics and birth control, see 'Vatican Watershed—A Special Report: Papal Birth-Control Letter Retains Its Grip', by Peter Steinfels, *New York Times*, 1 August 1993.

12. *Humanae Vitae*, Encyclical Letter of the Supreme Pontiff Paul VI to His Venerable Brothers the Patriarchs, Archbishops, Bishops and Other Local Ordinaries in Peace and Communion with the Apostolic See, to the Clergy and Faithful of the Whole Catholic World, and to All Men of Good Will, on the Regulation of Birth, 25 July 1968, www.vatican.va/holy_father/paul_vi/encyclicals/documents/hf_p-vi _enc_25071968_humanae-vitae_en.html; Catholic Church, Sacred Congregation for the Doctrine of the Faith, *Persona Humana*, Declaration on Certain Questions Concerning Sexual Ethics, 7 November 1975, www.vatican.va/roman_curia/congregations/cfaith/documents /rc_con_cfaith_doc_19751229_persona-humana_en.html.

13. Anthony Kenny, *A Path from Rome* (Oxford, 1985), 150.

14. *Ordo Paenitentiae*, Circular Letter Concerning the Integrity of the Sacrament of Penance, 20 March 1973, www.vatican.va/roman_curia /congregations/ccdds/documents/rc_con_ccdds_doc_20000630 _circolare-sulla-penitenza%20_en.html.

15. Mary Collins and David Power, eds., *The Fate of Confession*, Concilium Series 190 (Edinburgh, 1987); see also *Reconciliation and Penance*, Post-Synodal Apostolic Exhortation of John Paul II to the Bishops, Clergy, and Faithful on Reconciliation and Penance in the Mission of the Church Today, 2 December 1984, www.vatican .va/holy_father/john_paul_ii/apost_exhortations/documents/hf _jp-ii_exh_02121984_reconciliatio-et-paenitentia_en.html.

16. *Reconciliation and Penance*, Post-Synodal Apostolic Exhortation, 2 December 1984.

17. George Weigel, *Witness to Hope: The Biography of John Paul II* (New York, 1999), 473–474.

18. See *Kirchliches Amstsblatt der Diözese Münster 1977*, art. 236, cited in Collins and Power, eds., *Fate of Confession*, 65.

19. John Cornwell, *Breaking Faith* (London, 2002), 265ff. My interview with Cardinal Martini originally appeared in full in the *London Sunday Times Magazine*, 25 April 1993.

Twelve: Varieties of Confessional Experience

1. The testimonies quoted from my research throughout this chapter are from correspondence I received in response to my article in *The Tablet* on 18 August 2012 entitled "Where Are All the Penitents?" at www.thetablet.co.uk/article/163100, and are in my personal files.

2. Norbert Mette, 'Children's Confession', in Mary Collins and David Power, eds., *The Fate of Confession*, Concilium Series, vol. 190 (Edinburgh, 1987).

3. See, for example, John O'Donohue, *Anam Cara: A Book of Celtic Wisdom* (London, 1998).

Epilogue

1. Julia Kristeva, *New Maladies of the Soul*, trans. Ross Guberman (New York, 1995), 27ff.

2. Thomas à Kempis, *The Imitation of Christ: Four Books*, trans. William Benham (London, 1874), Chapter II: paragraph 2.

3. See Alasdair MacIntyre, *After Virtue: A Study in Moral Theory* (London, 1985).

4. See Hans Küng and David Tracy, eds., *Paradigm Change in Theology: A Symposium for the Future* (Edinburgh, 1989). In his opening remarks for the symposium, Jerald Brauer emphasised, for example, the new factor of 'pluralism in the modern world and in all forms of Christianity today.' He added: 'Some admit that fact grudgingly, and do everything possible to eliminate it. For others, pluralism is truth and practice of a tradition in the face of inevitable finite efforts to understand, appropriate and articulate their tradition' (p. 206).

5. Genesis 3.5. For further discussion, see Richard Kearney, *The Wake of Imagination: Ideas of Creativity in Western Culture* (London, 1988), 39ff.

6. William Golding, *Pincher Martin* (London, 1956). For discussion of the significance of *Pincher Martin* and the nature of sin, see Terry Eagleton, *On Evil* (New Haven, CT, 2010), 52.

7. Golding, *Pincher Martin*, 179.

8. In *On Evil*, Eagleton comments on *Pincher Martin*: 'There could no more be anyone "in" hell than there could be anyone in a material location called debt or love or despair. . . . The damned are those who experience God as a Satanic terror, since he threatens to prise their selves apart. His love and mercy loosen their hold on themselves, and in doing so risk depriving them of their most precious possession' (pp. 24–25).

9. See Nicholas Lash, 'Teaching or Commanding?', *America*, 13 December 2010.

10. *Lumen gentium*, Dogmatic Constitution on the Church Solemnly Promulgated by His Holiness Pope Paul VI, 21 November 1964, www.vatican.va/archive/hist_councils/ii_vatican_council /documents/vat-ii_const_19641121_lumen-gentium_en.html; Pope Paul VI, *Presbyterorum ordinis*, Decree on the Ministry and Life of Priests Promulgated by His Holiness Pope Paul VI, 7 December 1965, www.vatican.va/archive/hist_councils/ii_vatican_council/documents /vat-ii_decree_19651207_presbyterorum-ordinis_en.html; Henri de Lubac, *Catholicism: Christ and the Common Destiny of Man*, trans. Lancelot C. Sheppard and Elizabeth Englund (San Francisco, 1988), 37.

11. Karl Rahner, SJ, *Theological Investigations*, vol. 10 (London, 1984), 148.

12. Corneliu C. Simut, *The Ontology of the Church in Hans Küng* (Bern, 2007), 168ff; James Joyce, *A Portrait of the Artist as a Young Man* (London, 1992 [1916]), 172.

13. Herbert McCabe, OP, 'Self-Confessed Sinners', *The Tablet*, 5 March 2011, http://archive.thetablet.co.uk/article/5th-march-2011 /14/self-confessed-sinners; Karl Rahner, SJ, *Theological Investigations*, vol. 2 (London, 1963), 164.

INDEX